Light Bulb Baking

Light Bulb Baking

A History of the Easy-Bake® Oven

by Todd Coopee

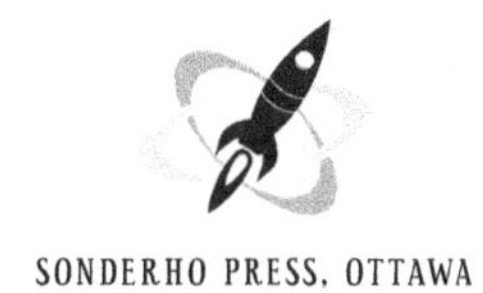

SONDERHO PRESS, OTTAWA

Sonderho Press, Ottawa K2P 0V4

Design, illustrations, and original photography by Denis Savoie, Savoie Photography and Design.

Edited by Maria Ford, Kaszas Marketing.

Printed in the United States of America.

ISBN: 978-0-9917484-0-2

This book is printed on acid-free paper.

"The most popular girl's toy since dolls."

Table of Contents

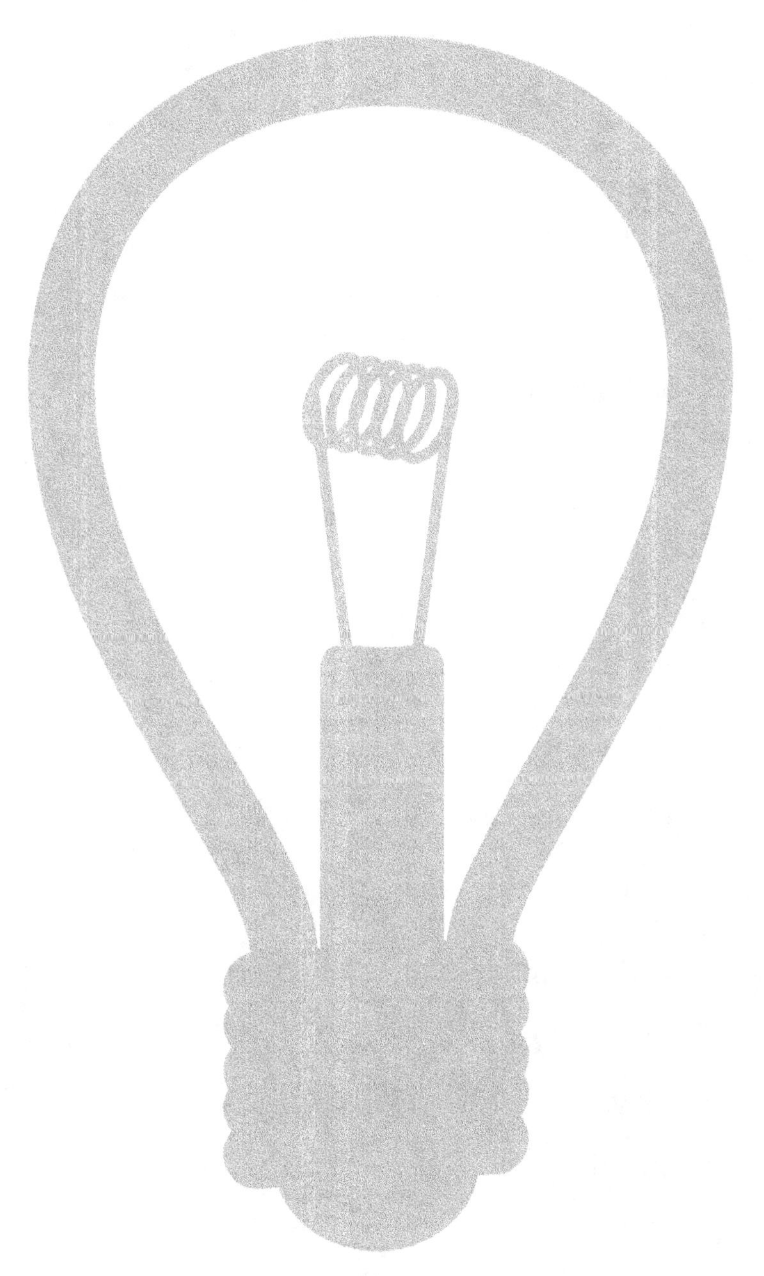

Author's Note

> *"A light bulb creates an environment by its mere presence."*
>
> — Marshall McLuhan

How has a plastic toy oven powered by a standard incandescent light bulb become a cultural icon? Pop-culture pundits often say that trends fade quickly and ultimately make a comeback every 20 years or so. The Easy-Bake Oven belies this notion. Its staying power has been consistent for 50 years, with more than 30 million ovens sold.

Nearly anyone born since 1955 has some memory of baking with an Easy-Bake. The oven allowed children to experience the delight of serving up miniature culinary concoctions while indulging in eating raw batter. For generations, the Easy-Bake Oven has taken and continues to take "playing house" to a level of realism that is nearly impossible for a child to hope for. The ability to bake and serve real food from a working oven without the supervision of a parent or the fear of fire is one of the most wonderful gifts a toy company (in this case, Kenner Products) has given to youth.

I was the youngest in a family of five children and did not have an Easy-Bake Oven to call my own. That honor fell to my three older sisters who, in 1971, were given reign over an avocado-green model (which made for quite a contrast

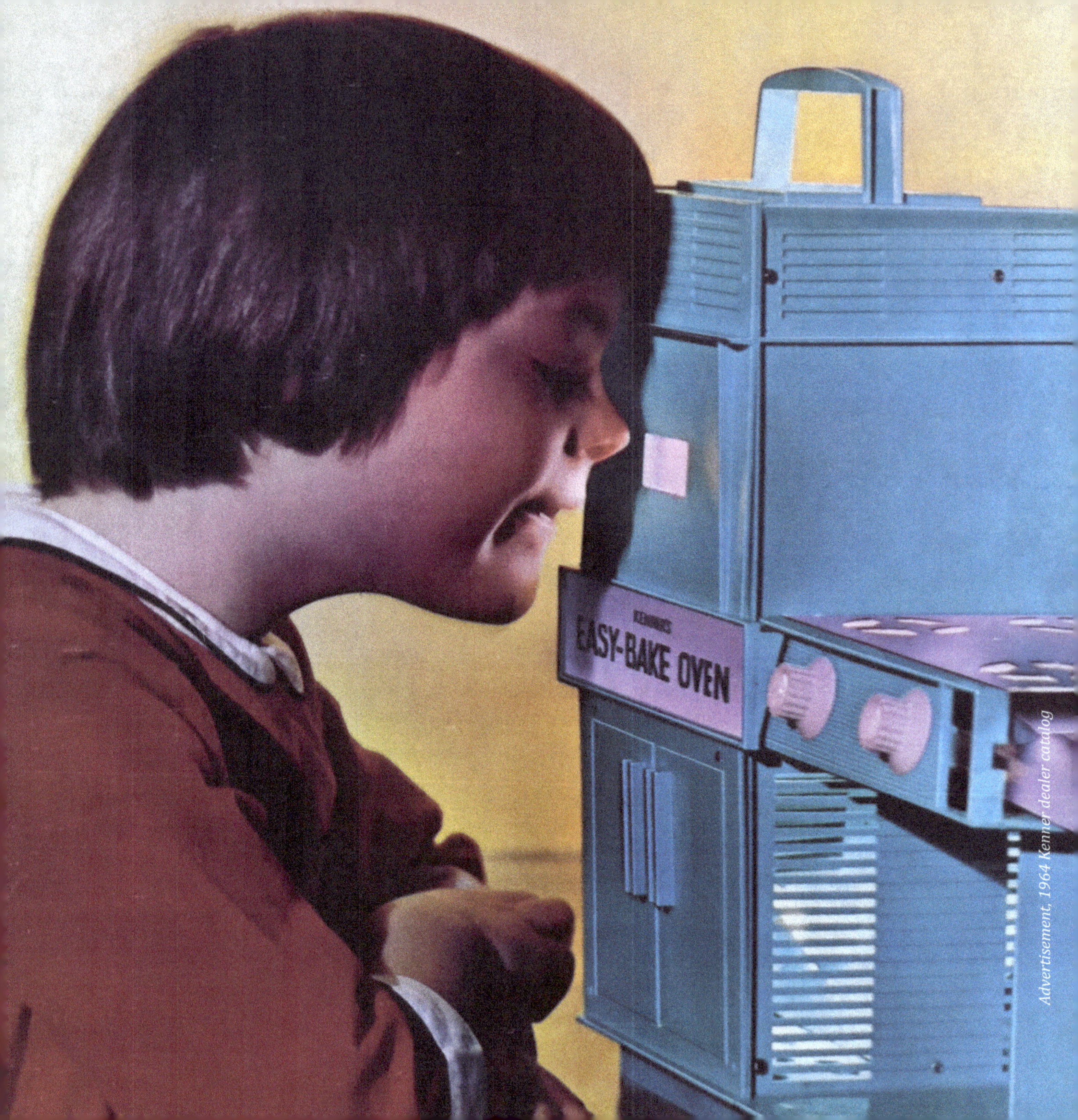

Advertisement, 1964 Kenner dealer catalog

with our harvest gold-themed kitchen). Despite ruling the Easy-Bake roost (and continually telling me that I was adopted—a story for another time), my sisters often let me participate in their baking sessions. I vividly recall peering through the watch-it-bake window, waiting impatiently as the light bulb worked its magic on the just-add-water mixes we had prepared. The results never looked like the pictures on the box, but they were delicious, and they were ours!

As I started to pay homage to those memories, this book rather unexpectedly became something more. It became an exploration of innovation, history, economics, commerce, advertising, and marketing. The story of the Easy-Bake Oven is a microcosm of post-war America. It demonstrates how the energies of technical innovation shifted after the war effort toward consumers. It traces the birth and evolution of a new popular culture that celebrated American invention and playfulness while reinforcing family-oriented values and traditional gender roles.

On a more personal note, this book also became a collage of many things that I enjoy: nostalgia, an affinity for vintage toys, a heavy dose of baking, and a love of dessert. My hope is that you will enjoy this retrospective as much as I have enjoyed bringing it to life.

Todd Coopee,
October 2013

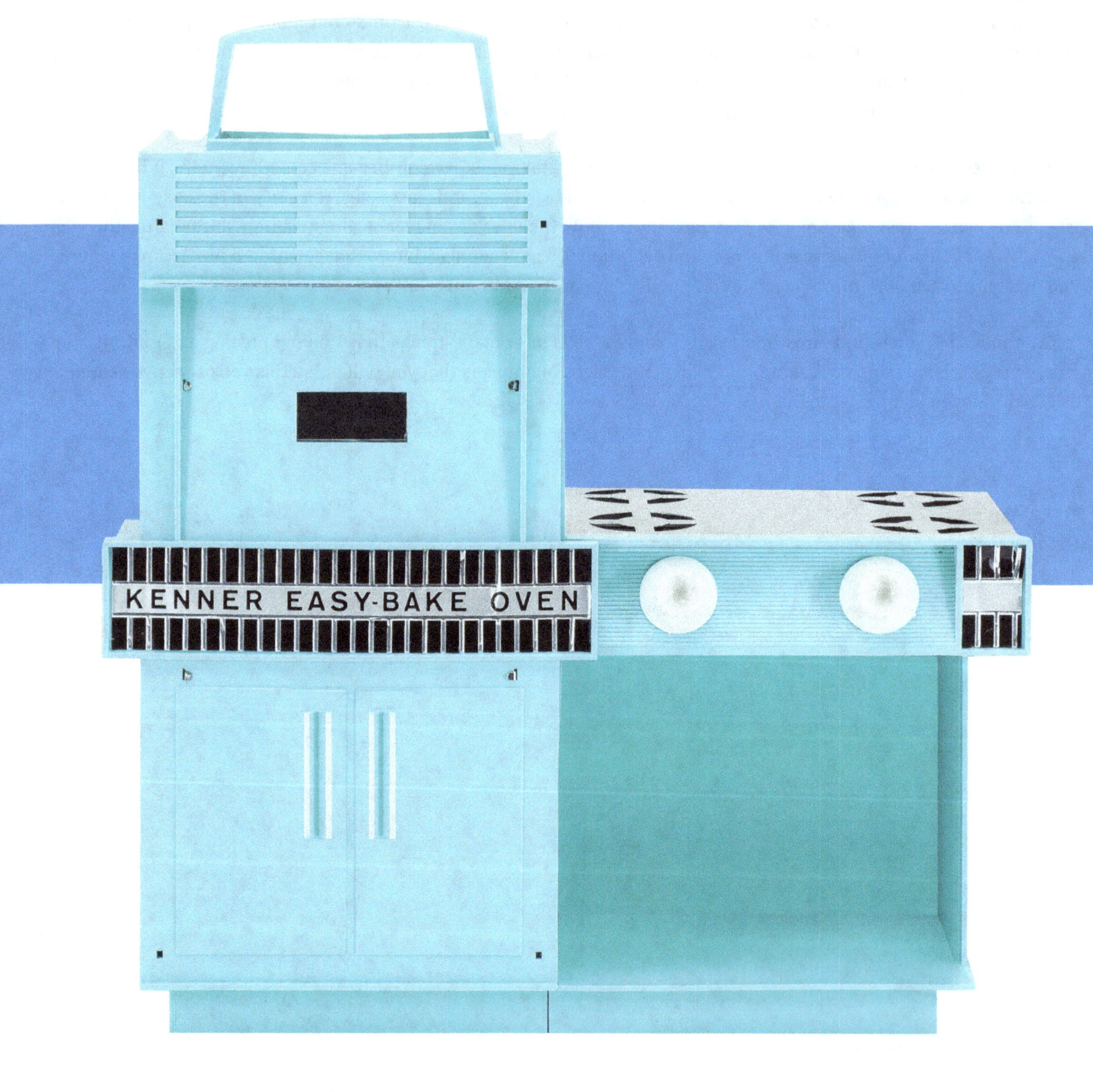

KENNER EASY-BAKE OVEN

Chapter 2

Brilliant Thinking

> "*No scientific discovery is named after its original discoverer.*"
>
> — *Stigler's Law of Eponymy*
>
> "*A great idea has no parents.*"
>
> — *Unknown*

As I contemplated writing a definitive history of the Easy-Bake Oven, a chapter on the oven's inventor seemed necessary. I longed to dig into the mind of the individual who had masterminded this toy of such mass appeal and longevity, perhaps discovering the brilliant "light bulb moment" (pun intended) that was the genesis of the Easy-Bake.

Research both dashed my hopes and expanded my horizons. Through conversations with the Steiner family (the founders of Kenner), various interviews, patent reviews, historical articles in trade publications, and internet research, it became clear that I would not find the answer to the question, "Who invented the Easy-Bake Oven?"

Instead, I discovered a group of enterprising post-war individuals and a toy company that fostered research and development, enabled innovation, and nurtured teamwork to bring new ideas to life. Inevitably, someone's name has to be assigned to a patent, and inevitably, someone or some group must become the champion for an idea to take wing. The more interesting story in this case is about the kind of environments and circumstances that become the wellspring for brilliant ideas.

Incubating Ideas

During its life, Kenner Products was a unique workplace and an ideal incubator of new toy ideas. Two aspects of its corporate culture in particular contributed to this. First, the company's leaders were receptive to new ideas and had no interest in copying or trying to "one-up" toys already on the market. Second, the company focused its innovations. Specifically, Kenner sought to produce small, realistic, working versions of things that kids saw their parents use—such as an oven.

Research and development at Kenner was a complex process that involved all aspects of the company, including manufacturing, sales, marketing, and product development. During the development of a new toy, Kenner would typically hold weekly meetings. James "Jeep" Kuhn, Vice President, Research & Development (and the man whose name appears as the inventor on the original Easy-Bake Oven patent) ran a meeting at Kenner. Albert Steiner, the President and dynamic leader of the company, ran another at his home in Cincinnati, usually in the evenings.

These meetings were open forums where anyone interested in a specific toy could come together to brainstorm, discuss ideas, identify issues, and solve problems. The Easy-Bake Oven was just one of countless toy designs and delivery strategies that were honed by a diverse team of individuals.

The Light-Bulb Moment

James Kuhn is widely credited with shepherding the Easy-Bake Oven through the development process and Ronald Howes, a member of Kuhn's team, is often referred to as the inventor. However, the genesis of the light-bulb-baking idea came from Norman Shapiro, Kenner's sales manager in New York City. Shapiro was a toy demonstrator with frequent gigs at Macy's flagship department store at Herald Square in Manhattan. Sharp and innovative[1], Shapiro was struck by the small ovens that street vendors used to cook and heat pretzels. He pitched the idea of manufacturing a children's version of the pretzel oven to the executives at Kenner's Cincinnati head office.

---

[1] During a telephone conversation, Bob Steiner recalled Norman Shapiro as "sharp and innovative."

Refining the Concept

Kenner executives liked the idea—it fit well with the company's culture and its approach to toy making. It was an original idea and it would allow children to recreate an adult experience: cooking and baking. The idea was immediately refined to bake items that were more appealing to kids, like cakes and cookies. Team members also determined that the oven would be fully functional, and early Kenner marketing literature dubbed it as "just like Mom's— bake your cake and eat it too!"

Surely there were countless individuals at Kenner who, during those weekly meetings, contributed to what we now know as the Easy-Bake Oven. Although no one I spoke with completely agreed with Howes' status as the oven's inventor, most believed that he played a major role in the creation and testing of the various mixes and mix sets that the oven used. This coincides with comments that his wife made in his obituary indicating that he was always testing things in the family garage during the time the Easy-Bake Oven was being developed.

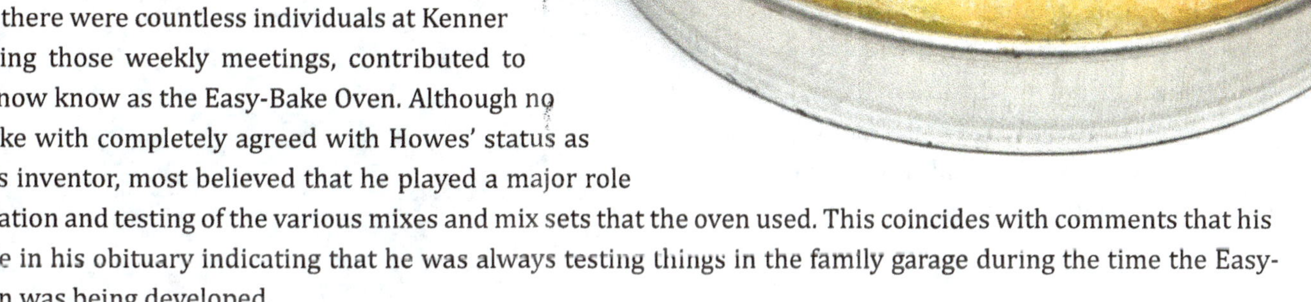

The team would have also worked together to overcome a key challenge with the idea of a toy oven: convincing parents that it was safe for their kids to use. To ease those concerns, a common incandescent light bulb was selected as the energy source rather than a traditional heating element, like what you would find in a toaster oven today. Talk about brilliant thinking! Although the toy oven could become as hot as a conventional oven, the fact that a potentially hazardous cooking element was replaced by a common household object that kids were around every day—a light bulb—made the Easy-Bake Oven appear virtually harmless.

Launching the Product

The idea blossomed until Kenner's three owners at the time, Al, Phil, and Joe Steiner, were so enamored with the product that they wanted to call it the Safety-Bake Oven. The National Association of Broadcasters—a trade association representing radio and television broadcasters in the United States—vetoed that name, telling Kenner that it implied the existence of a safety track record that didn't yet exist.

After some additional internal deliberation, Kenner moved ahead with the name Easy-Bake Oven, augmenting early product promotions with the phrase: "with built-in safety features". Launched in November 1963, the oven that let children bake by light bulb couldn't keep up with demand in its first year, selling all 500,000 pieces produced for the holiday season. Kenner tripled production the next year. Some reports from the time tell of female consumers literally fighting each other to get their hands on one.

Part of the success of the Easy-Bake Oven can be attributed to the fact that, in 1963, most activity based toys were designed for boys, widely thought to be more hands-on and productive than girls. Debunking that assumption is just one of the many ways that the Easy-Bake Oven was pivotal in the emergence of a new popular culture in North America.

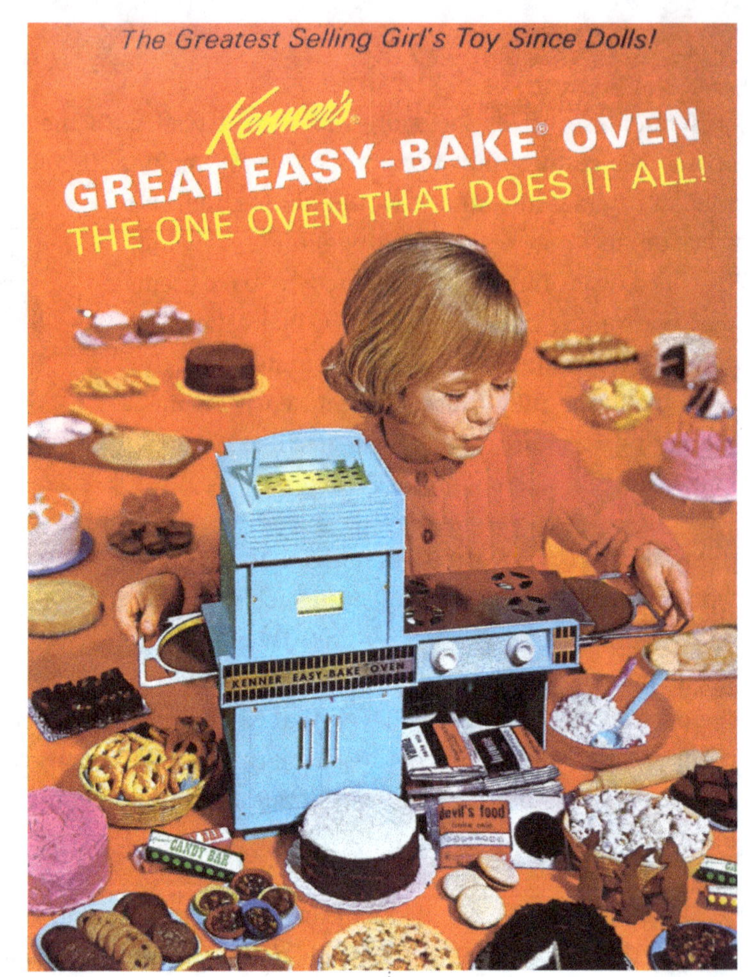

1968 advertisement featuring the original Easy-Bake Oven.

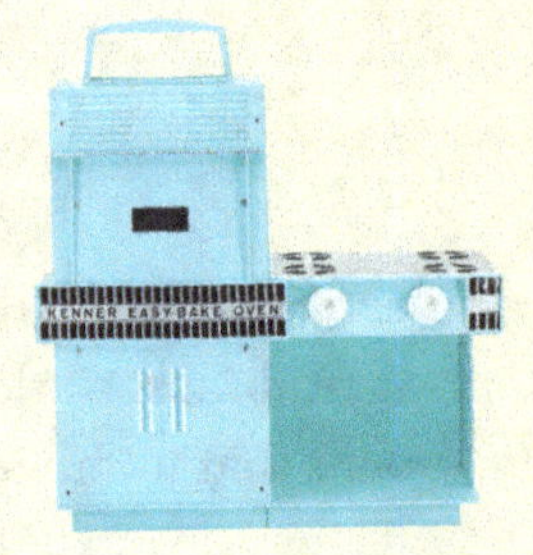

Did you know?

Kenner sold 500,000 Easy-Bake Ovens in the first year.

Light Bulb Basics

*F*or more than 40 years, the Easy-Bake Oven was powered by a simple incandescent light bulb. More recently, Hasbro began dabbling with light-bulb-free models, starting with the release of the Easy-Bake Real-Meal Oven in 2003. Ironically, it is the incandescent bulb's lack of energy efficiency which makes it an ideal energy source for the Easy-Bake.

Light Bright

A standard incandescent light bulb consists of these main parts:

- A metal base that supports the bulb, screws into the electrical source, and contains electrical contacts that safely conduct electricity into the bulb.
- The filament, a coiled piece of metal commonly made from tungsten.
- A glass globe filled with low-pressure, inert gases (argon and/or nitrogen) which also houses and protects the filament.

These parts work in concert to provide a safe, reliable light source.

When an incandescent bulb is screwed into an electrical socket and turned on, a simple loop circuit is created, allowing for a continuous flow of electricity from the base of the bulb through the filament. Electrical current passing through the filament causes it to heat up and

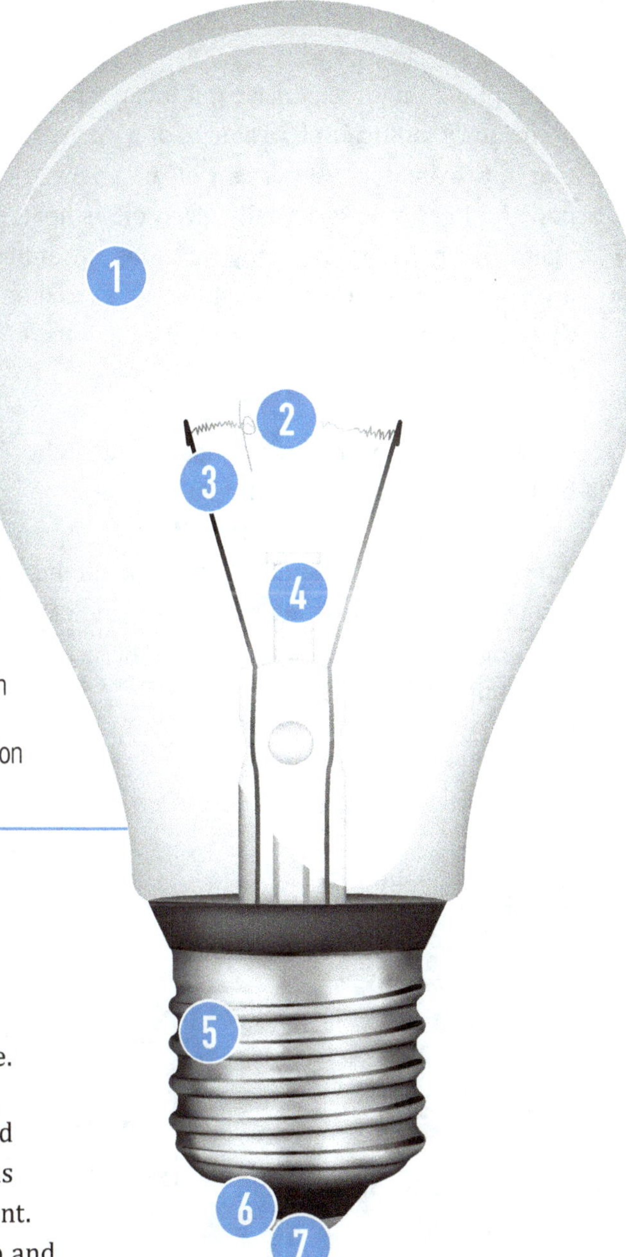

glow, a concept known as incandescence. The gases contained in the globe keep the heat of the filament in check, allowing it to emit a steady stream of light without getting too hot and burning out.

Heat Source

Despite being inexpensive, an incandescent light bulb is notoriously inefficient as a source of light. It is estimated that approximately 90 percent of the energy used to power a light bulb is actually given off as heat, not light. This is the reason why incandescent bulbs are so hot to the touch. It is also what makes them a suitable energy source for the Easy-Bake Oven.

Depending on the oven model, the light bulbs required to power the Easy-Bake have varied between 60 and 100 Watts. Watts, named after inventor James Watt, are a number rating assigned to a light bulb that indicates how much energy it uses. Higher wattage bulbs have longer filaments to emit more light and burn brighter.

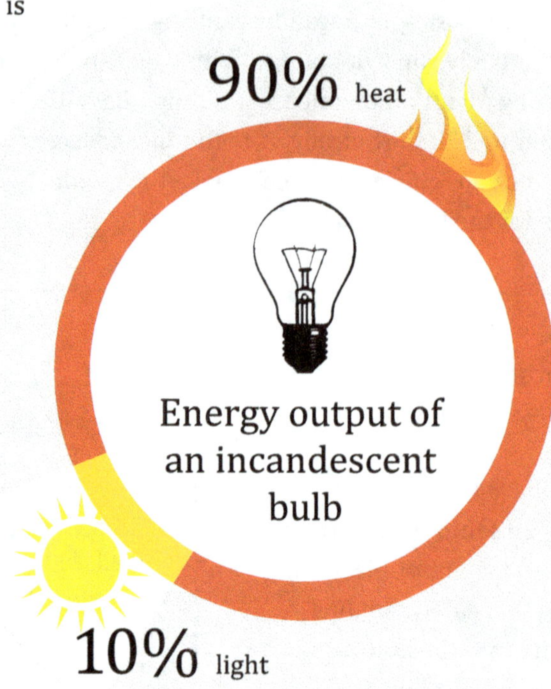

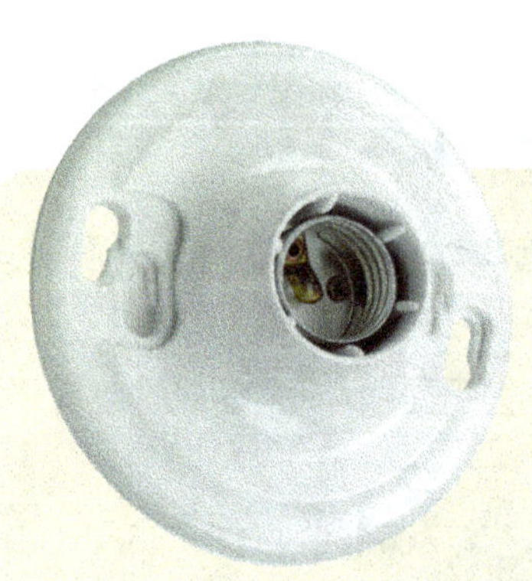

Did you know?

A typical American home contains between 50 and 100 light bulb sockets.

Inside the Original Easy-Bake Oven

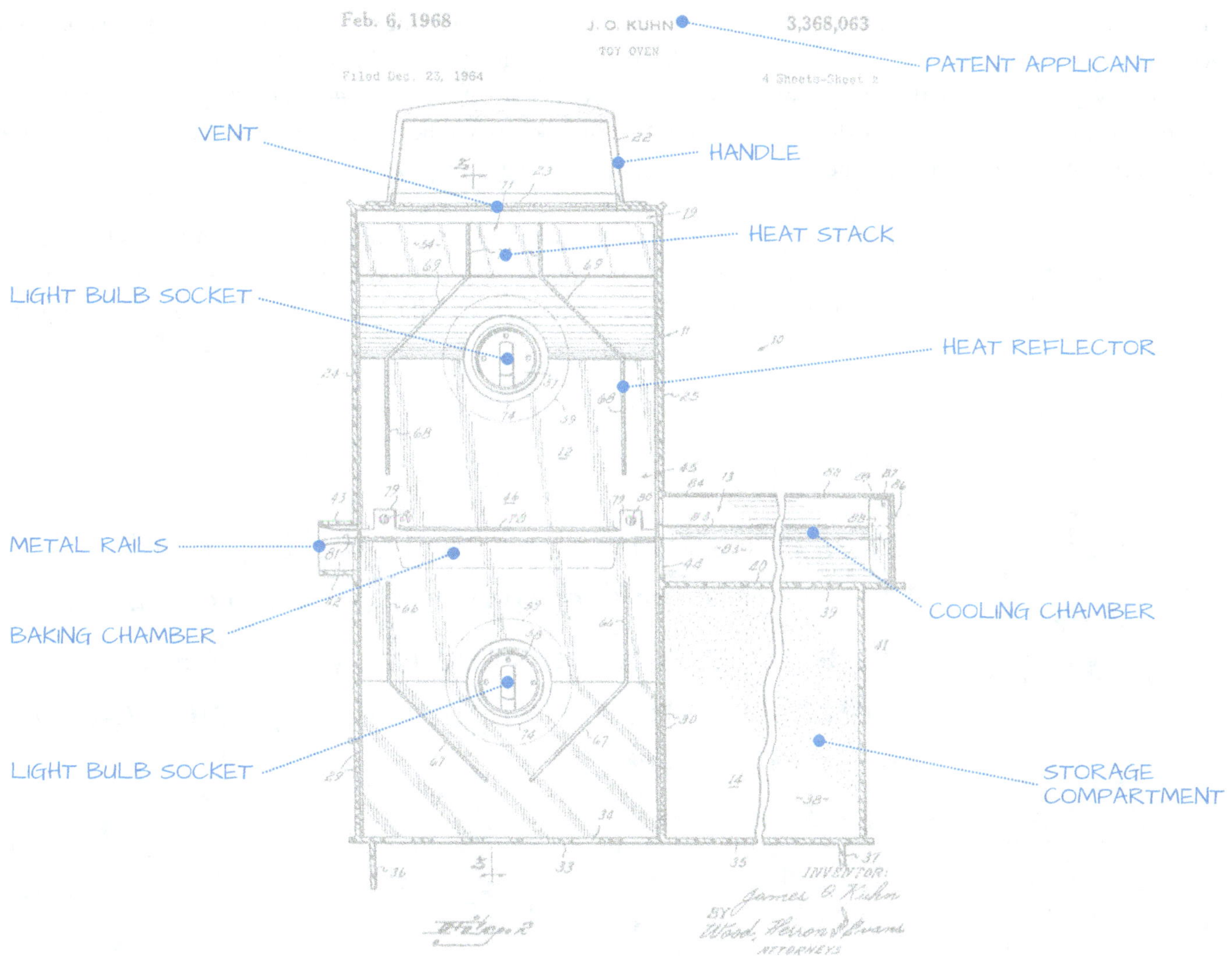

The ingenuity behind the Easy-Bake Oven's core technology is revealed in United States Patent #3,368,063, filed December 23, 1964 under the name James O. Kuhn and assigned to Kenner Products Company. Separate, side-by-side baking and cooling chambers are encased in heat- and impact-resistant plastic that is vented at the top.

Horizontal openings at both ends of the oven provide access to opposing grooved metal rails that run the entire width of the toy. These rails allow the metal baking pans to be pushed into the oven, moved through each chamber successively, and removed from the oven on the other side.

The magic happens inside the baking chamber. 100-Watt light bulbs are mounted above and below the horizontal track. Metal plates installed around each bulb act as heat reflectors and focus radiant heat downwards (in the case of the bulb above) to the top of the baking pan and upwards (in the case of the bulb below) to the bottom of the baking pan. Once plugged in and warmed up for about 15 minutes, the baking chamber temperature can rise to approximately 350 degrees Fahrenheit—probably the world's most common baking temperature.

On the flip side, the cooling chamber is equipped with adequate venting to promote airflow that cools baking pans pushed into it within 10 to 15 minutes. Not shown in the patent diagram is a wire rack that attaches to the end of the cooling chamber. This addition allows finished pans to be pushed onto the cooling rack before being completely removed.

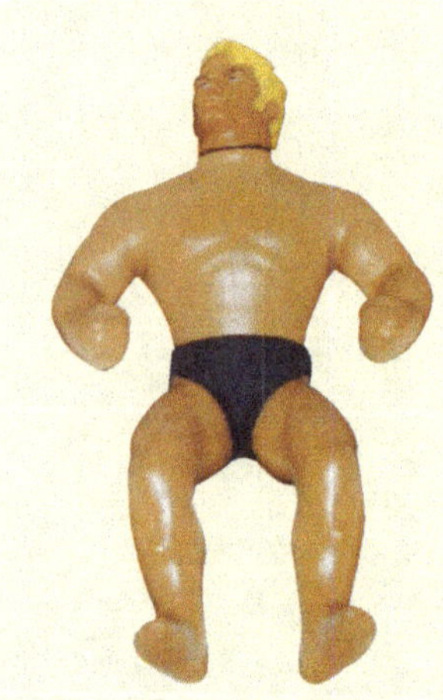

Did you know?

James O. Kuhn is also listed on U.S. patent #4169336 A as the inventor of a "Stretchable figure exhibiting slow recovery"—a.k.a. Stretch Armstrong—a popular toy released by Kenner in the mid 1970s.

Inside the Easy-Bake Mini-Wave Oven

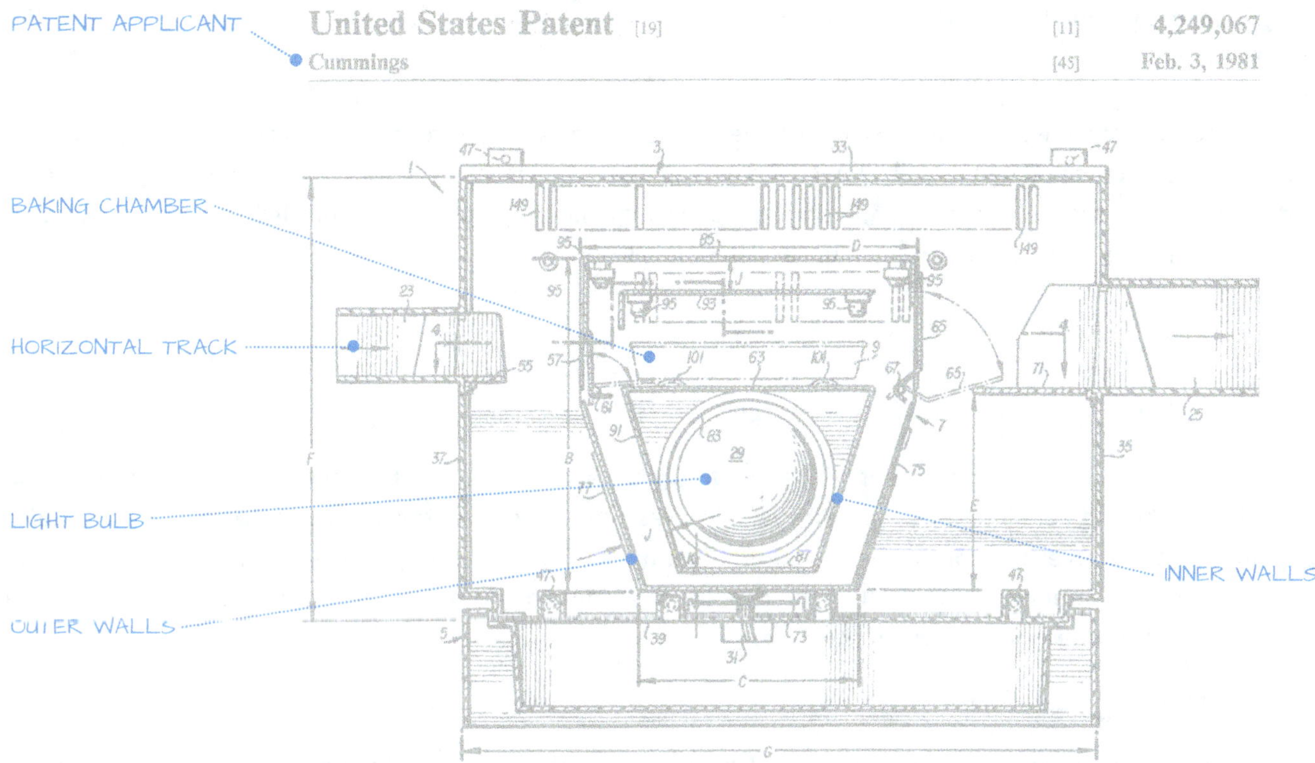

*I*n 1978, Kenner introduced the Easy-Bake Mini-Wave Oven, touting a new "oven-in-oven" construction that allowed it to cook faster than competing toy ovens. United States Patent #4,249,067, filed under the name of Charles A. Cummings, documents the science behind the claim and illustrates how Kenner improved upon the original design.

Like its predecessor, the Mini-Wave consists of separate side-by-side baking and cooling chambers surrounded by heat- and impact-resistant plastic. Cooling and ventilation is accomplished through a series of strategically placed fins, cooling slots, and tiny holes in the oven's outer shell.

Openings on either side of the toy provide access to a continuous horizontal track that allows baking pans to be placed in one side of the oven, moved through the baking and cooling chambers, and out of the oven on the other side.

The most noticeable changes are found inside the baking chamber. It is smaller than the original Easy-Bake Oven and houses a single 100-Watt incandescent light bulb (reducing the power requirements by 50 percent of the original) surrounded by an inner and outer metal shell. This dual-wall construction allows the oven to heat the surrounding air between the two walls and generate a convection current that flows through the chamber and cooks the food. Once plugged in and warmed up for 10-15 minutes, the oven maintains a relatively uniform temperature of 325-350 degrees Fahrenheit.

Five years after the introduction of the first Mini-Wave, Kenner added a simple venting system to the baking chamber. A temperature lever on the updated model allowed the user to determine if the oven's internal temperature should be set to high or low. When set to low, the vent opening is smaller, allowing less heat to enter the enclosed baking chamber. This updated model was released in 1983, as the Easy-Bake Dual-Temp Oven.

Catching Up with Charles Cummings

As an engineer in the Product Concepts & Design group at Kenner from 1968 to 1995, Charles Cummings had a self-described "dream job" for nearly 30 years. He was a full-time inventor for one of the top toy companies in the United States. Over the course of his career, Cummings amassed an impressive array of patents and his fingerprints are on a number of successful products from Kenner, including two popular toys that are still sold today: the Baby Alive doll and the Easy-Bake Oven.

In fact, Cummings was at the center of a key milestone in the Easy-Bake Oven's evolution.

Kenner's corporate culture encouraged exploration and innovation, especially around product lines that were successful, like the Easy-Bake. "The toy was already a success, but no one thought you could bake a cake using just one light bulb," recalls Cummings. He took up this challenge and started an initiative to develop a new baking chamber for the oven that would bake items faster, using one light bulb instead of two.

Cummings spent months developing and tweaking a mathematical model for the new baking chamber, which was smaller and used convection to allow the toy to maintain a steady temperature using a single 100-Watt bulb. The reduced size meant that the form factor of the oven could also be changed, and a design was created to resemble a new kitchen appliance: the microwave oven.

After a series of prototypes yielded promising results—it was baking cakes in 10 minutes using a single bulb— the group Cummings worked with approached Bernie Loomis, Kenner Products President at the time, with the

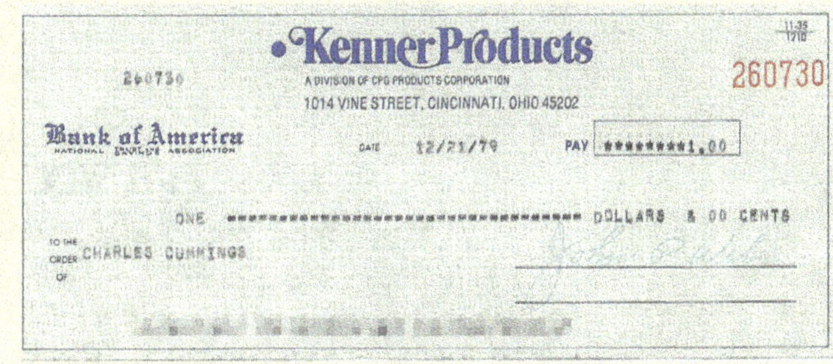

Kenner Products had a policy of issuing a one-dollar check to an employee in recognition of a patented invention.

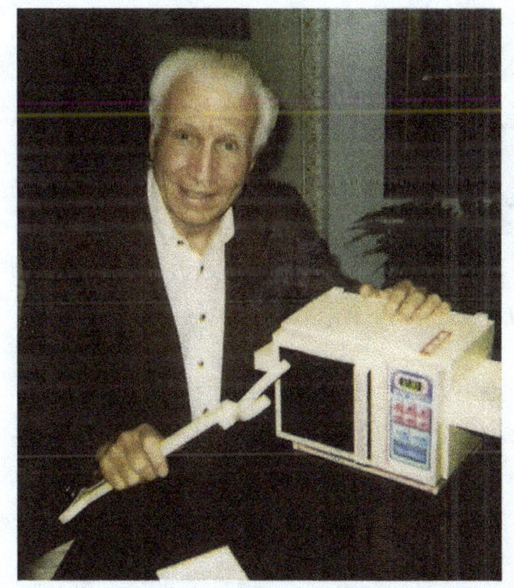

Charles Cummings, 2000

results. Loomis was excited but remained skeptical. His skepticism led to one of the seminal moments in the history of the toy.

Cummings was asked to present the one-bulb prototype at a board meeting, where he added water to one of the standard cake mixes and placed it in the oven. Loomis began the meeting and said that they would check in on the progress of the cake shortly. After 10-minutes, Cummings removed the cake from the oven and placed the finished and fully baked item on a plate for everyone to see. "Everyone just started clapping," he remembers.

From that moment, Kenner began work to convert the prototype into a product that could be mass-produced, pass safety requirements, and be sold at a reasonable price. In 1978, the 15th anniversary Betty Crocker Easy-Bake Mini-Wave Oven hit store shelves. Sales for the oven remained strong, and in 1981 Cummings was granted a patent for his invention.

After retiring in 1995, Cummings remains active in the toy industry. He formed a partnership with 10 others called AT Insights and continues to develop new products and provide consulting services to start-up toy companies.

Lights Out

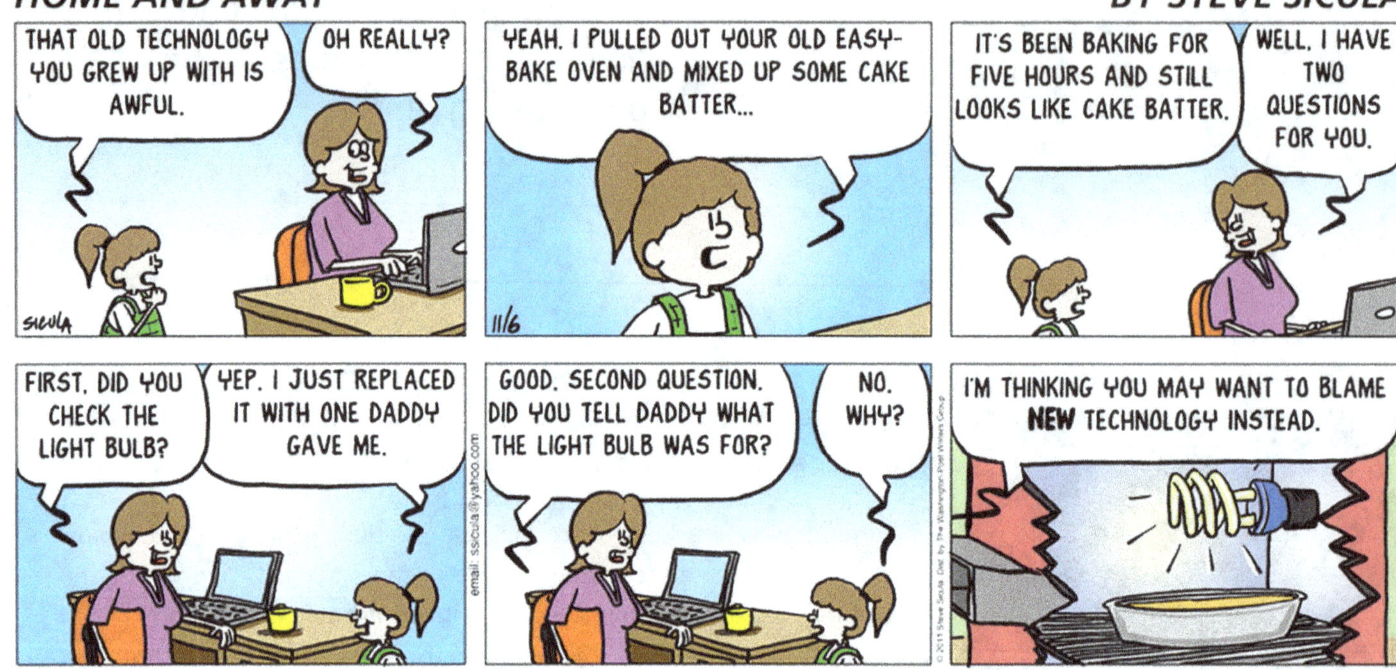

© Copyright Steve Sicula, distributed by Washington Post Writers Group.

In 2007, the United States Government set new efficiency standards for light bulbs, and the future of the Easy-Bake Oven was thrown into upheaval. Part of the *Energy Independence and Security Act* (EISA) requires that all screw-based light bulbs must be 27 percent more efficient by 2014. For example, a light bulb that used to consume 75 Watts of electricity to function must now use fewer than 53.

Houston, We Have a Problem!

The first phase of EISA went into effect in 2012 and targeted 100-Watt bulbs, including the incandescent light bulbs that were used to power the Easy-Bake Oven. Unfortunately, only about 10 percent of the electricity used to power an incandescent bulb is actually given off as light, making these bulbs incapable of reaching the required efficiency targets.

Easy-Bake Oven: The Next Generation

Rather than end 47 years of toy history, Hasbro seized on the demise of the 100-Watt bulb as an opportunity to completely re-invent the oven. Introduced in 2011, the Easy-Bake Ultimate Oven was the product of this re-tooling. At the core of the re-design is the use of a light-bulb-free heating element that's more akin to a conventional toaster oven.

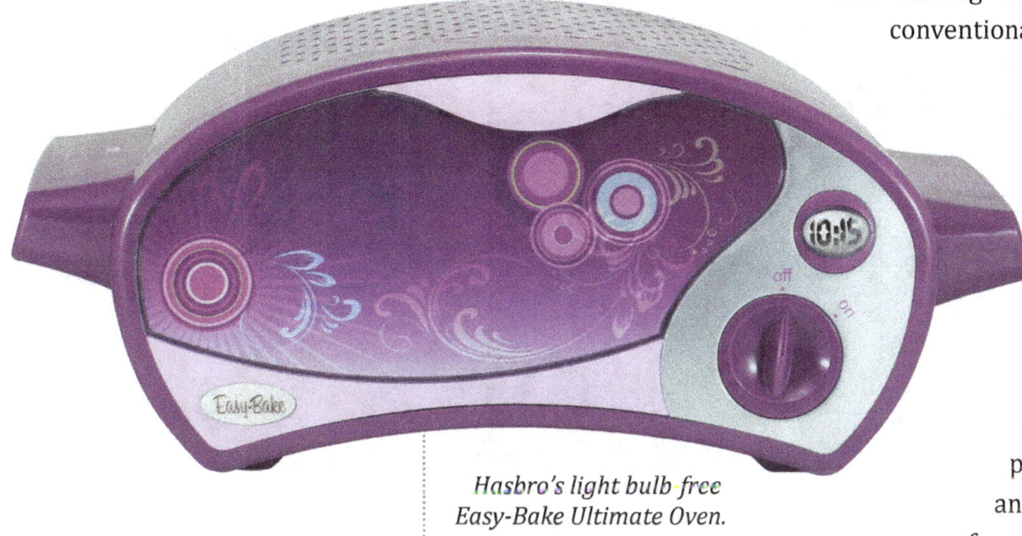

Hasbro's light bulb-free Easy-Bake Ultimate Oven.

Bulb-Free Baking

Even before EISA, Hasbro twice flirted with Easy-Bake Oven models that were light bulb-free. In 2003, the company introduced the Easy-Bake Real-Meal Oven, which was powered by a heating element and remained on the market for four years. Soon after that, Hasbro officially retired the light bulb from the Easy-Bake Oven line with the release of the Easy-Bake Classic Oven in 2006. Unfortunately, this model was recalled for safety reasons, forcing Hasbro to pivot back to incandescent bulbs in 2008, with the release of the Easy-Bake Oven & Snack Center.

Did you know?

Three Easy-Bake Oven models have swapped out the incandescent light bulb for a heating element.

Total Recall

Five years after Hasbro acquired Tonka Corporation, Kenner's parent company, it overhauled the Easy-Bake Oven. Two key changes of the re-design included replacing the traditional light bulb with an electric heating element, and switching the oven's entry point from the side to the front. Decked out in dark lavender and pink, the new oven resembled a contemporary kitchen range, complete with a backsplash and four "burners" on top, one of which served as a warming element.

Unfortunately, the new design led to the first major crisis in the toy oven's then 43-year history.

Uneasy Baking

After the release of the new model in May 2006, Hasbro received reports of 29 children getting their hands or fingers caught in the front-loading door, including five reports of burns. In February 2007, the company issued a voluntary recall of the oven, advising parents to take the oven away from children under the age of eight and contact the company for a free retrofit kit.

The kit, approved by the United States Consumer Product Safety Commission (CPSC), consisted of a pink plastic grate that fit over the oven door, and a warning notice. The grate allowed the oven to continue to function as designed while providing an additional barrier to keep small fingers out.

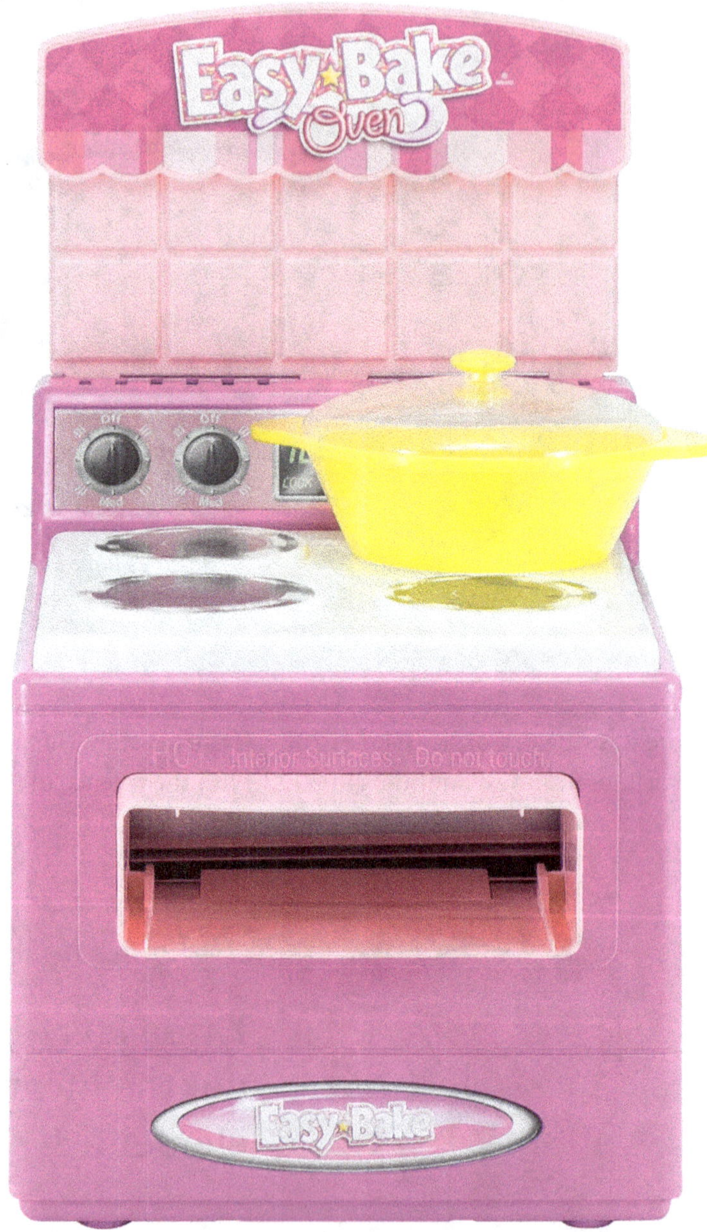

Despite the retrofit program, the problems persisted. According to data from the CPSC, an additional 249 reported incidents included 77 burns, 16 of which were second- or third-degree in nature. In July 2007, Hasbro re-issued its voluntary recall of the Easy-Bake after learning that part of a five-year-old girl's finger had to be amputated because of a severe burn.

Hasbro and the CPSC recommended that consumers stop using the oven immediately. The company allowed consumers to return the toy free of charge and provided a $32 voucher towards the purchase of another product from Hasbro's online store.

Back to the Bulb

The recall affected almost one million of the redesigned ovens sold between May 2006 and July 2007. Ovens sold prior to May 2006 were not part of the recall, leaving the more than 25 million side-entry/light bulb models in circulation unaffected.

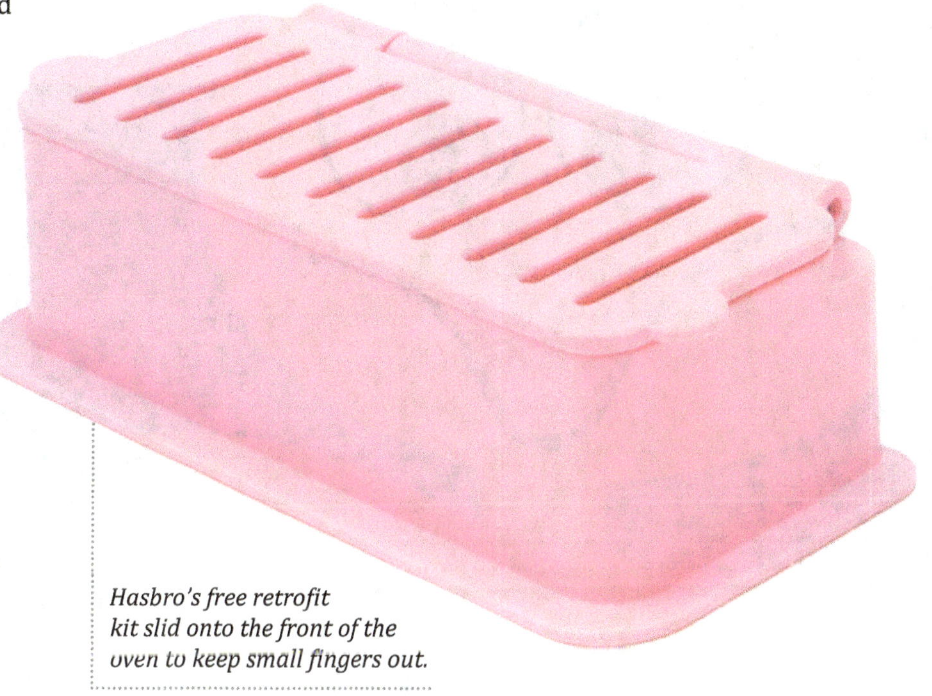

Hasbro's free retrofit kit slid onto the front of the oven to keep small fingers out.

Hasbro returned to the Easy-Bake Oven's incandescent light bulb roots with the release of the Easy-Bake Oven & Snack Center in 2008.

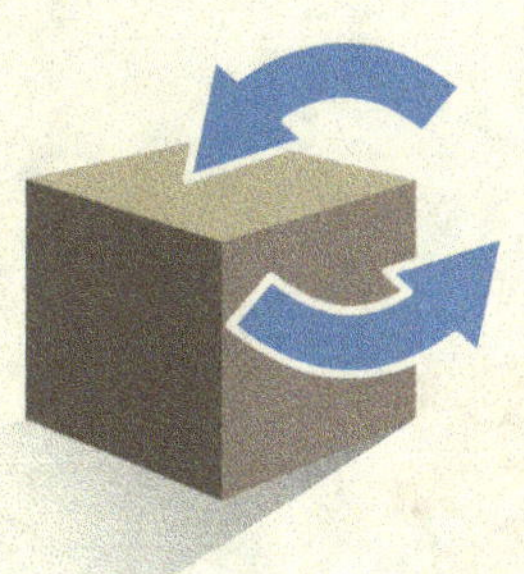

Did you know?

The recall affected almost one million ovens sold between May 2006 and July 2007.

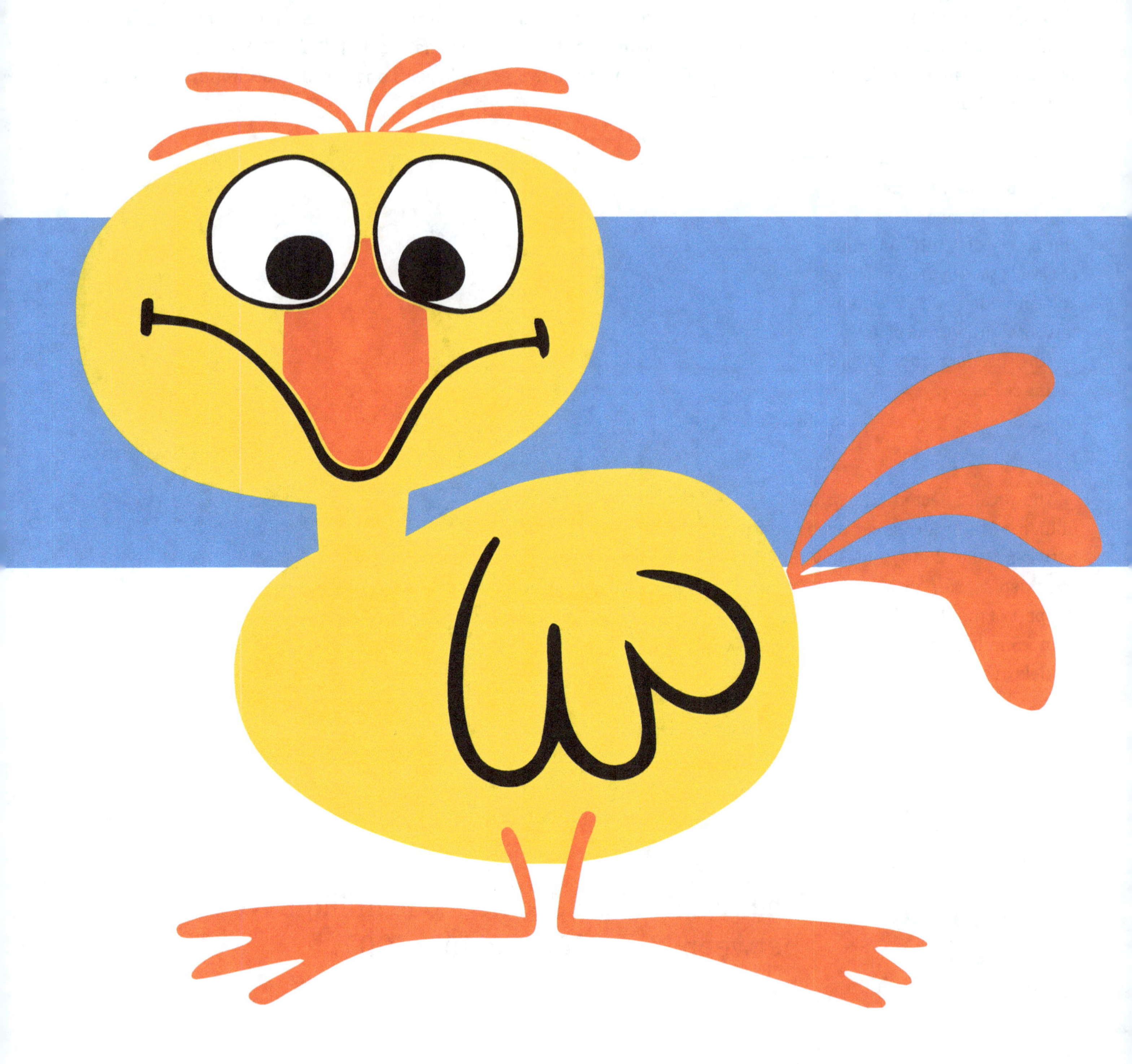

It's Kenner, It's Fun!

> "It is a happy talent to know
> how to play."
>
> — *Ralph Waldo Emerson*

Cincinnati, 1946

Post-WWII Cincinnati, Ohio was a city in pursuit of a dream. With a population hovering around half a million, the former industrial powerhouse had undertaken an ambitious plan of modernization and renewal. The city was bustling with new development, art, and culture. Post-war confidence was evident in proposed enhancements to public transit and a renewed commitment to community restoration in the downtown core. During this decade, three Cincinnati brothers founded a family business that would soon become a dominant player in the toy industry.

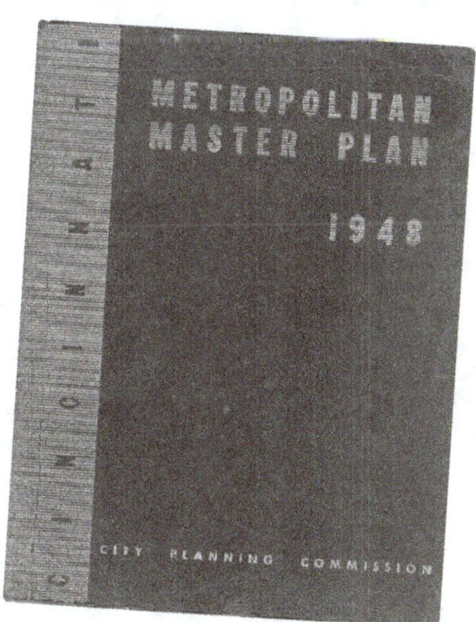

Soap & Bubbles

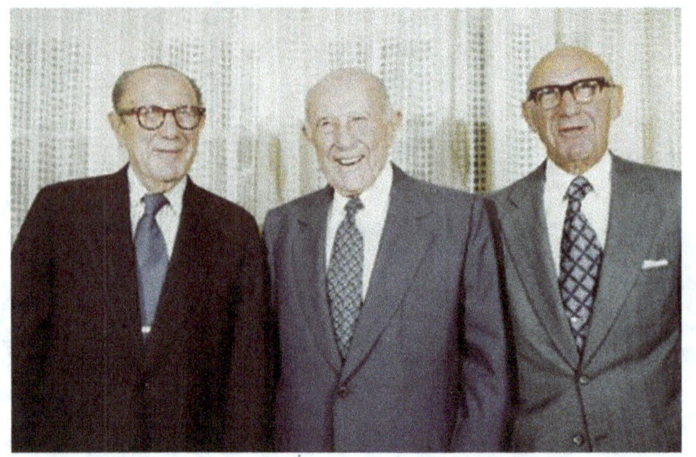
Phil, Albert and Joseph Steiner, 1987

In 1946, Phil, Albert, and Joseph Steiner were an enterprising trio running the Grandpa Soap Co., a soap, flavoring, and extract business with offices on Kenner Street. Legend has it that soap led to the inspiration for the brothers' next venture. After seeing a young boy dipping a wand into soapy water, then waving the wand to create giant bubbles, Albert Steiner was apparently inspired to create the firm's first toy product: the Bubbl-Matic Gun.

A silver, quasi-squirt gun that shot a stream of bubbles instead of water, the Bubbl-Matic was distributed in boxes of soap and was so well received that the company switched businesses. The Bubbl-Matic is perhaps most notable for leading to the development of a second product, the Bub-L-Rocket. The Rocket sold more than a million units in Kenner Products' second year and launched the fledgling business onto the path that would eventually see it become one of the top toy makers in the nation.

Toyetic: The Secret Sauce

Bernard Loomis, Kenner's President from 1970-1978, coined the term "toyetic" to describe characters and concepts that are appealing to children and can be easily mass-produced. Every decade saw Kenner produce memorable, toyetic brands. Three of the company's biggest hits—Play-Doh, the Easy-Bake Oven, and Star Wars figures—have been inducted into the National Toy Hall of Fame.

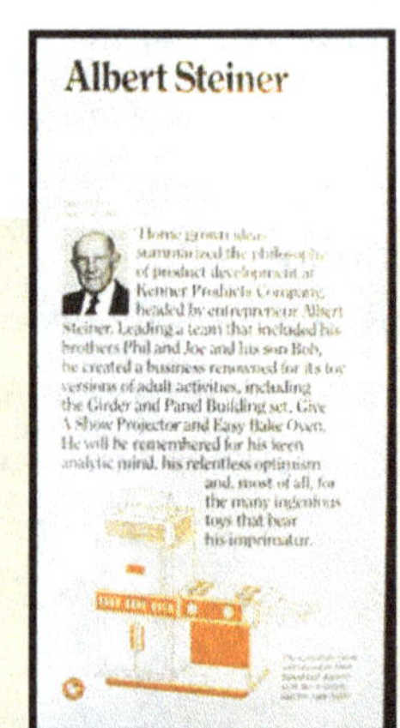

Did you know?

Although Albert Steiner was inducted into the Toy Industry Hall of Fame (posthumously in 1993), Kenner was a true collaboration. Phil was the financial brains who also managed the company's real estate acquisitions, while Joseph was exceptional at sales and business development.

Drive for Innovation

A bird's-eye view of the Kenner Products toy line reveals the drive for innovation that permeated the company. In fact, this characteristic was critical to the firm's longevit in the competitive toy business. Kenner developed a reputation for actively seeking out new ideas, encouraging employees to think "outside the box", and focusing on the research and development of toys based on new concepts and inventions.

Kenner also distinguished itself by avoiding trends and fads. Instead, the company focused on building volume and customer loyalty across product lines that sold year after year—a trait that continues to endear them to collectors and nostalgic adults.

One of Kenner's specialties was recreating adult activities at a child's level. Many Kenner toys enabled children to do what they saw their parents doing or talking about, spurring the imagination and encouraging discovery.

The Easy-Bake Oven is an exceptional example of this winning formula. It empowers children to manage their own kitchens. They learn to read recipes, mix ingredients, use kitchen tools, and produce finished food items that they can serve to friends and family.

The Bub-L-Rocket sold more than one million units.

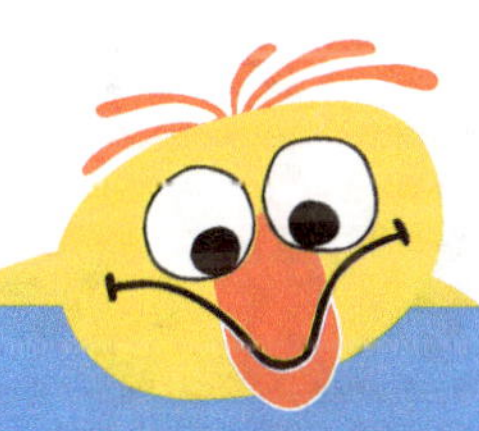

A Bird's Eye View – Hit Toys Year After Year	
'40s	Bub-L-Rocket
'50s & '60s	Play-Doh, Give-a-Show Projector, Easy-Bake Oven, Close'n Play Phonograph, Girder & Panel and Bridge & Turnpike Building Sets, Spirograph
'70s	Jukebox, Baby Alive, Star Wars figures, The Six-Million Dollar Man action figures
'80s	Care Bears, The Real Ghostbusters action figures, Strawberry Shortcake, MASK – Mobile Armored Strike Kommand
'90s	Toys from the Batman and Jurassic Park films, Starting Lineup action figures

Playing Out the American Dream

The founding, growth, evolution, and eventual sale of Kenner Products played out like a microcosm of the American dream. Started as a family business, the company established itself through home-grown ideas, grew through key acquisitions, and was sold three times (to General Mills, Tonka, and Hasbro)—all the while producing hit toys year after year.

Once a stronghold in its hometown of Cincinnati, Kenner was eventually absorbed into larger companies and product lines. In 2000, Hasbro closed Cincinnati operations and with it, an era in American toy history. Many of the early Kenner toys—including the Easy-Bake Oven—live on today under a very modern type of family: the Hasbro brand.

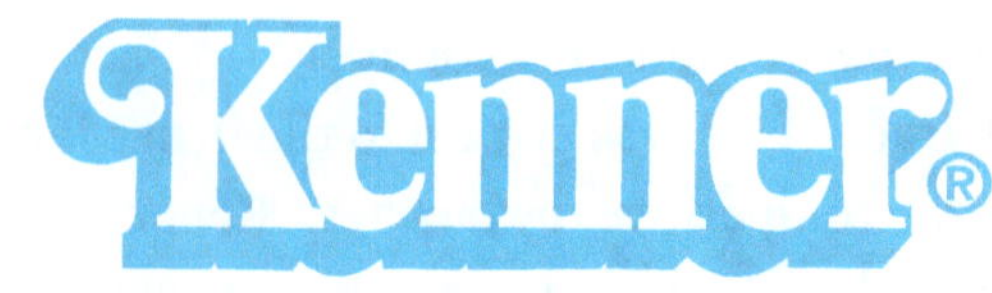

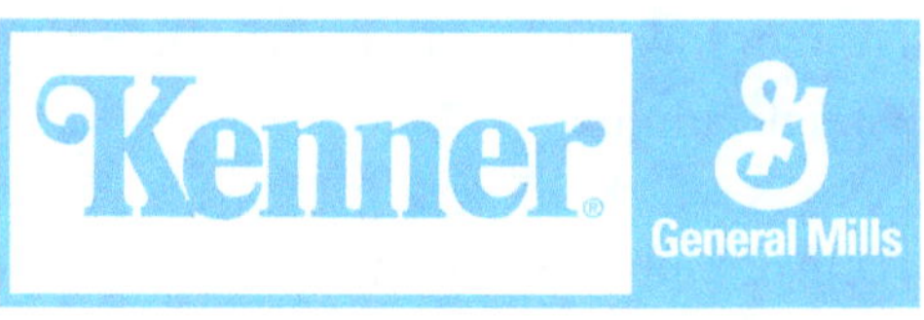

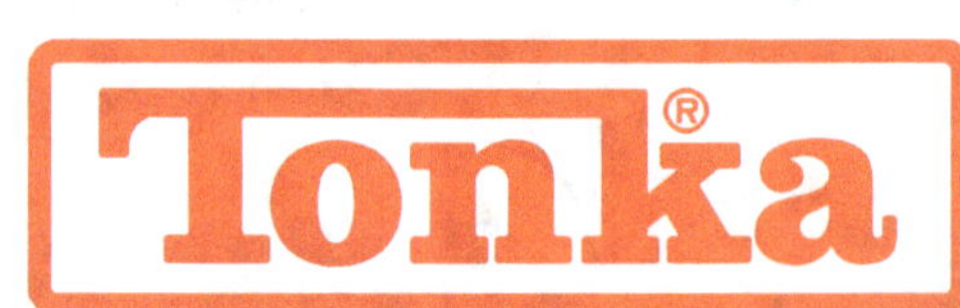

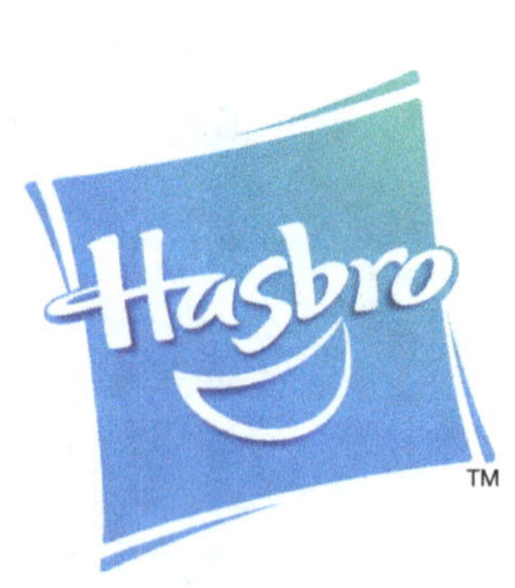

Did you know?

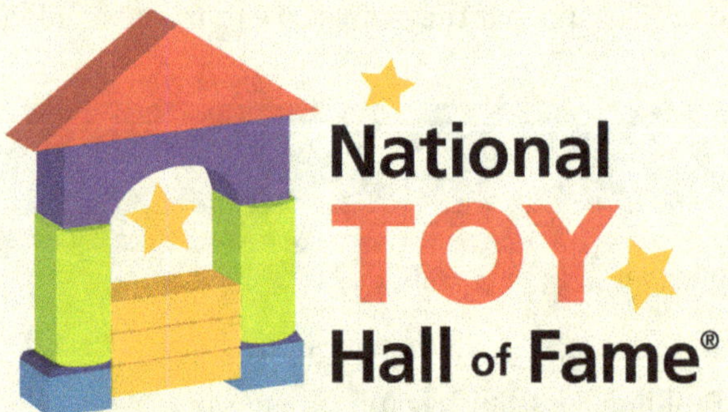

Three Kenner Products toys have been inducted into the National Toy Hall of Fame: Play-Doh, the Easy-Bake Oven, and Star Wars figures.

The Gooney Bird

In 1962, the Kenner brand became tightly associated with a squat yellow bird with an orange beak and feet. Designed by Bob Grannan of Leonard Sive and Associates, the deliberately gender-neutral corporate mascot, known as the Kenner Gooney Bird, was used as part of the company logo on most product packaging along with the company slogan, *"It's Kenner, It's Fun!"* and periodically in trade publications and ads with the tagline, *"This bird means business!"*

In 1968, the Gooney Bird was brought to life in the form of a Muppet designed by Jim Henson and built by Don Sahlin and Kermit Love. The Muppet Gooney Bird was used in a now-famous commercial for the Easy-Bake Oven in which it interacted with child actress Barbara Price, pulling stunts like snacking on the sweets she baked, popping out of her pies, and flying into a wall of Kenner products while squawking the company slogan. Reaction to the Gooney Bird was so positive that Henson later refurbished him as Little Bird, a sidekick to Big Bird in early seasons of the ground-breaking *Sesame Street* television show.

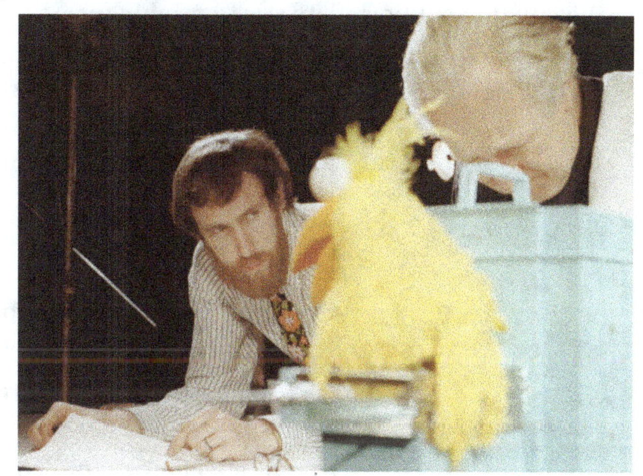

Jim Henson on set with the Gooney Bird and the Easy-Bake Oven.

The Gooney Bird dabbled as a character actor as well, making appearances in animated TV commercials from Kenner, warbling the company slogan while performing various comedic stunts. He also made several cameo appearances in Kenner's *Talking Show Projector* and *Give-a-Show Projector* toy sets.

Kenner slowly phased out the Gooney Bird's public appearances by 1974, although the icon remained in use internally. When Hasbro merged Cincinnati operations in 2000, employees were given caps and watches with the Gooney Bird logo as thank-you gifts.

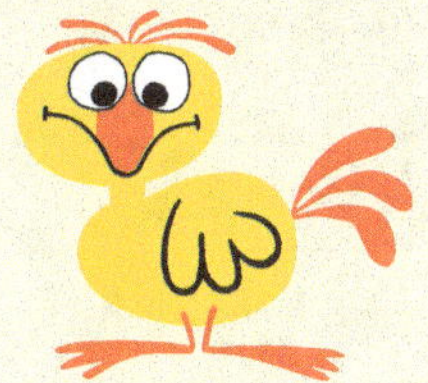

Did you know?

The Kenner Gooney Bird mascot appeared in print and media campaigns from 1962-1974.

Home Grown Ideas

" *H* ome grown ideas" is the inscription on Albert Steiner's plaque in the Toy Industry Hall of Fame. Those three words summarize the philosophy of product development at Kenner Products and can aptly be applied to Kenner's presence and impact on the city of Cincinnati as well. Over the course of 54 years, Kenner blossomed into one of the most respected and top-grossing toy makers in the industry, while at the same time remaining deeply rooted in the city that supported its rise to prominence.

During Kenner's heyday, it employed more than 3,000 employees at multiple locations in the Cincinnati area.

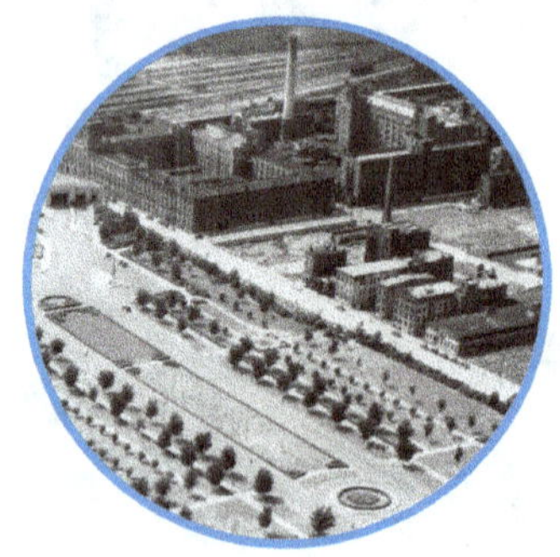

1024 Kenner Street

Location of The Grandpa Soap Co., a soap, flavoring, and extract business run by the Steiner brothers, Albert, Phil, and Joseph.

After selling a chunk of the soap business to Proctor & Gamble in 1938 and being flooded out of the Kenner Street location in 1945, the Steiners moved offices to 912 Sycamore Street and formed Kenner Products in 1946.

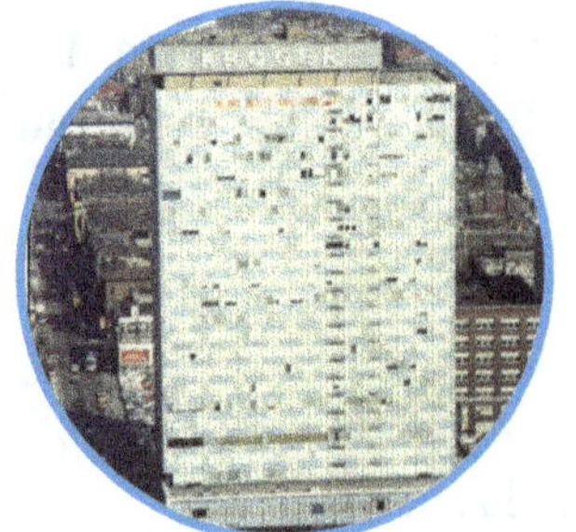

1014 Vine Street – The Kroger Building

In 1976, during a period of expansion, Kenner moved its corporate headquarters here, where the company soon topped 3,000 employees.

Cincinnat

2950 Robertson Avenue – The Oakley Commerce Center

This manufacturing plant was a product of Kenner's expansion in 1976 and closed shortly after Hasbro acquired Kenner in 1991.

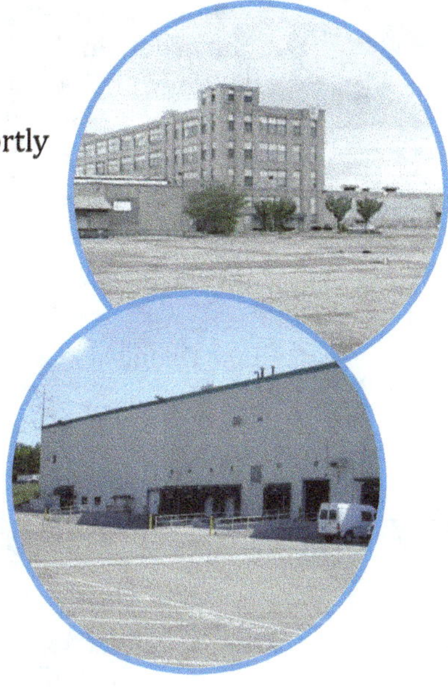

2940 Highland Avenue – Norwood Distribution Center

When General Mills acquired Kenner in 1967, the cash infusion was used to expand production facilities in Cincinnati. In 1969, the company built a 250,000 sq ft distribution center on Highland Avenue. In 1974, the company doubled the size of its automated shipping plant to support truck and train shipping.

615 Elsinore Place

Kenner's final corporate headquarters was acquired shortly after Hasbro purchased Tonka Corporation (and along with it, the Kenner Products division) in 1991. The company remained here until Hasbro pulled all operations from Cincinnati in 2000, as part of a nationwide consolidation of its toy groups.

912 Sycamore Street

From 1946-1976, toys were designed and produced in three separate buildings at Kenner Products headquarters.

Local Cincinnati designers, Barbara and David Day, designed the abstract mural of a child playing marbles that appeared on the building. The mural was also featured on the cover of the 1973 Kenner Toy Fair Catalog. The building has since been demolished and replaced with a municipal court building.

Corporate Timeline: The Kenner Years

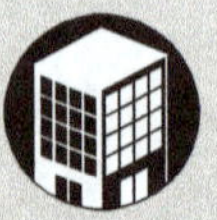 Kenner establishes a year-round showroom in the "Toy Center" building on 200 Fifth Avenue in New York City's Manhattan borough.

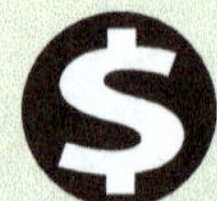 Kenner breaks the $100 million sales mark.

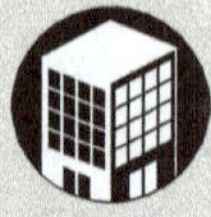 Kenner establishes manufacturing operations in Tijuana, Mexico.

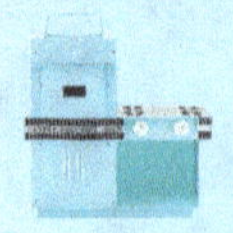 Kenner introduces the Easy-Bake Oven.

 Kenner is sold to General Mills.

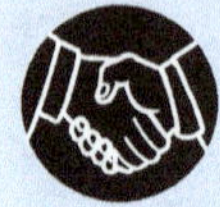 Kenner negotiates a license for Star Wars products, which becomes one of the company's most successful toy lines.

1946 1960 1963 1966 1967 1970 1975 1976 1977 1978 1983

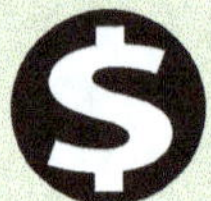 Kenner breaks the $25 million sales mark.

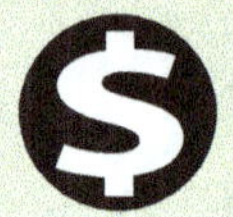 Kenner breaks $200 million in sales.

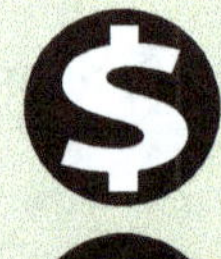 Kenner breaks the $1 million sales mark.

Kenner partners with Irwin Specialties, forming Kenner Products (Canada) Limited to distribute Kenner Products in Canada.

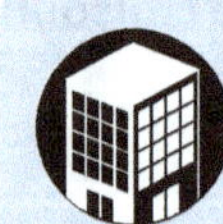 Kenner moves headquarters to 1014 Vine St., Cincinnati, Ohio.

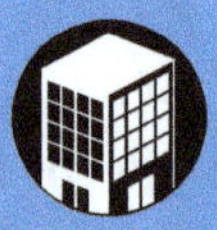 Kenner Products founded in Cincinnati, Ohio by brothers Albert, Phil, and Joseph Steiner.

 Rainbow Crafts is merged into Kenner Products and Play-Doh becomes part of the Kenner line.

Bernard Loomis is appointed president of Kenner.

 Kenner Parker Toys Inc., the country's fourth largest toy company, is spun off from General Mills.

 Albert Steiner is inducted into the Toy Industry Association Hall of Fame.

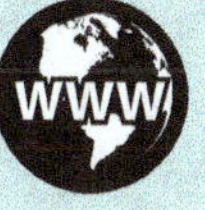 Kenner-branded products are featured on Hasbro's first website at hasbrotoys.com.

 Hasbro Purchases Tonka Corporation and makes Kenner a division of the largest toy company in the world.

1985 1986 1987 1988 1991 1992 1993 1994 1996 2000

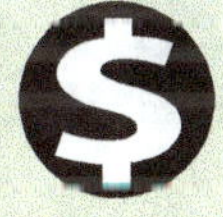 Kenner Parker Toys sales exceed $500 million.

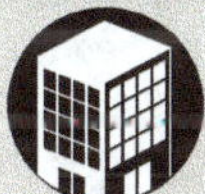 Kenner moves headquarters to 615 Elsinore Place, Cincinnati, Ohio.

 As part of a nationwide consolidation of its toy group, Hasbro pulls all operations from Cincinnati, ending 54 years of Kenner history in the city.

Kenner's legacy—and the Easy-Bake Oven product line—continue under the Hasbro brand.

 Tonka Corporation establishes four operating divisions: Kenner Products, Parker Brothers, and Tonka Products serving the U.S.; and Tonka International.

 Tonka Corporation acquires Kenner Parker Toys Inc.

 Hasbro restructures into two groups: Hasbro Toy Group (Kenner, Tonka, and Playskool), and Hasbro Game Group (Parker Brothers and Milton Bradley).

Canada Eh!

*I*t wasn't long before Kenner sought to market the popular Easy-Bake Oven in new international markets, such as Mexico and the United Kingdom. Canada also represented a significant enough opportunity for Kenner to pursue entry into the Great White North. But, before the age of comprehensive free-trade agreements, breaking into the Canadian marketplace was a daunting task for both large and small toy companies in the United States.

Canada was large but relatively sparsely populated, making it difficult to justify the marketing and development expenses required to gain a foothold there. Tariffs on imports served as a further disincentive. The only viable way for foreign companies to get their toys into Canada was to find a local distributor. Toronto, Ontario-based Irwin Toy saw an opportunity and seized it.

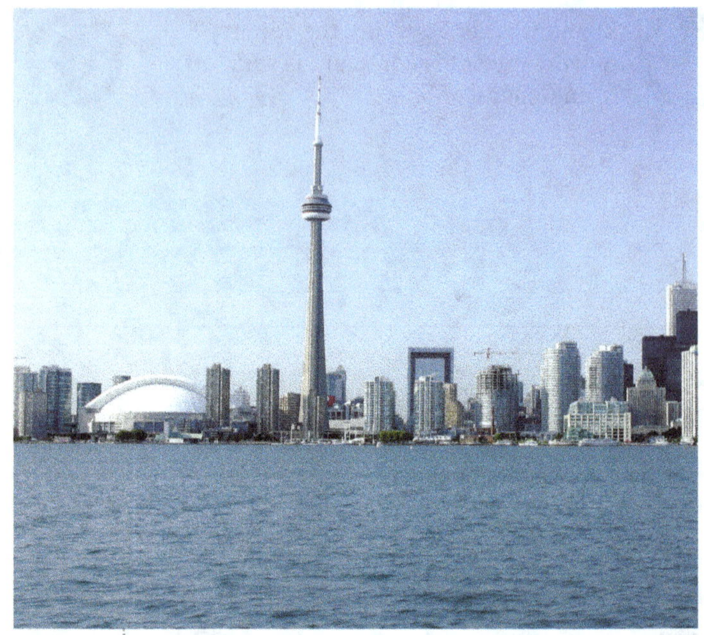

The headquarters of Kenner Products (Canada) Limited were located in Toronto, Canada.

Playtime in the North

Founded as a tourist and souvenirs specialties business, after 1958 Irwin began acting as a Canadian broker for a variety of American toy manufacturers. In 1969, the company changed its name to Irwin Toy Limited and an IPO soon followed. These developments, coupled with a series of shrewd business deals, elevated Irwin to a dominant position in the Canadian toy industry.

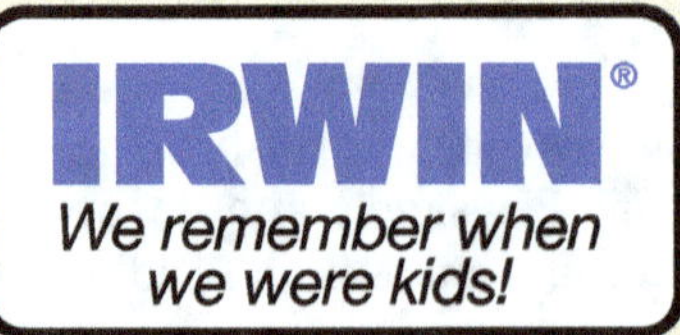

Did you know?

The Irwin Toy logo often appeared on packaging with the tagline, *"We remember when we were kids!"*

Irwin also formed jointly owned companies with several foreign toy makers. In one such partnership, Irwin Toy partnered with Kenner Toys in 1960 to own a 50% stake in the newly formed Kenner Products (Canada) Limited.

This new joint venture exposed Canadian children to some of Kenner's most popular toys, including Care Bears, Star Wars action figures, and the Easy-Bake Oven.

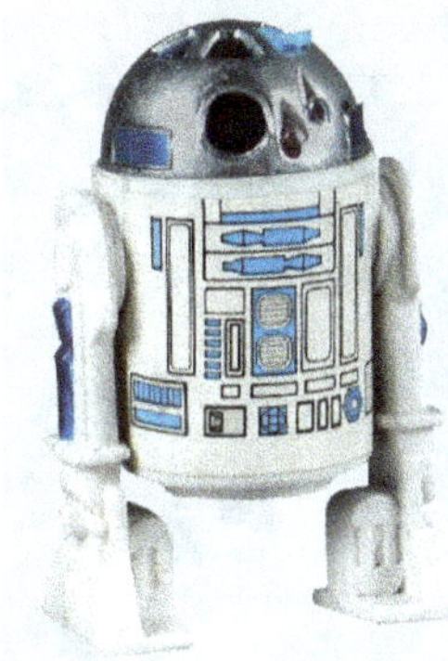

A Collector's Dream

Kenner Canada products are some of the most desirable for collectors today. The products were produced at much lower volumes than their United States counterparts and packaging and instructions were bilingual to support both of Canada's official languages (English and French). These characteristics, along with subtle production differences and naming conventions, make these vintage products more difficult to find—especially in the Star Wars universe.

Free Trade Fallout

In the late 1980s, Irwin Toy's stronghold in Canada began to erode. The Canada-United States Free Trade Agreement of 1988 and the Canada-United States-Mexico North American Free Trade Agreement of 1994 reduced tariffs and made it much less costly for American companies to form Canadian branches and take distribution in-house. Kenner Products (Canada) Limited was officially dissolved on January 1, 1987.

In April 2001, Irwin Toy was sold to a private investment group for $55 million. Just 18 months later, the company declared bankruptcy and went into liquidation after 76 years in business. The original factory on 43 Hannah Avenue—once the workplace of 350 employees—was sold and converted into loft condominiums.

In 2003, the Irwin Toy name, patents, and a part of its product line were re-purchased by two of the former owners, George and Peter Irwin, and re-launched under a new name: itoys inc.

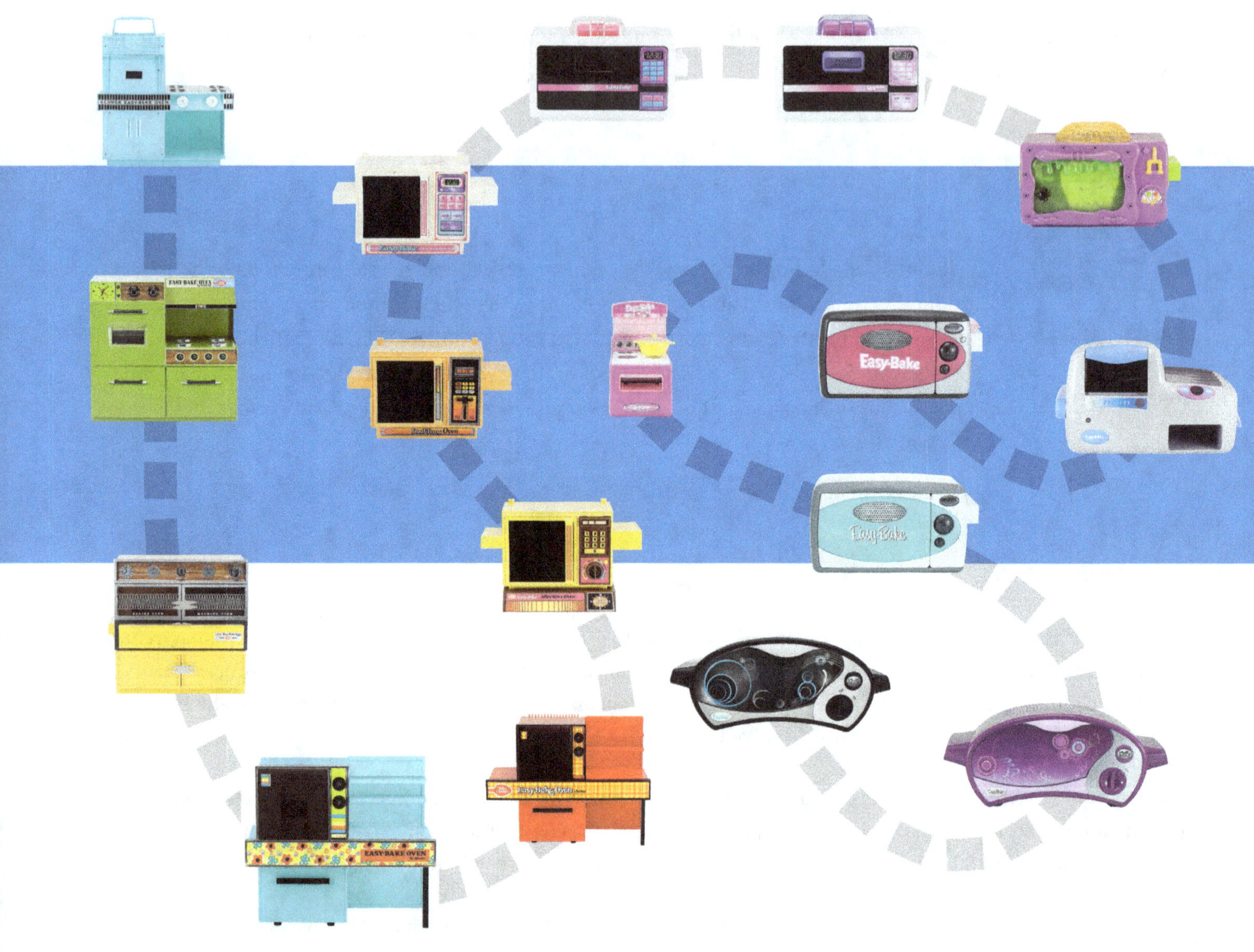

Chapter 4

A Visual History

> *"The most effective kind of education is that a child should play amongst lovely things."*
>
> — Plato

Since 1963, the Easy-Bake Oven has been through numerous model changes. Many of these reflect the color palettes and appliance styles of the time, while others are telling of larger changes, such as the integration of electronics into daily life, interest in gender neutrality, and increasing sensitivity to energy consumption.

While the design of the oven has constantly evolved, its popularity and durability as a pop culture icon has never waned. This chapter illustrates the story of a toy that has sold more than 30 million pieces over its 50 years.

Original retail prices for each model are provided for context, even though many stores sold the Easy-Bake at a discounted rate, especially during the peak buying period leading up to the Christmas season.

50 Years in Color

It's interesting to observe how the Easy-Bake Oven's color palette has evolved over 50 years. From the 1960s to the 1980s, Easy-Bake Ovens were generally designed to reflect popular kitchen appliance colors of the time.

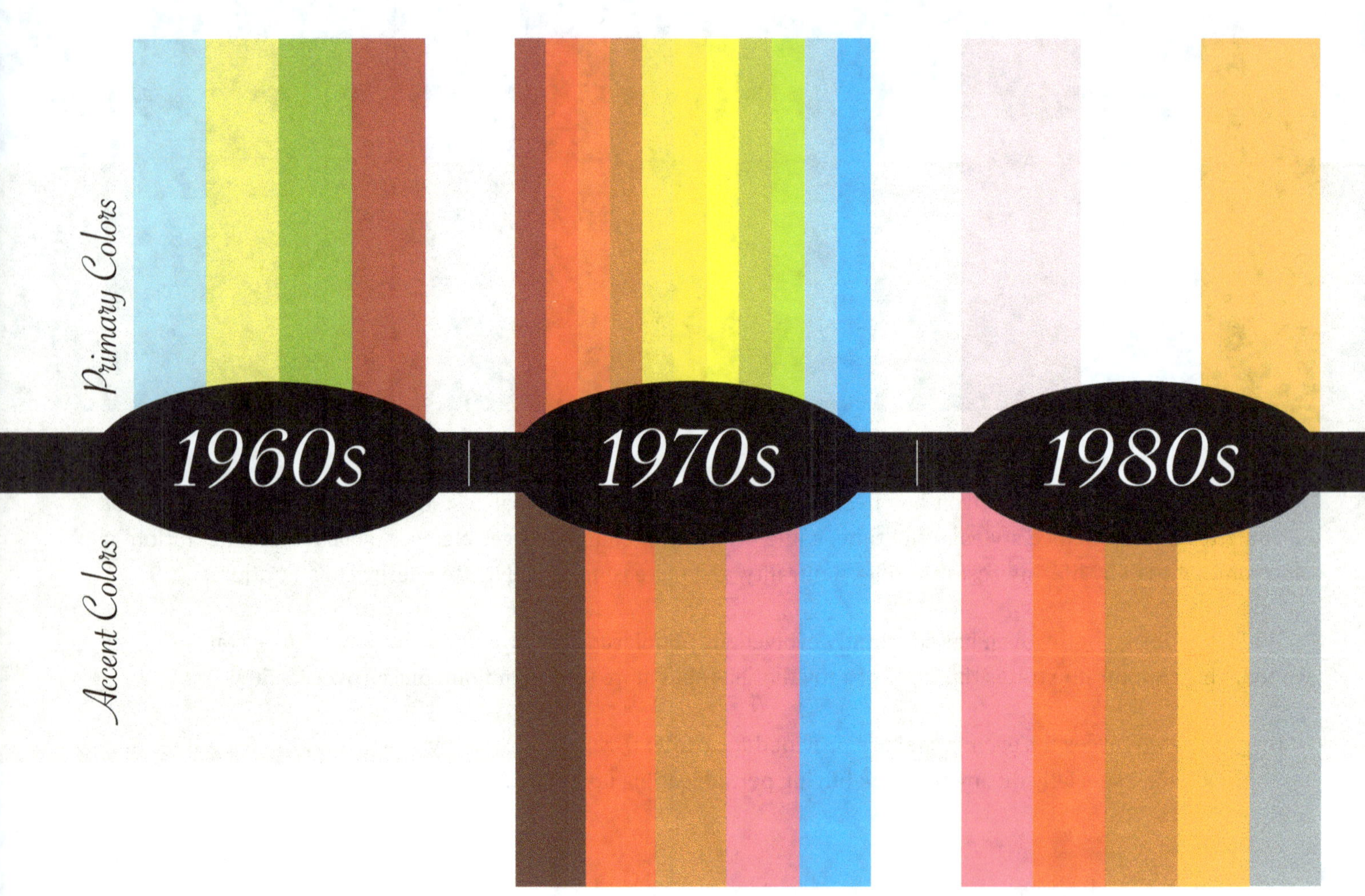

But starting in the 1990s, the oven's palette became distinct from a "real" kitchen and instead began to reflect color trends that could be seen in other contemporary toys—and particularly (but not exclusively) girls' toys.

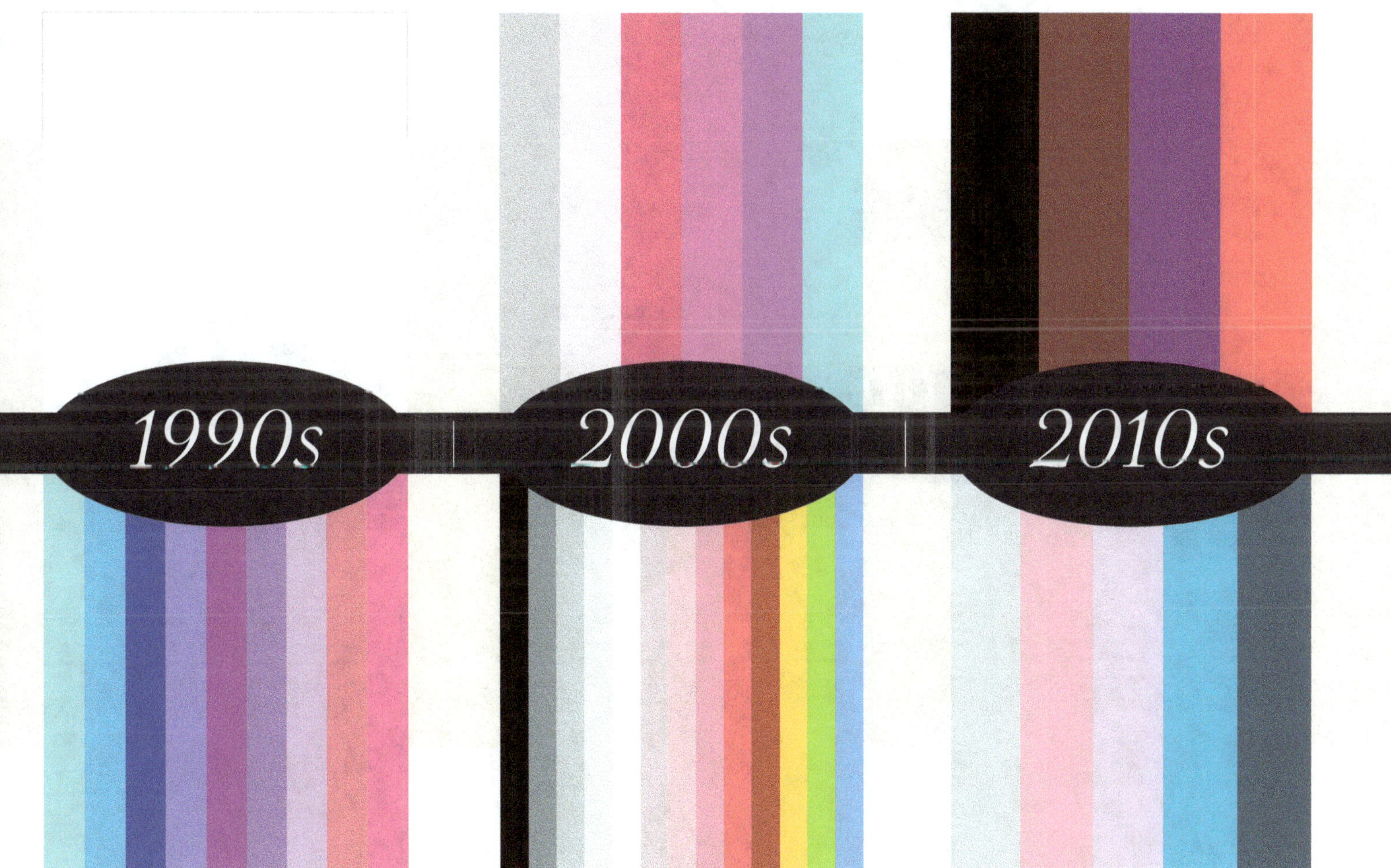

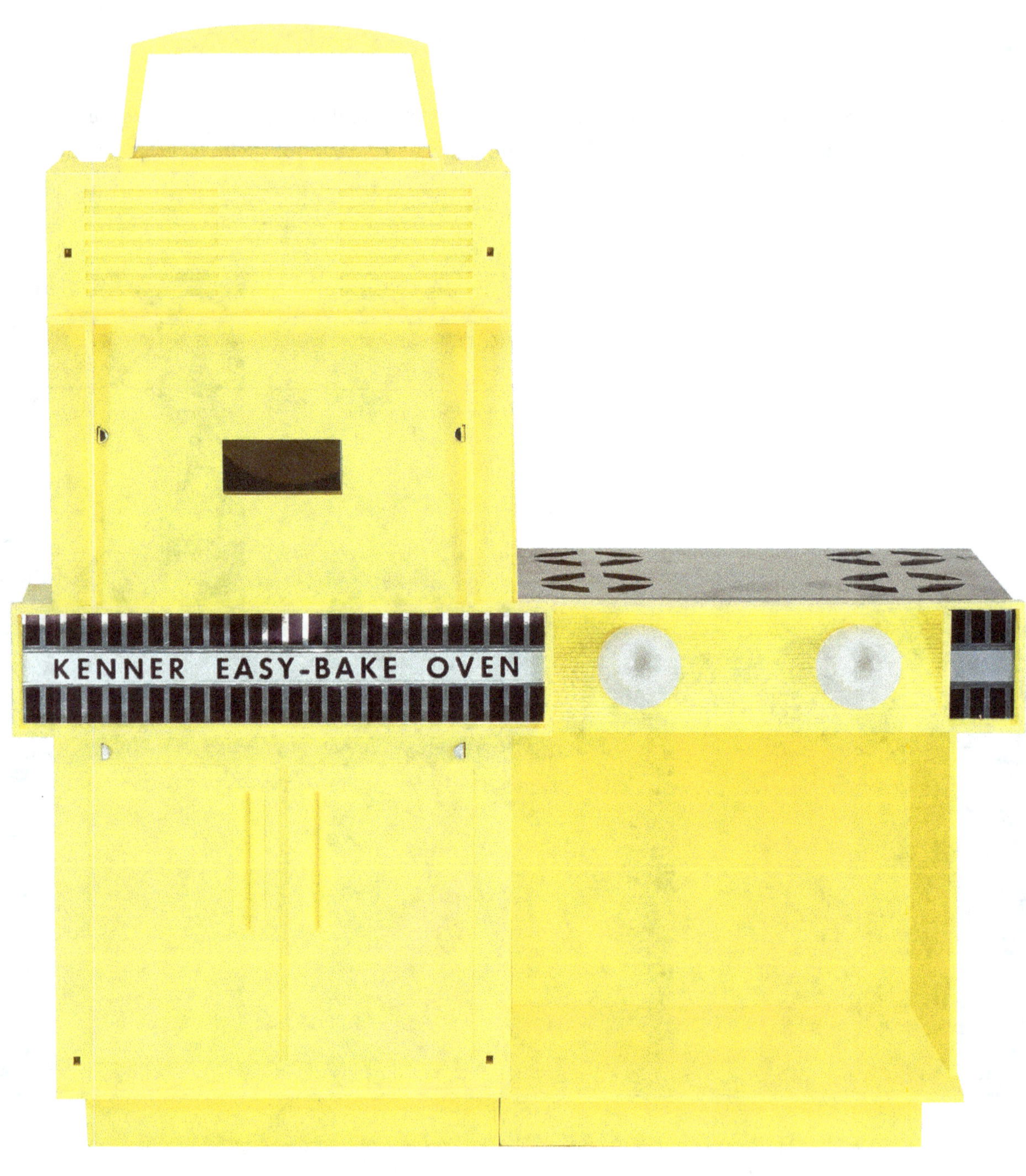
KENNER EASY-BAKE OVEN

Kenner Easy-Bake Oven

The original Easy-Bake Oven came in turquoise and bright yellow and quickly became an instant hit for Kenner, selling out over the 1963 Christmas holiday and causing the company to triple production in 1964.

The oven was powered by two 100-Watt light bulbs that were housed in an enclosed baking chamber with a vent at the top. A small "watch it bake" window was cut into the front of the oven.

Did you know?

The original Easy-Bake Oven hit store shelves on November 4, 1963 and was an instant hit.

Original retail price: **$15.95**

Powered by: **2x** 100W light bulbs

Available in *Yellow*

Available in *Turquoise*

In the box:

- 12 mixes
- 3 baking pans
- Bowl
- Spatula
- Rolling pin
- Teaspoon
- Cookbook

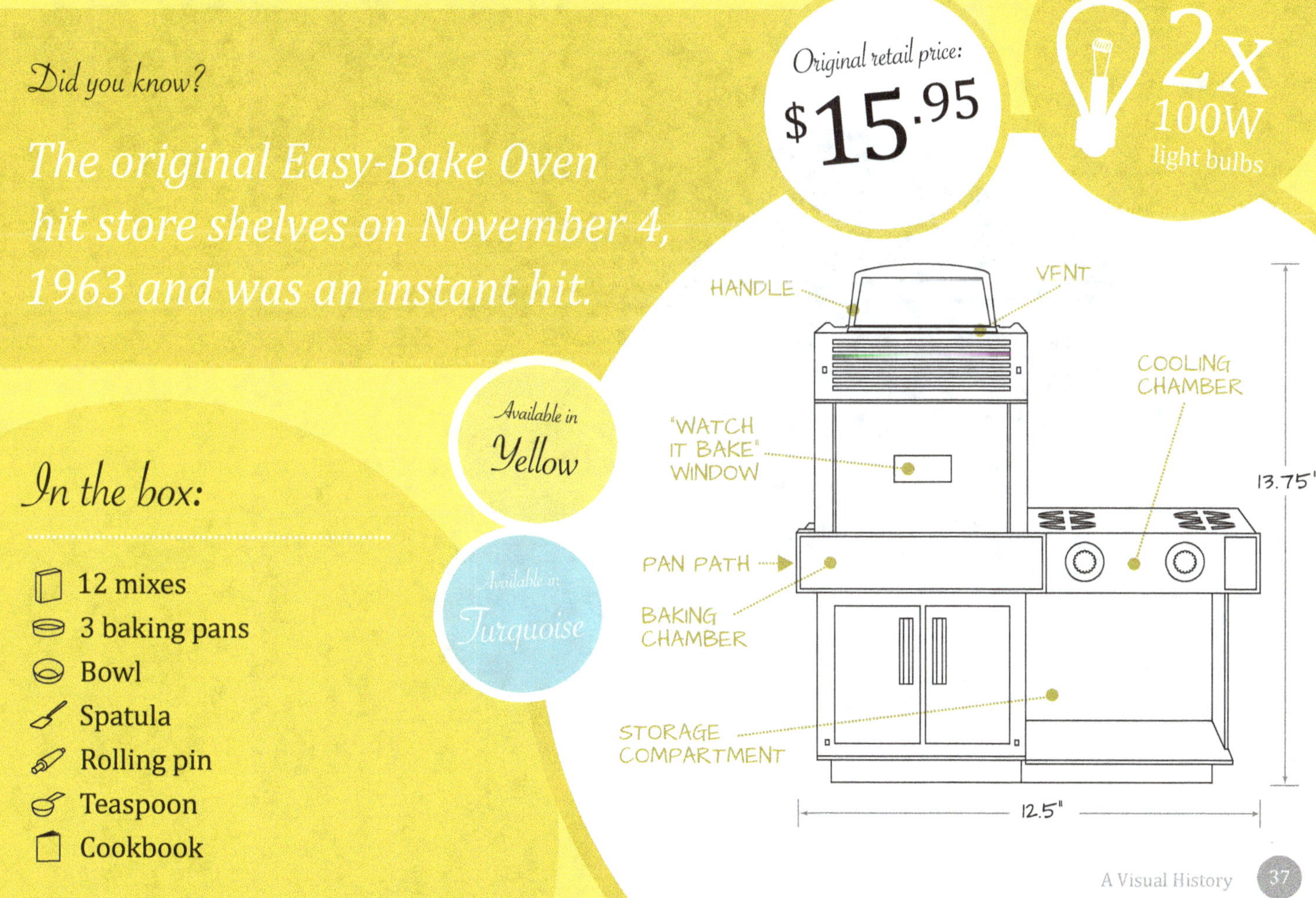

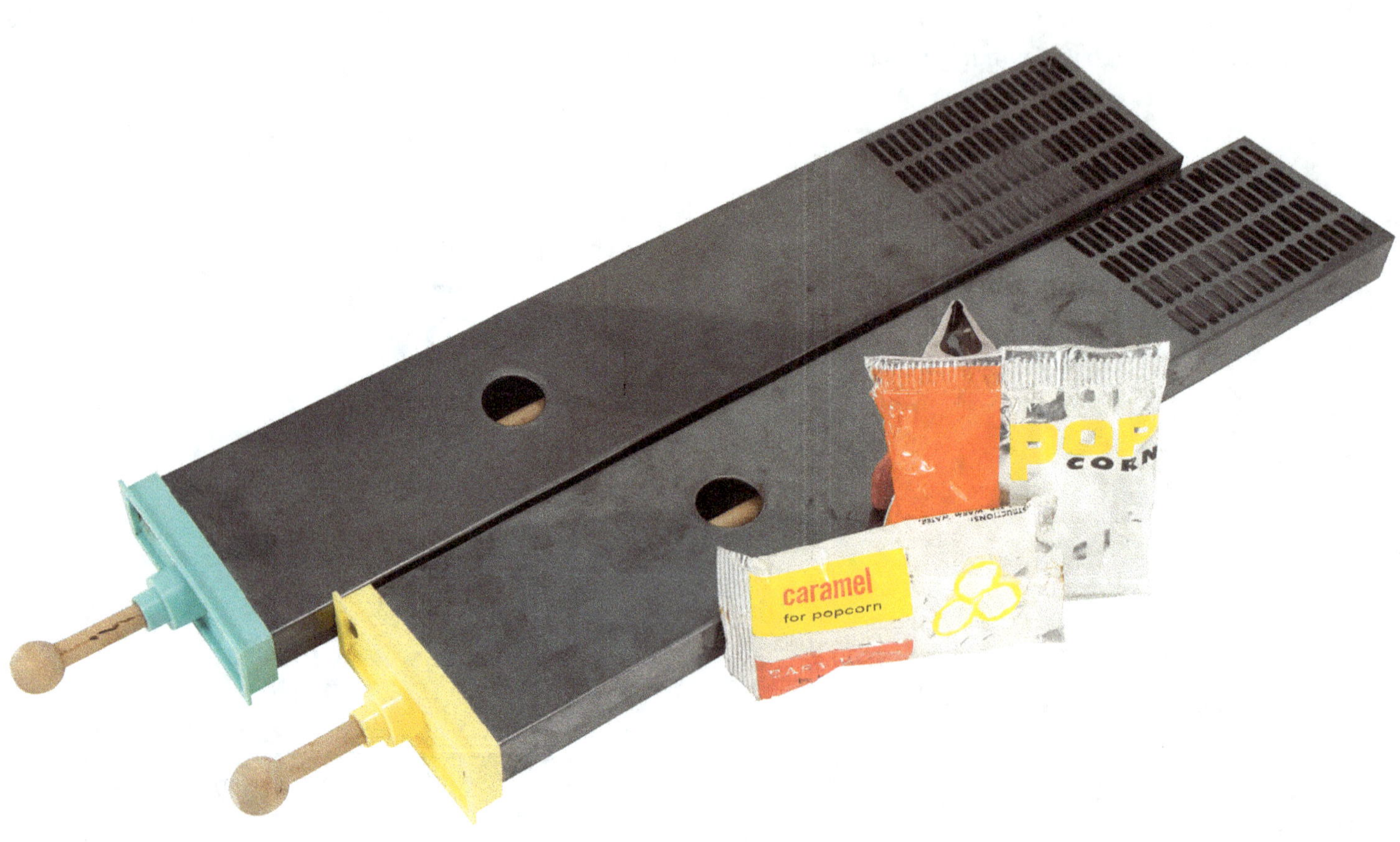

POP
CORN
caramel
for popcorn

Easy-Pop Corn Popper

The Easy-Pop Corn Popper came in two colors to match the Easy-Bake Oven during this time period: yellow or turquoise.

The popper slipped inside the oven and popcorn was added through a hole in the top of the Easy-Pop. The whole apparatus was then pushed inside the oven via its wooden handle. Pulling back the knob automatically emptied the corn through a much larger hole in the bottom, depositing it into a bowl below. Popcorn was ready in about four minutes.

Did you know?

The Easy-Pop Corn Popper was one of the first attempts by Kenner to widen the appeal of the Easy-Bake to boys.

Original retail price:

$3.98

Powered by:

In the box:

- 2 bags of popcorn
- Caramel syrup mix
- Recipe sheet

Available in **Yellow**

Available in **Turquoise**

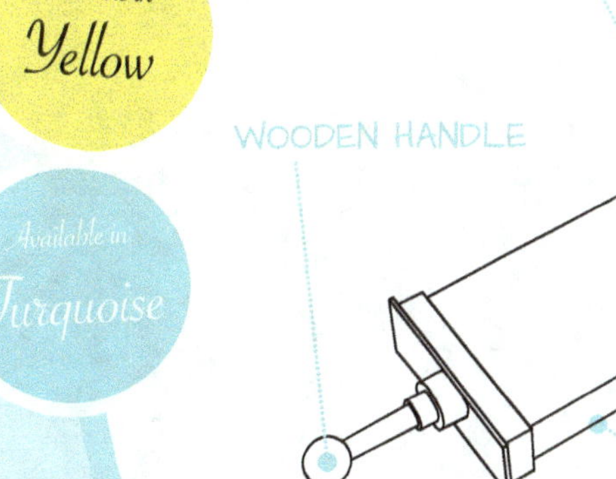

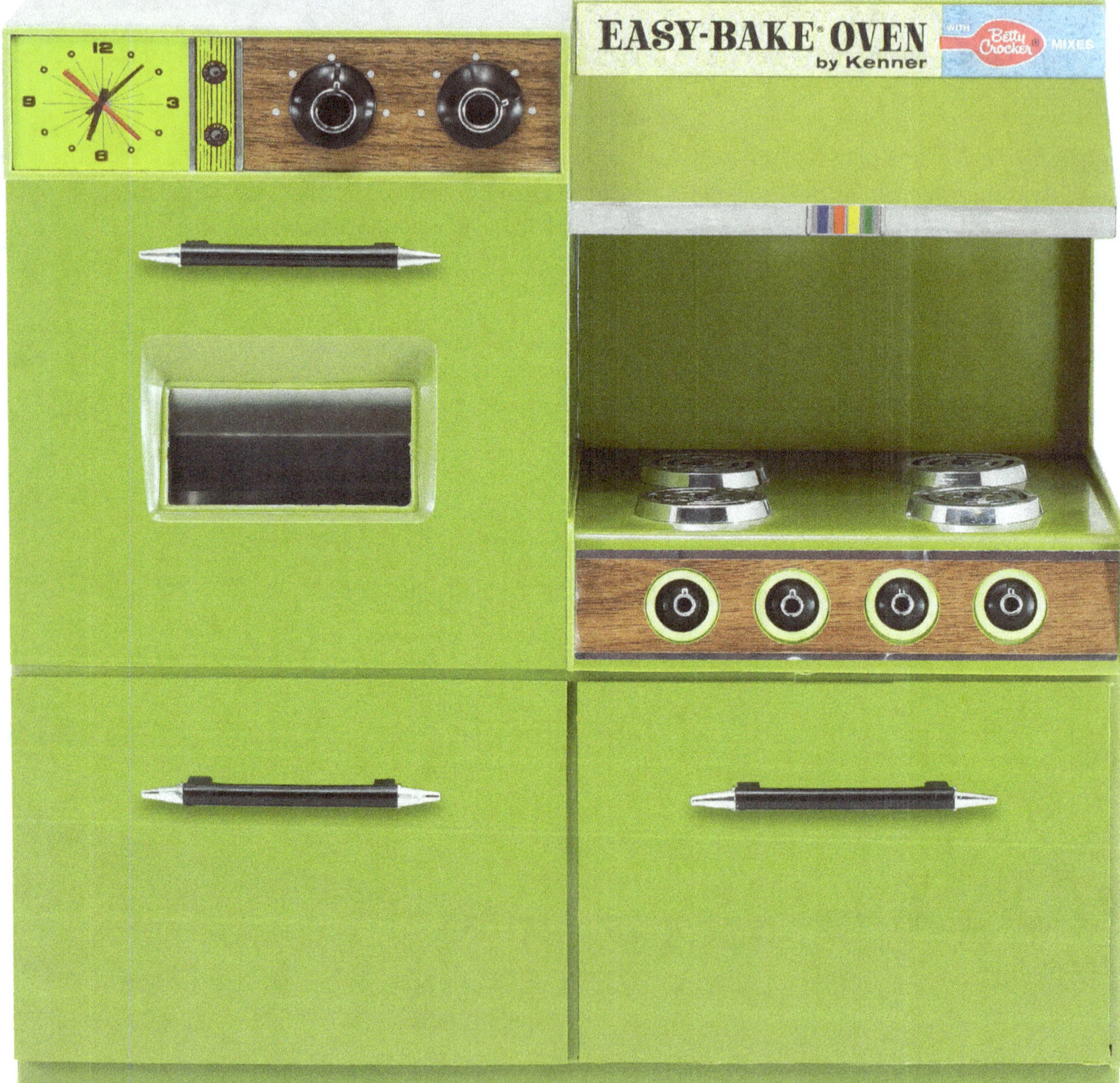

EASY-BAKE® OVEN
by Kenner
WITH Betty Crocker® MIXES
12
3
6
9

Betty Crocker Easy-Bake Oven

Soon after General Mills purchased Kenner in 1967, the parent company began shipping miniature, boxed versions of Betty Crocker products for the Easy-Bake Oven.

A new Betty Crocker-branded oven was also introduced. Avocado green and deep red joined turquoise as hip color choices, reflecting popular style trends of the day. This new Premiere Model also sported additional dials, a faux clock, Partridge-Family-inspired stick-on wood-grain panels, chrome accents, and an oven hood.

Betty Crocker coupons were included with each oven, reflecting their popularity. In fact, one in three households in the United States was clipping them at the time.

Original retail price:
$19.99

Powered by:
2x
100W
light bulbs

Sales to date:

4 million ovens
67 million mixes

Available in
Avocado Green

Available in
Turquoise

Available in
Deep Red

Faux-Color
Wood Grain

In the box:

- 5 Betty Crocker mixes
- 3 baking pans
- Bowl
- Spoon
- Betty Crocker cookbook
- Betty Crocker coupons

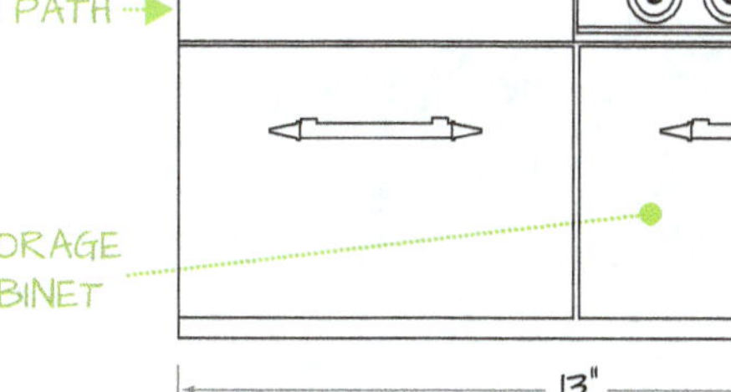

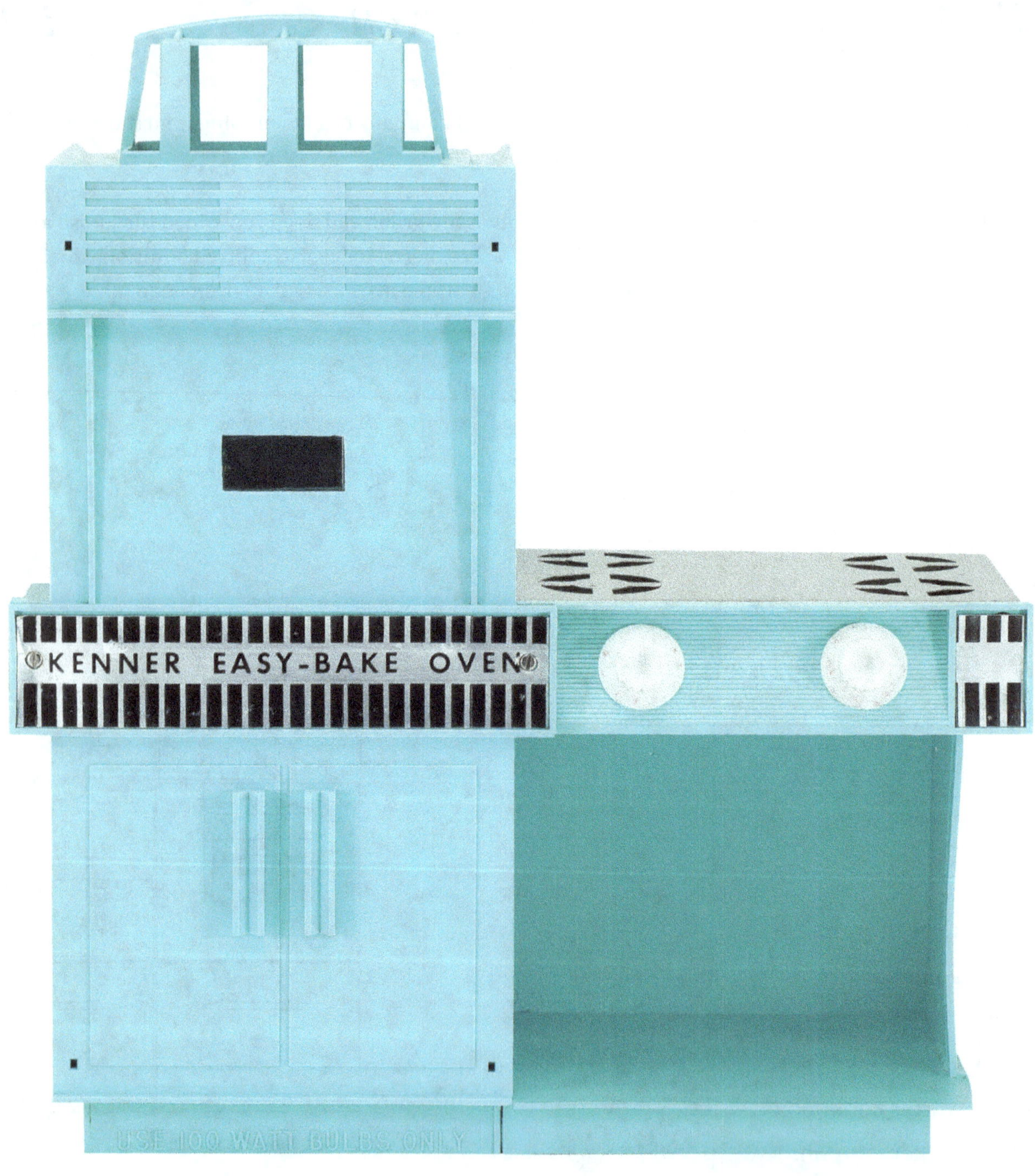

KENNER EASY-BAKE OVEN
USE 100 WATT BULBS ONLY

Kenner *Easy-Bake Oven*

In 1969, Kenner made a minor design update to the first Easy-Bake Oven. The original handle was swapped out for a new version that further shielded the vent at the top of the oven—making it more difficult for small fingers to touch it while the toy was in operation.

The oven continued to be powered by two 100-Watt light bulbs housed in an enclosed baking chamber.

Did you know?

The original Easy-Bake Oven mixes had a two-year shelf life.

Original retail price:
$15.95

Powered by:
2x 100W *light bulbs*

Available in **Yellow**

Available in **Turquoise**

In the box:

- 12 mixes
- 3 baking pans
- Bowl
- Spatula
- Rolling pin
- Teaspoon
- Cookbook

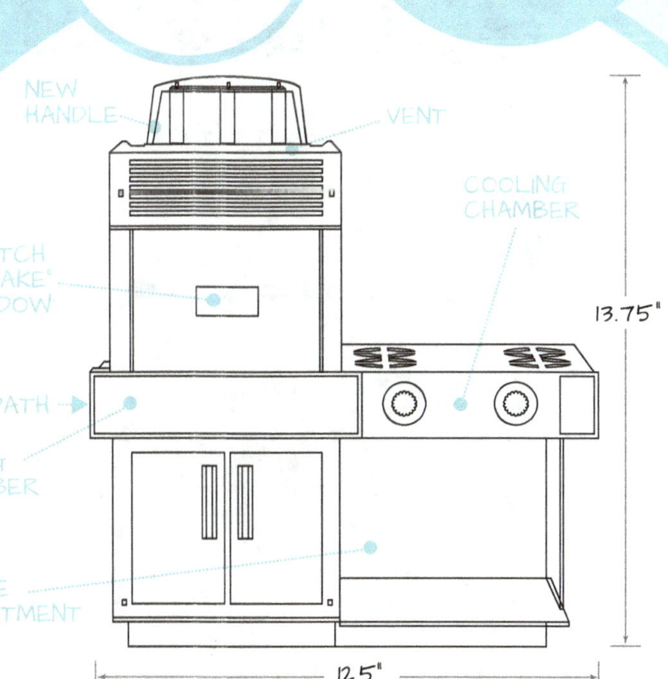

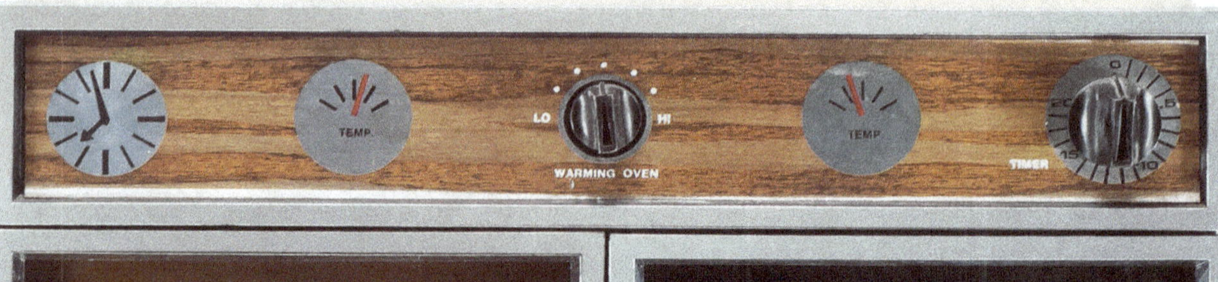

TEMP.
LO   HI
WARMING OVEN
BAKING OVEN

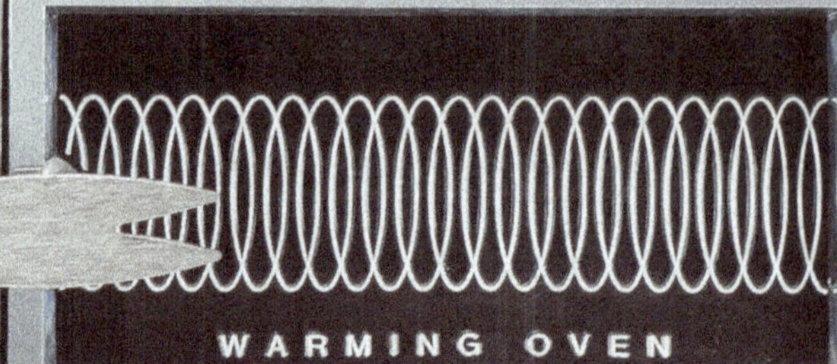

TEMP.
TIMER
WARMING OVEN

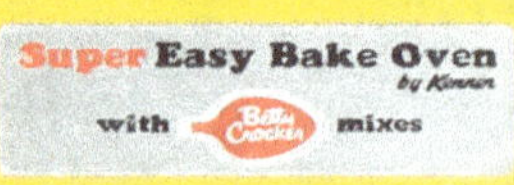

Super Easy Bake Oven
by Kenner
with Betty Crocker mixes

Super Easy-Bake Oven

The 1970s iconic harvest gold color was introduced into the product line with the Super Easy-Bake Oven. Advertised as "two ovens in one", it was packaged with eight Betty Crocker mixes and two different pan sizes. New double-sized pans baked cakes twice as large as before.

A working 20-minute timer was complemented by a built-in warming oven that was controlled via a functional temperature control knob. An enclosed storage cabinet was provided to store extra pans and accessories. The black "Magi-Glas" viewing window was also super-sized, allowing kids to see into the oven when both 100-Watt light bulbs were on.

Original retail price:
$24.95

Powered by:
2x
100W
light bulbs

Did you know?
The Super Easy-Bake Oven came packaged with 55 Betty Crocker coupons.

In the box:

- 8 Betty Crocker mixes
- 4 baking pans (2 large, 2 regular)
- Mixing bowl
- Spatula
- Cookbook
- Betty Crocker coupons

Available in
Harvest Gold

Trim Color
Wood Grain

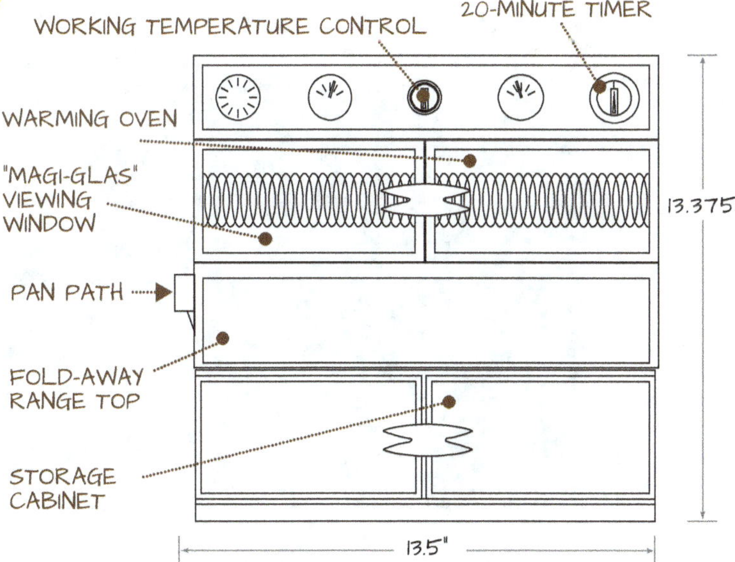

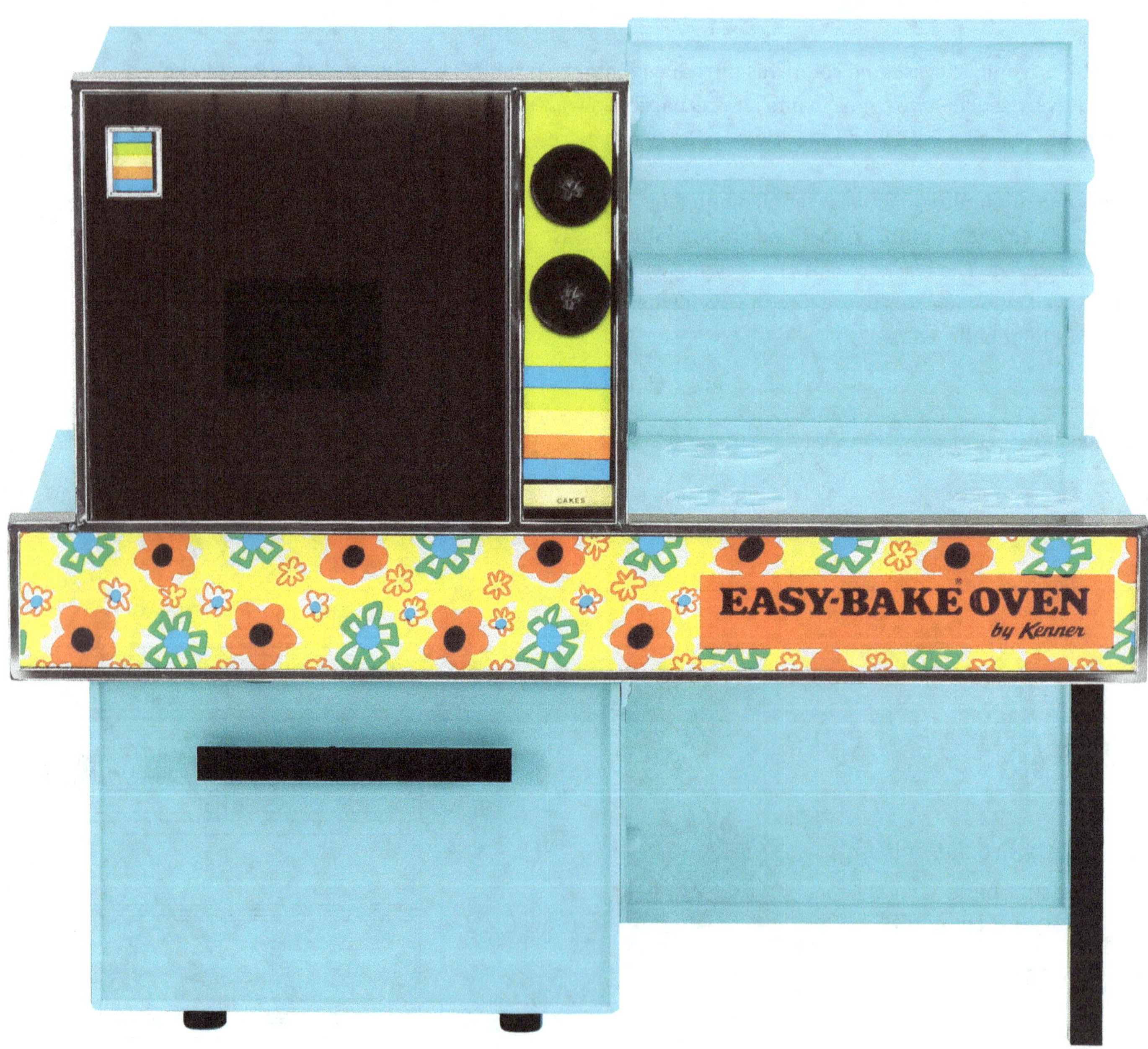

CAKES
EASY-BAKE® OVEN
by Kenner

Contemporary Easy-Bake Oven

1971

The Contemporary Easy-Bake Oven is an homage to the '70s. Advertised as combining "...the 'right-on styling' and 'right now' features that little girls (and their mothers) want...", the oven came in a variety of colors, including sunshine yellow, lime green, sky blue, and burnt orange. Complementary flower decals completed the design.

Additional features included a revamped "Magi-Glas" viewing window and a timing guide that could be used to find recommended baking times for cakes, pies, cookies, and brownies.

This was also the first model to bake with cooler 60-Watt bulbs.

Original retail price:

$**15**.99

Powered by:

2X 60W *light bulbs*

Sales to date:

5 million ovens
80 million mixes

In the box:

- 3 baking pans
- 3 mixes
- Cookbook

Available in
Sunshine Yellow

Available in
Lime Green

Available in
Sky Blue

Available in
Burnt Orange

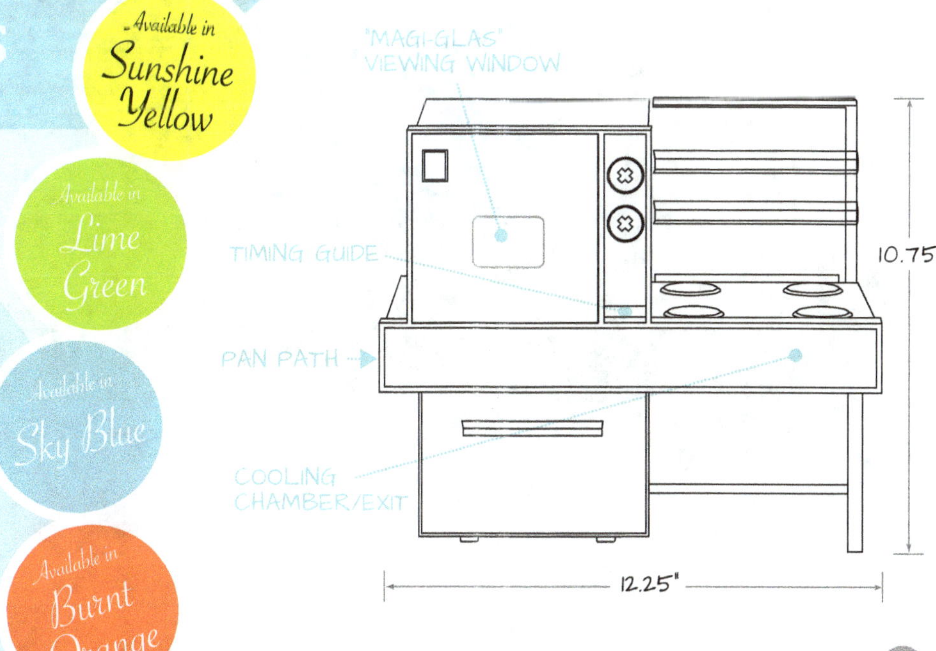

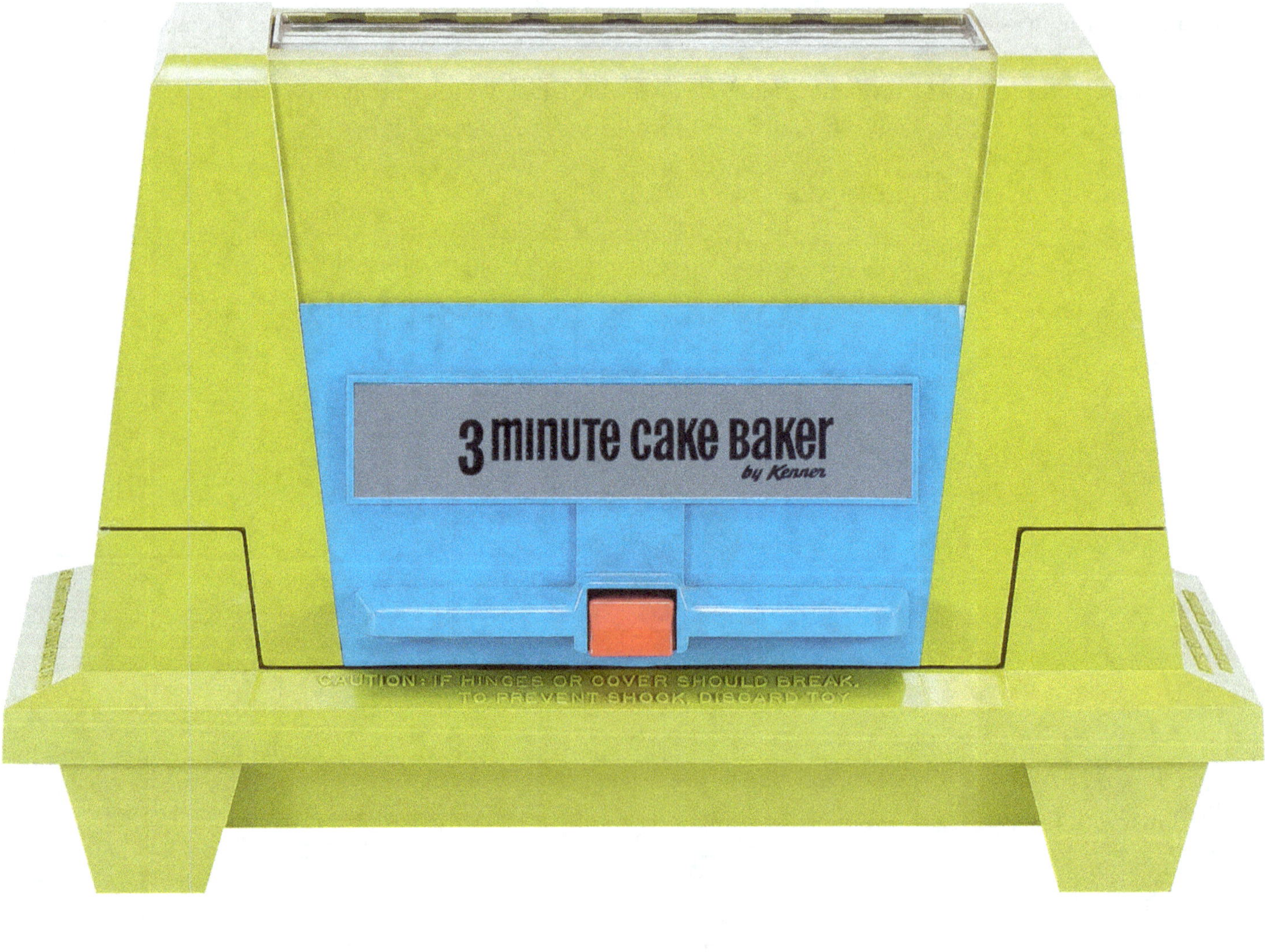

3 minute cake baker
by Kenner
CAUTION: IF HINGES OR COVER SHOULD BREAK,
TO PREVENT SHOCK, DISCARD TOY

3 Minute Cake Baker

With the appearance of a toaster with a flip-up lid, the 3 Minute Cake Baker was the first attempt by Kenner to broaden the appeal of baking to a younger demographic than the Easy-Bake Oven's recommended "8 years+".

The 3 Minute Cake Baker used no light bulbs or heating coil, relying instead on heat generated from the special stainless-steel baking tray to evaporate moisture from the batter. It literally baked a cake in three minutes—a process that Kenner referred to in its marketing material as "revolutionary" and "miraculous".

Original retail price:
$10.99

Powered by:
AC POWER

Did you know?

The 3 Minute Cake Baker was marketed to children aged 4 years and older.

In the box:

- Baking tray
- 10 Betty Crocker mixes
- Timer
- Mixing bowl
- Measuring spoon
- Betty Crocker coupons

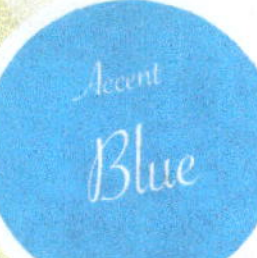

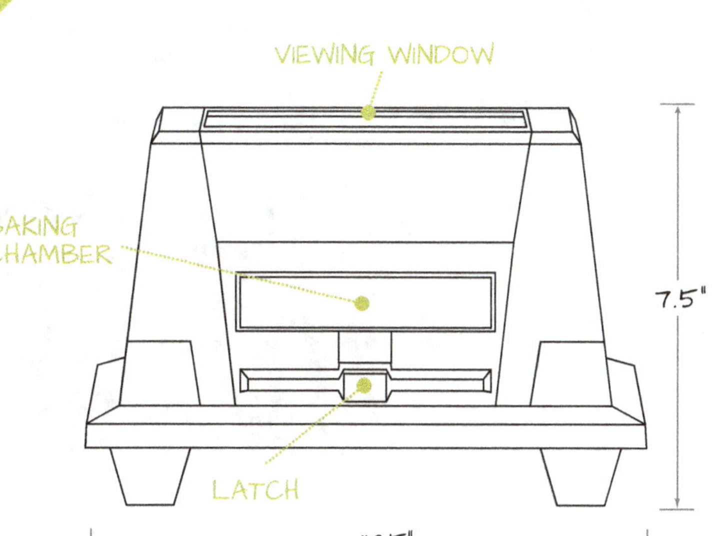

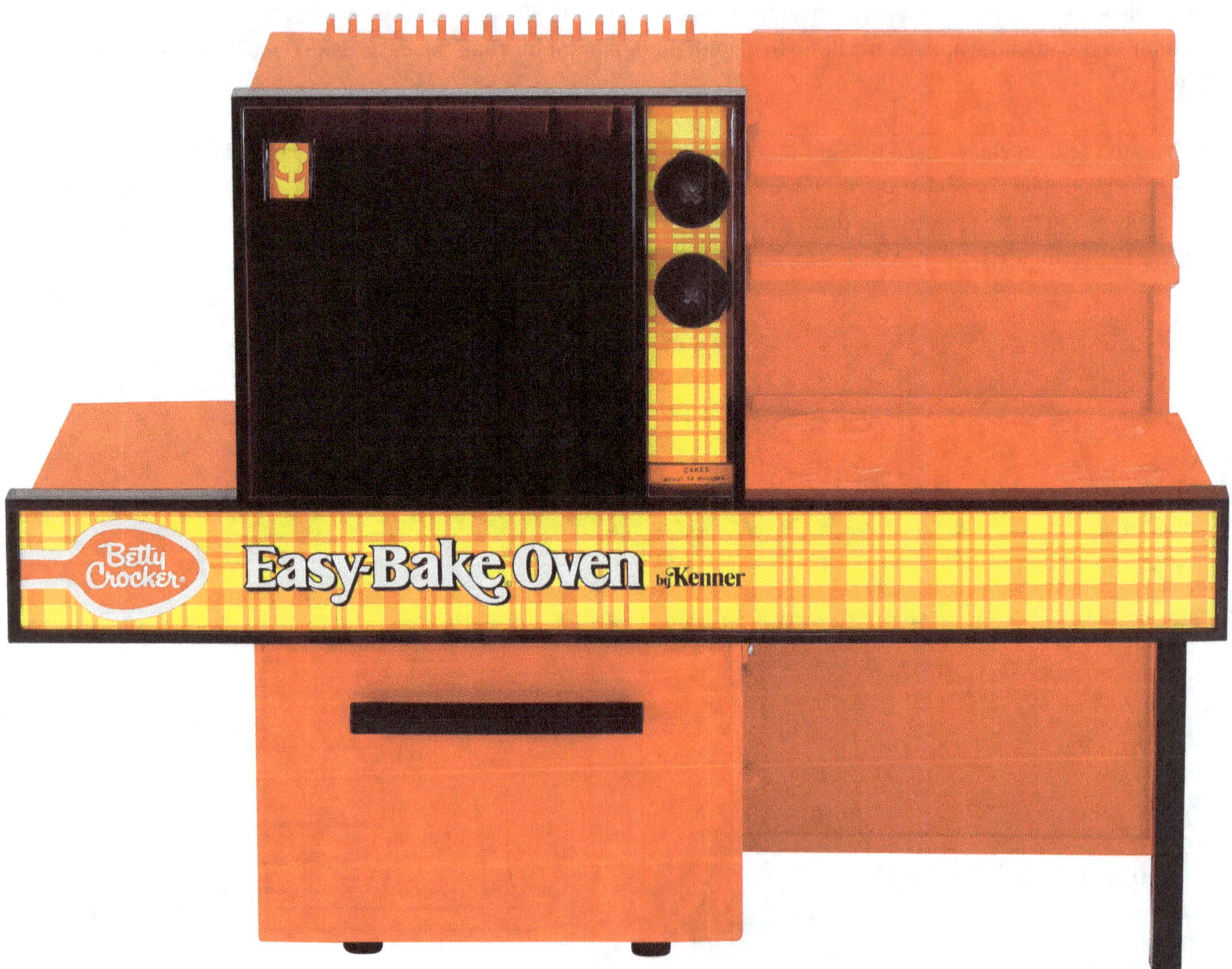

CAKES
about 14 minutes
Betty Crocker
Easy-Bake Oven by Kenner

Betty Crocker Easy-Bake Oven

For the 10th anniversary of the Easy-Bake Oven, the 1971 Contemporary model was officially re-branded the Betty Crocker Easy-Bake Oven. A new color was also added to the mix: poppy red. Flower decals were replaced with "Scotch-Plaid" decals.

This model introduced a new safety feature: the pan pusher. This hard plastic tool allowed amateur bakers to slide their creations in and out of the oven more easily (and more safely) than before.

The footprint of the oven was altered to accommodate the pusher tool, extending it by two inches in width.

Did you know?

With more than 5 million ovens sold, Kenner estimated that the Easy-Bake Oven had provided at least 19 million hours of baking fun.

In the box:

- 3 baking pans
- 3 Betty Crocker mixes
- Pan pusher
- Betty Crocker coupons
- Cookbook

Original retail price:
$19.99

Powered by:
2x 60W light bulbs

Available in
Poppy Red

Available in
Lime Green

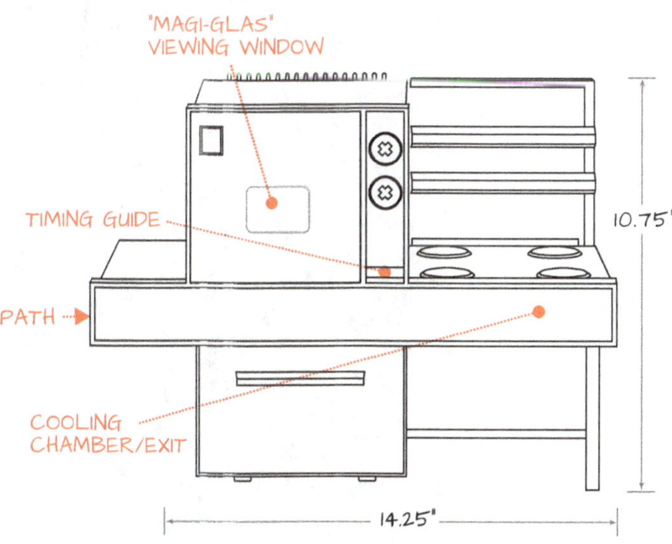

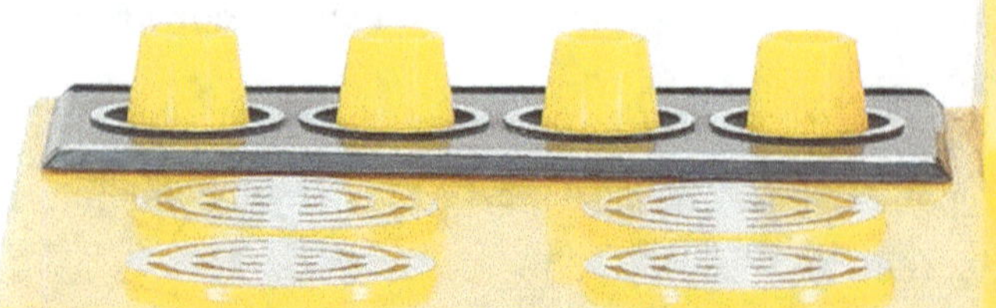
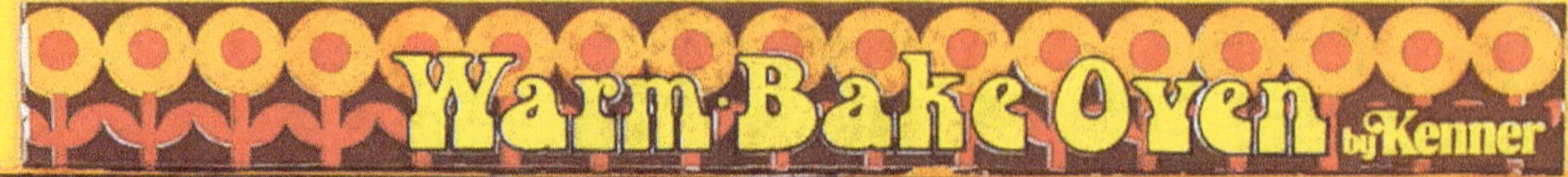

Warm·Bake Oven
by Kenner

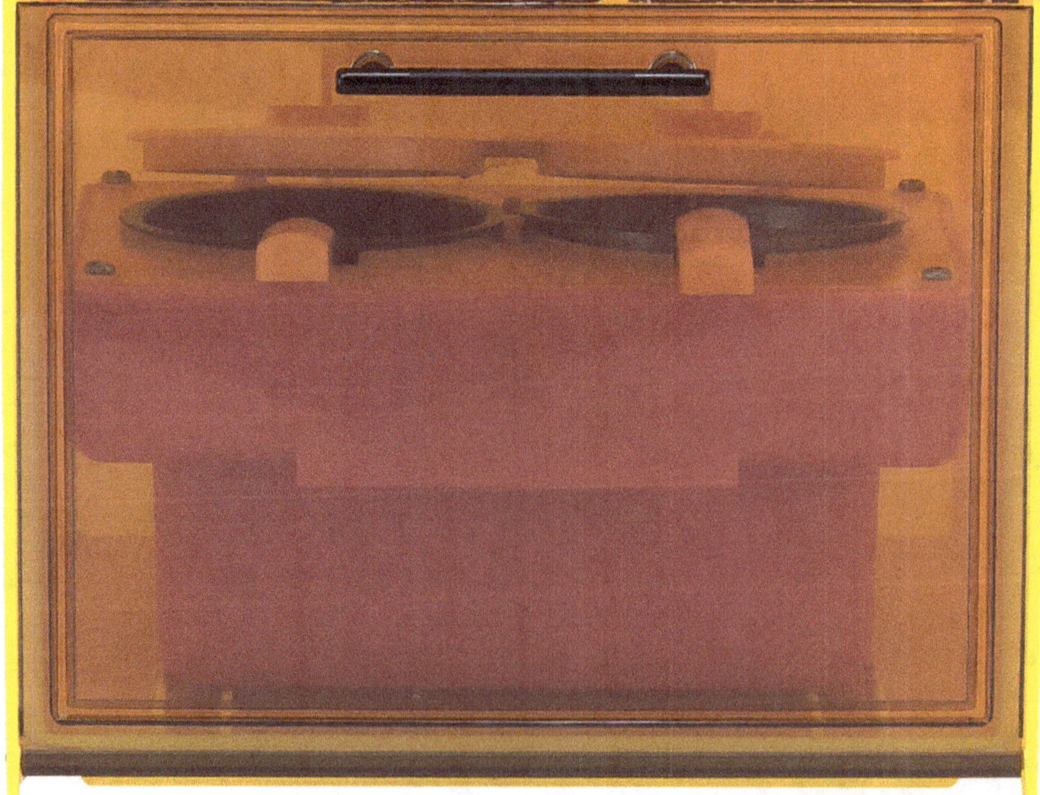

Warm-Bake Oven

Replacing the 3 Minute Cake Baker, the Warm-Bake Oven was Kenner's second attempt to appeal to a younger set of bakers (ages four and up) and their safety-conscious parents.

The oven used specially formulated mixes that, when placed in round metal baking pans and inserted into a reservoir filled with hot water, caused the batter to rise and bake in a short period of time.

After its introduction in 1973, the Warm-Bake Oven remained on the market for three years.

Original retail price:
$8.99

Powered by:
Hot water

Did you know?

The Warm Bake Oven replaced the 3 Minute Cake Baker for children ages 4+.

In the box:

- 2 baking pans
- 2 mixing bowls
- Spatula
- Measuring cups
- 10 Warm-Bake mixes
- Cookbook

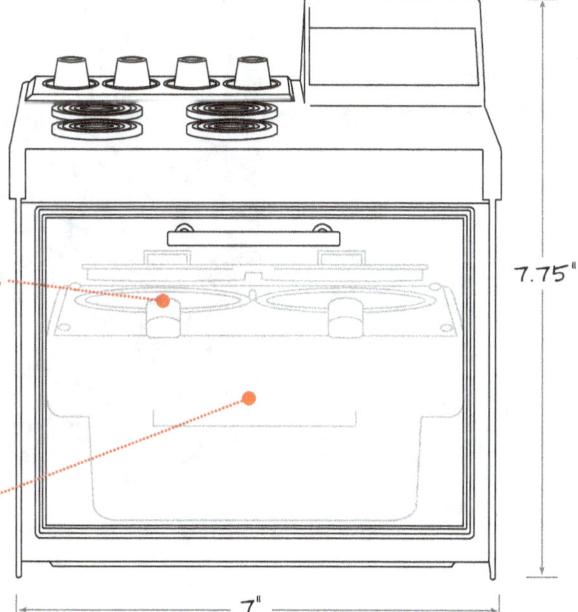

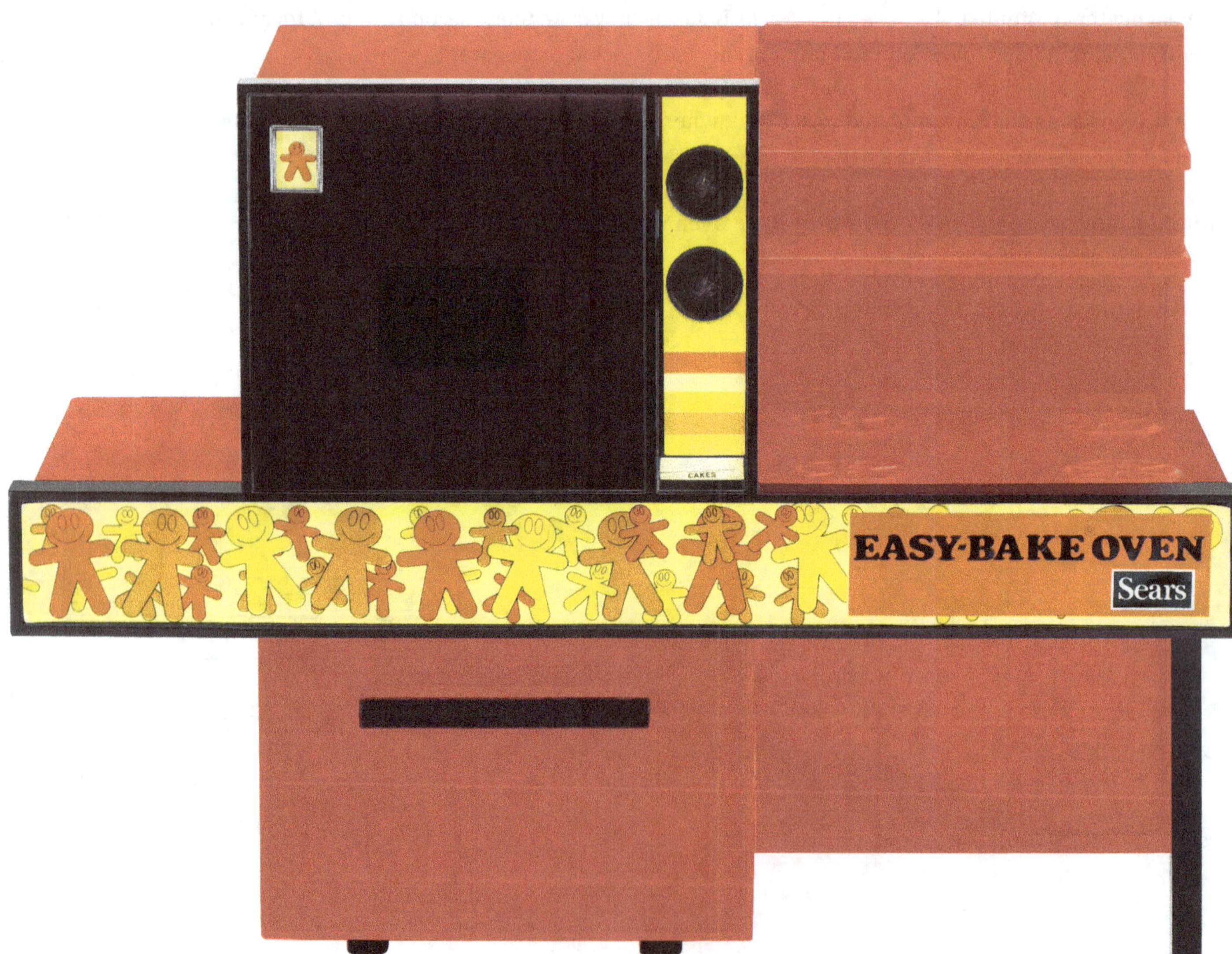

CAKES
EASY-BAKE OVEN
Sears

Easy-Bake Oven – Sears, Roebuck and Co. 1974

This Easy-Bake Oven was sold exclusively through Sears, Roebuck and Co. stores and catalogs. A re-branded version of the Betty Crocker Easy-Bake Oven, it featured a darker color scheme and different sticker set.

The *Sears Wishbook* featured the Easy-Bake Oven alongside several competing toy ovens, including the Magic-Cool Electric Oven, the Funtime Oven, and the Kenmore Microwave Electric Bake Oven.

Did you know?

This oven was sold exclusively at Sears, Roebuck & Co.

Original retail price:

$19.99

Powered by:

2x 60W light bulbs

Available in

Deep Red

In the box:

- 3 baking pans
- 3 mixes
- Pan pusher
- Cookbook

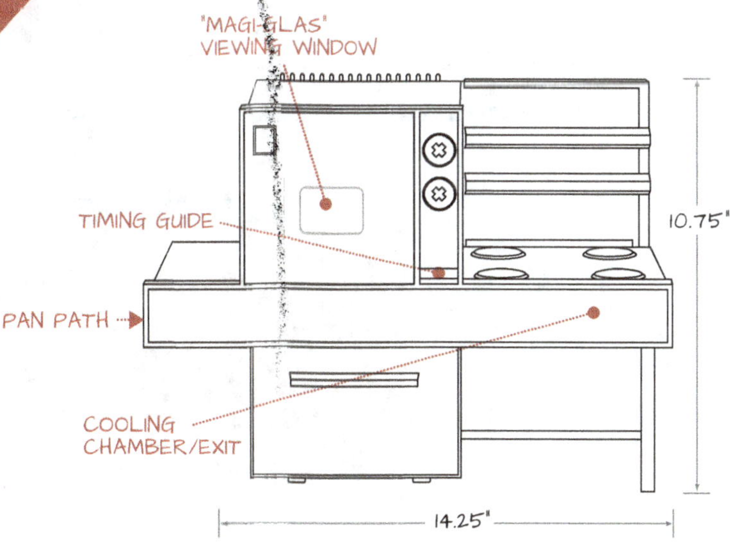

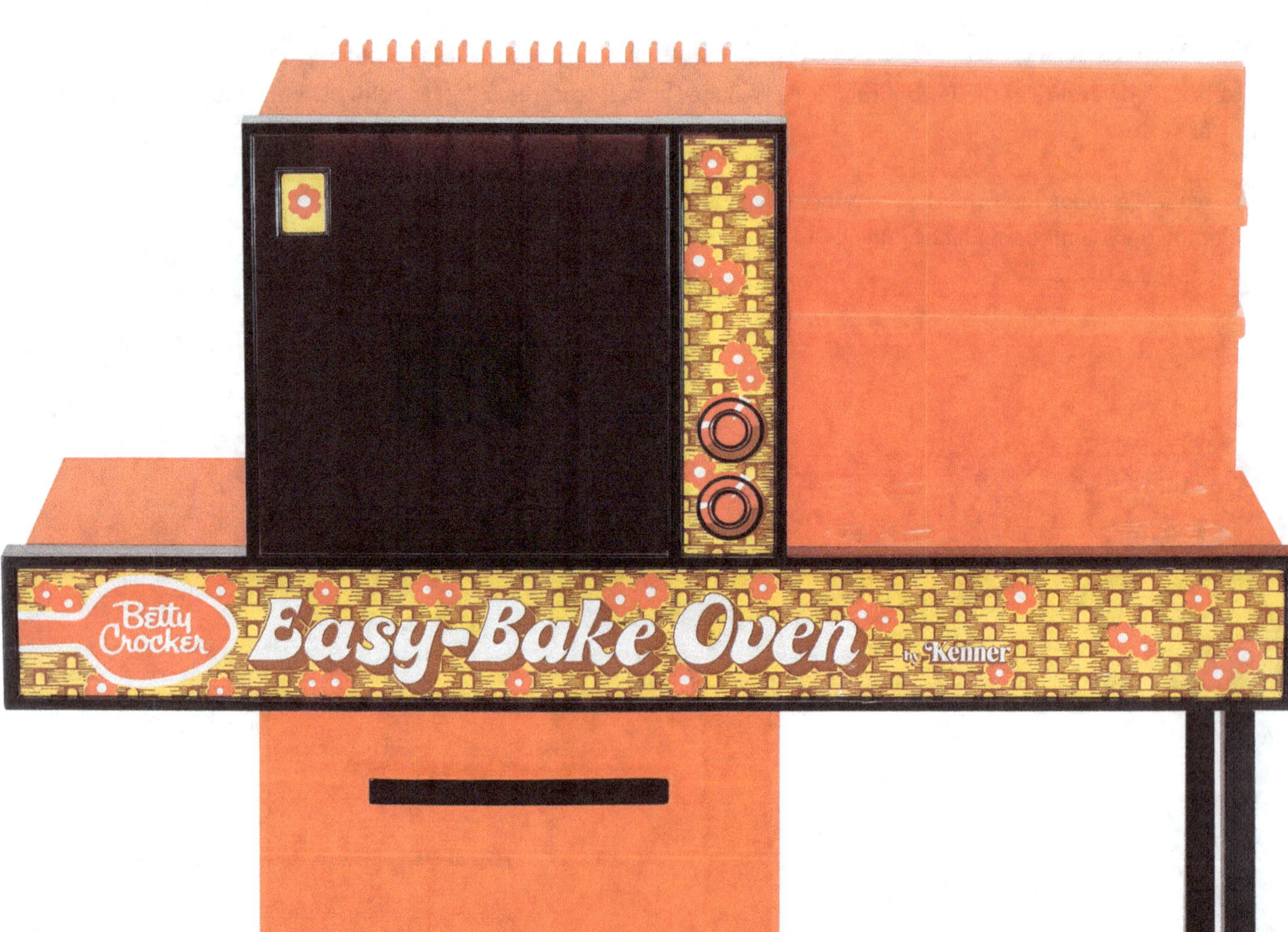

Betty Crocker
Easy-Bake Oven
by Kenner

Betty Crocker Easy-Bake Oven

In its 13th year, the Easy-Bake Oven received a new streamlined design. The timing guide and knobs were replaced with a set of flowery accent stickers that complemented the toy's poppy red color and mimicked ratan home accents.

Kenner launched a series of new food options for the Easy-Bake Oven at this time: the Easy-Bake Potato Chip Maker and the Easy-Bake Pizza Maker.

Did you know?

This oven was advertised as "A Little Girl's First Real Oven."

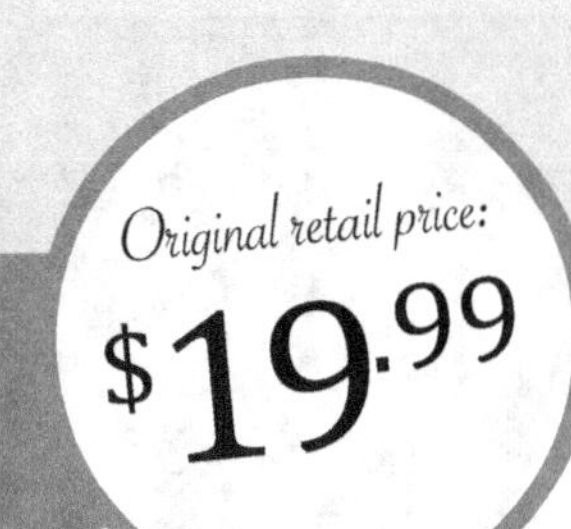

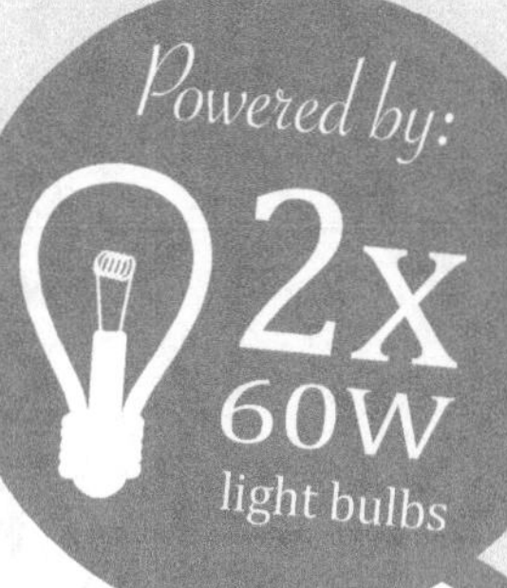

In the box:

- 3 baking pans
- 3 Betty Crocker mixes
- Pan pusher
- Cookbook

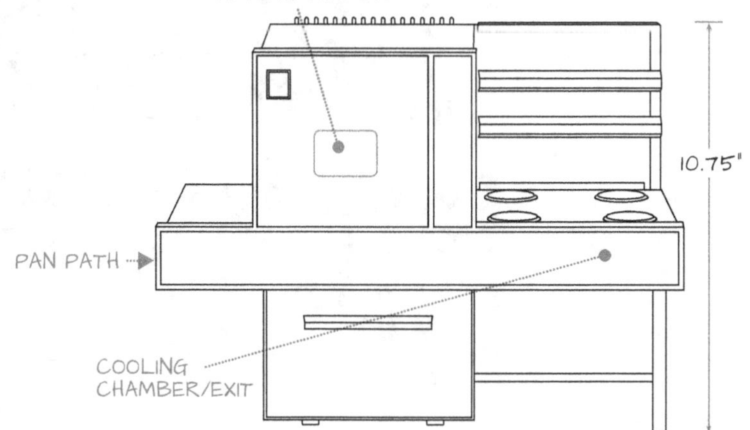

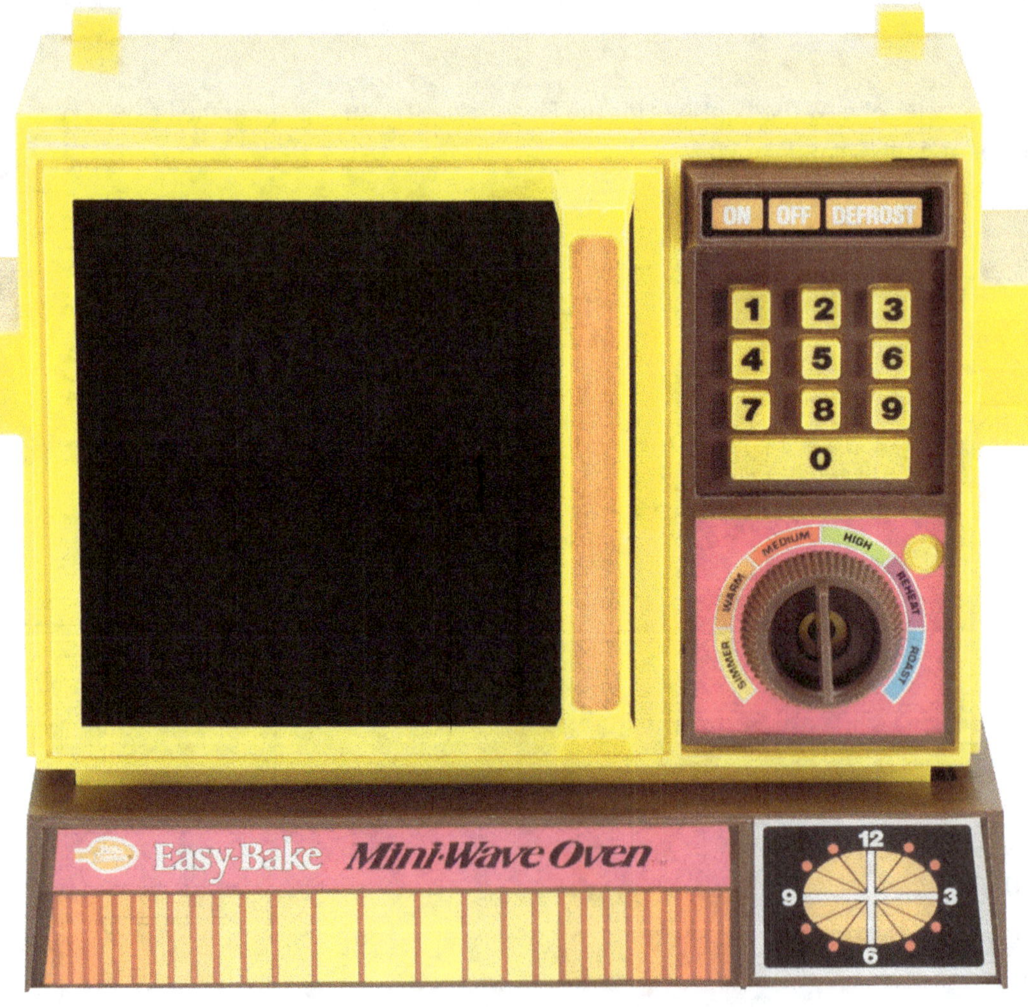

ON OFF DEFROST
1 2 3
4 5 6
7 8 9
0
WARM MEDIUM HIGH
SIMMER REHEAT ROAST
Easy-Bake Mini-Wave Oven
12
9 3
6

Betty Crocker Mini-Wave Oven

A new "Mini-Wave" model was introduced to celebrate the Easy-Bake Oven's 15th anniversary.

The inner workings of the oven were revamped to include a modified enclosed baking chamber that used only one 100-Watt light bulb. Kenner patented this new "oven-in-oven" construction and claimed that it allowed the Mini-Wave to cook faster than competing toy ovens.

The pan pusher tool was also revamped to be longer, making it even easier to move baking pans in and out of the toy.

Did you know?

The Mini-Wave was the first Easy-Bake to bake with a single light bulb.

Original retail price:
$19.99

Powered by:
1x 100W light bulb

In the box:

- 2 baking pans
- 3 Betty Crocker mixes
- Pan pusher
- Cookbook

Available in **Yellow**

Accent **Brown**

Accent **Pink**

Accent **Orange**

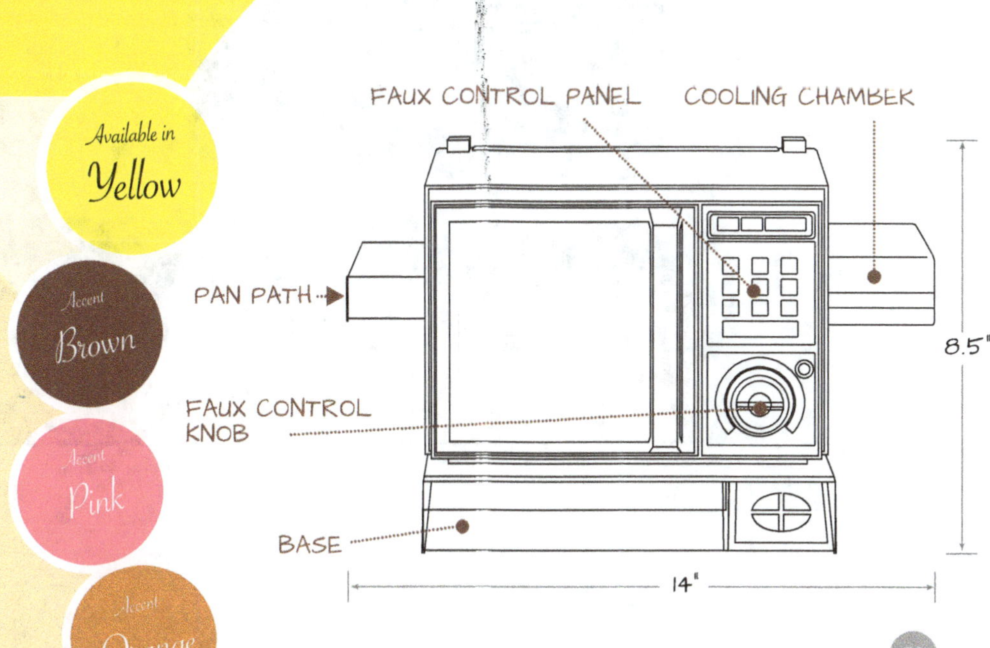

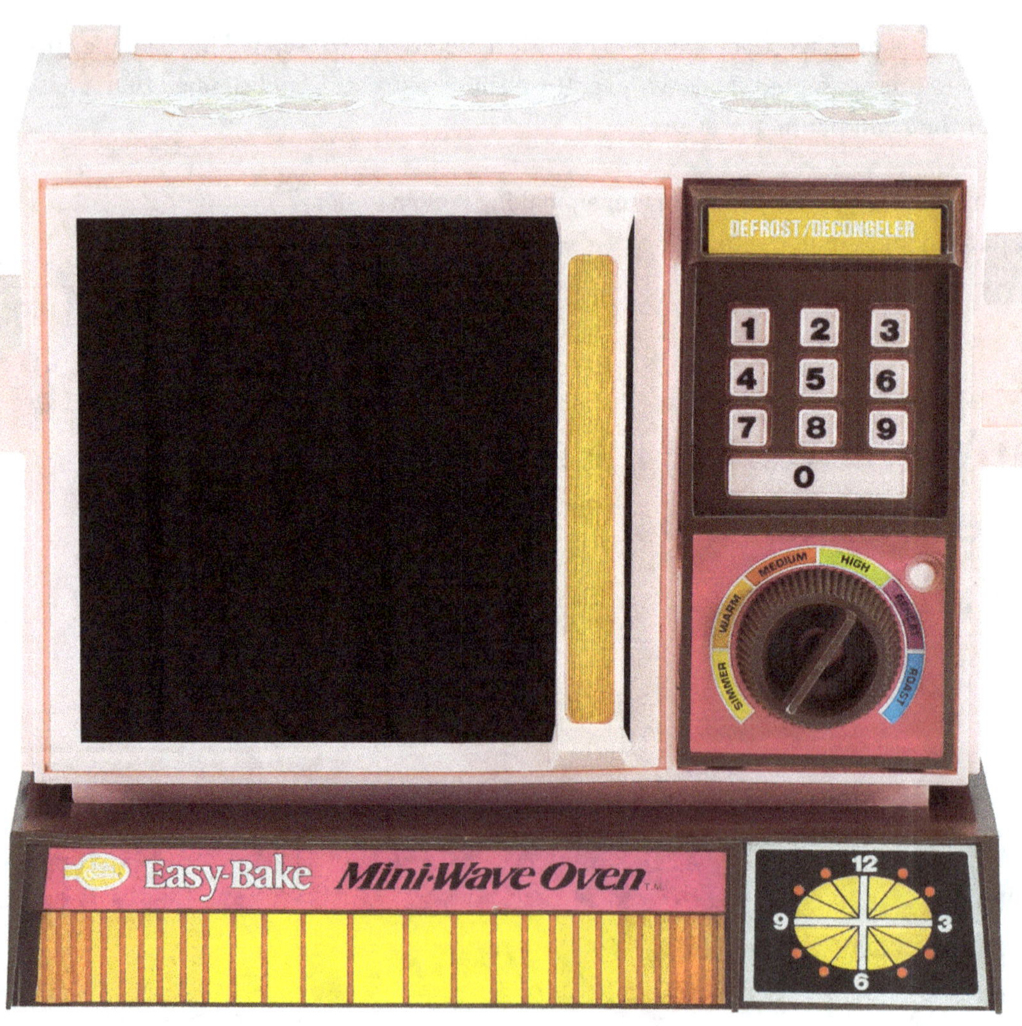

DEFROST/DECONGELER
1 2 3
4 5 6
7 8 9
0
WARM MEDIUM HIGH
SIMMER ROAST
Easy-Bake Mini-Wave Oven T.M.
12
9 3
6

Strawberry Shortcake Mini-Wave Oven

Kenner's parent company, General Mills, licensed Strawberry Shortcake from American Greetings and began cross-promoting the character within the Easy-Bake Oven product line.

A Strawberry Shortcake bake set was introduced first, followed soon after by the Betty Crocker Strawberry Shortcake Mini-Wave Oven. It was predominantly pink in color and included a set of Strawberry Shortcake stickers and a matching pan pusher.

Did you know?

In 1977, American Greetings juvenile artist, Muriel Fahrion, designed Strawberry Shortcake and her cat, Custard.

Original retail price:
$19.99

Powered by:
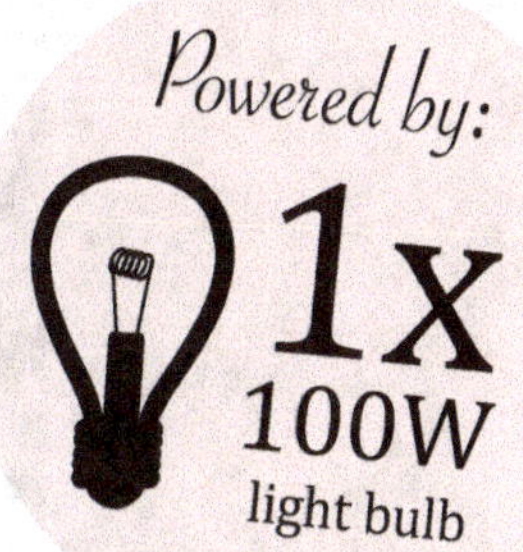
1x
100W
light bulb

In the box:

- 2 baking pans
- 3 Betty Crocker mixes
- Pan pusher
- Cookbook

Available in
Pink

Accent
Brown

Accent
Fuchsia

Accent
Orange

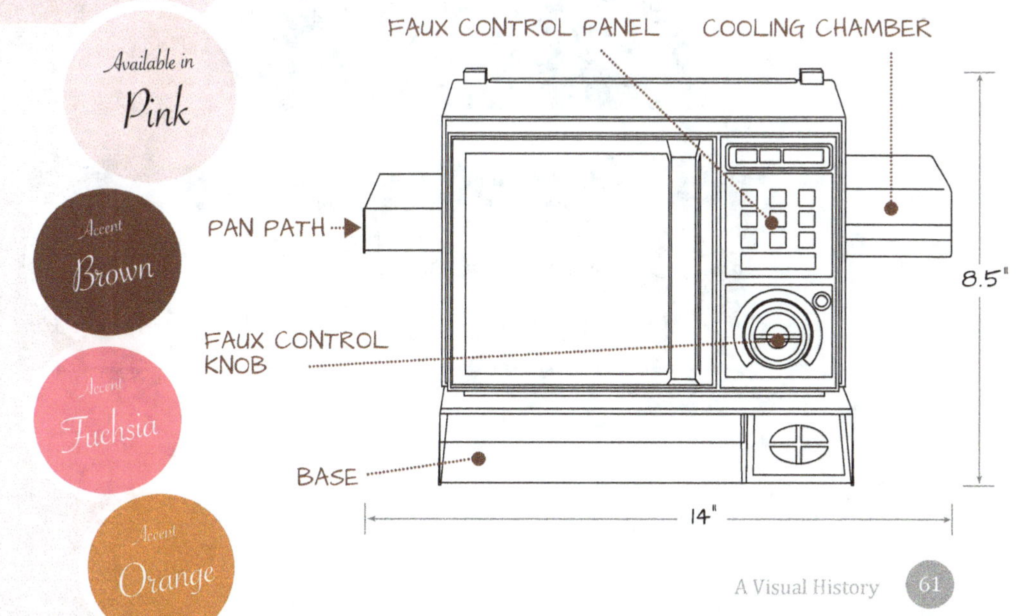

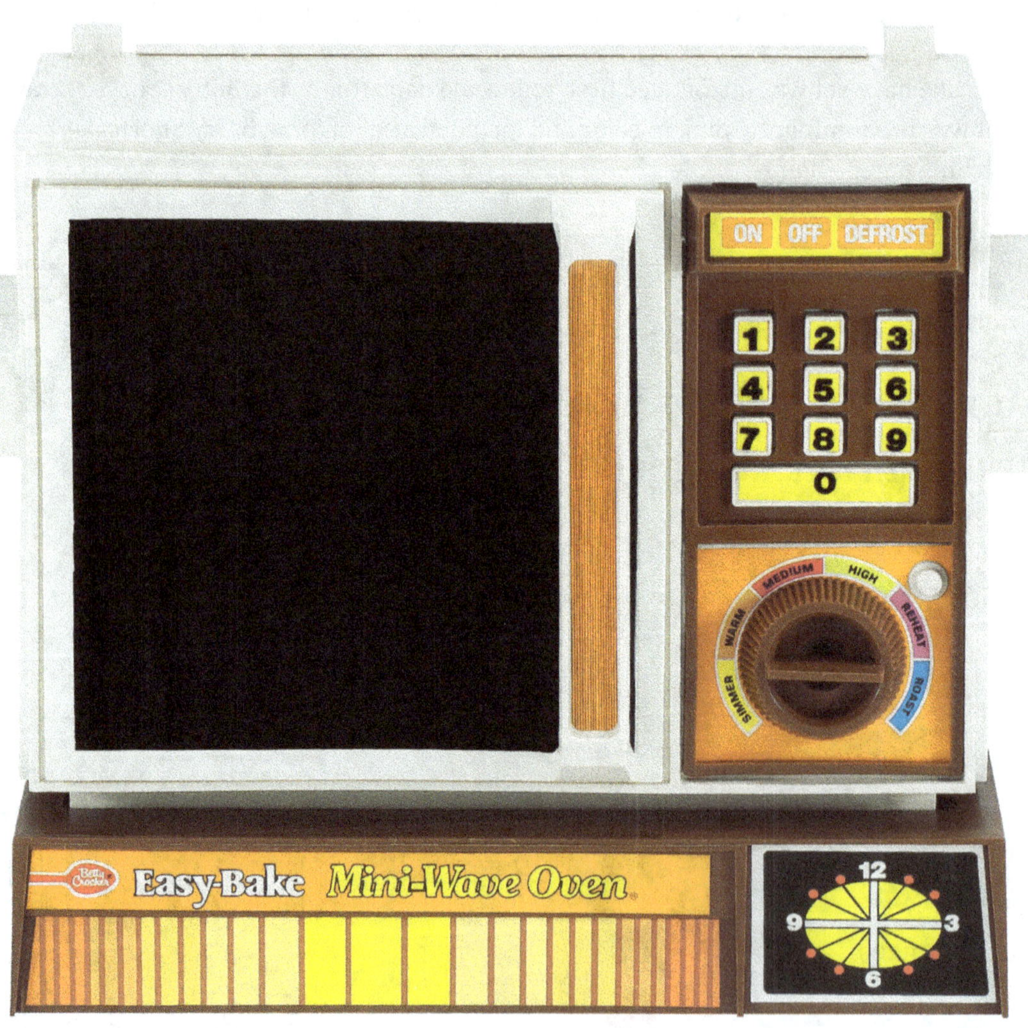

ON OFF DEFROST
1 2 3
4 5 6
7 8 9
0
SIMMER WARM MEDIUM HIGH REHEAT ROAST
Betty Crocker
Easy-Bake Mini-Wave Oven
12
9   3
6

Betty Crocker Mini-Wave Oven

In the '80s, a trend towards the use of neutral colors in the kitchen was reflected in the 18th anniversary edition of the Easy-Bake Oven, which offered a more subdued white, brown, and orange palette.

The pan pusher was again redesigned to be longer and wider than previous versions, making it easier and safer to push and pull baking pans through the oven.

Did you know?

Kenner's patent on the "oven-in-oven" construction used in Mini-Wave Ovens was granted in 1981 (U.S. patent #4,249,067).

Original retail price:
$19.99

Powered by:
1x
100W
light bulb

In the box:

- 2 baking pans
- 3 Betty Crocker mixes
- Pan pusher
- Cookbook

Available in
White

Accent
Brown

Accent
Orange

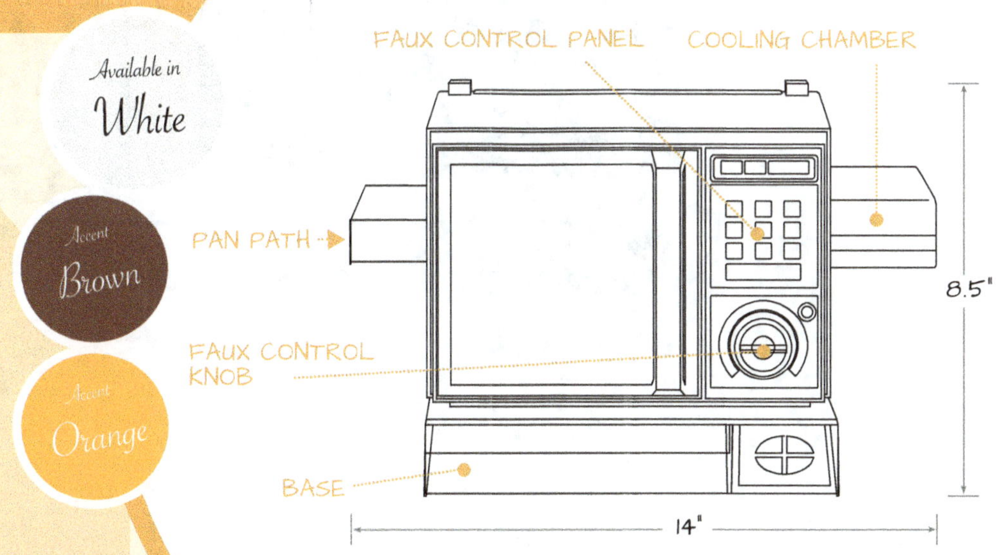

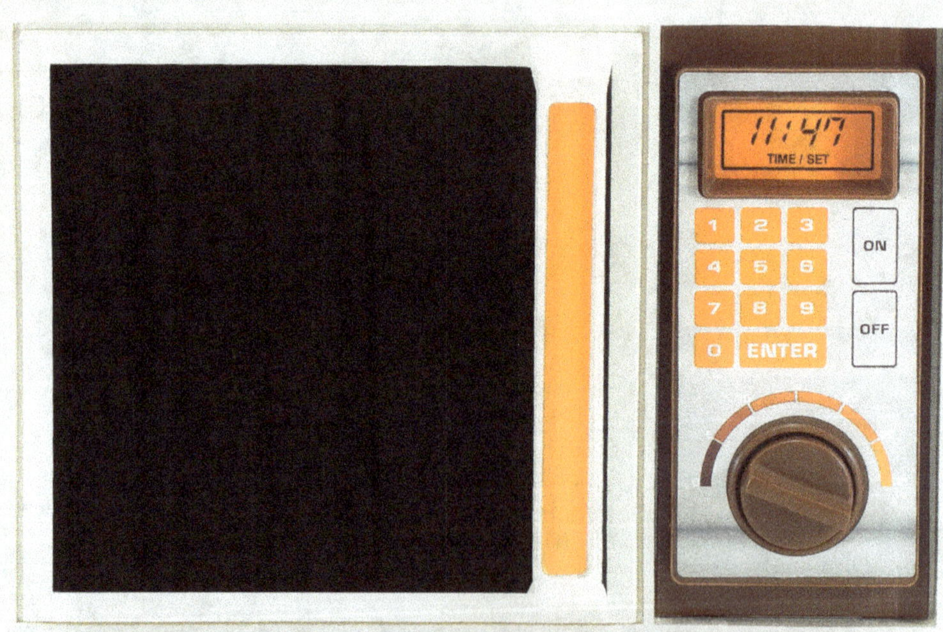
11:47
TIME / SET
1 2 3
4 5 6
7 8 9
0 ENTER
ON
OFF
Betty Crocker Easy-Bake. Mini-Wave Oven.

Betty Crocker Mini-Wave Oven

In the 1980s, electronic technology was becoming part of everyday life. The 1982 edition of the Easy-Bake Oven reflected this new reality, as it was the first model to sport a faux digital clock (which was permanently set to the time of 11:47).

This version also included a faux touch keypad, on/off buttons, and a power setting dial. The marketing materials described the oven's "sleek, chrome, micro-wave look".

Did you know?

The 19th anniversary edition of the Easy-Bake Oven continued to be marketed by Kenner as the "best-selling girl's toy since dolls".

Original retail price:

$**19**.99

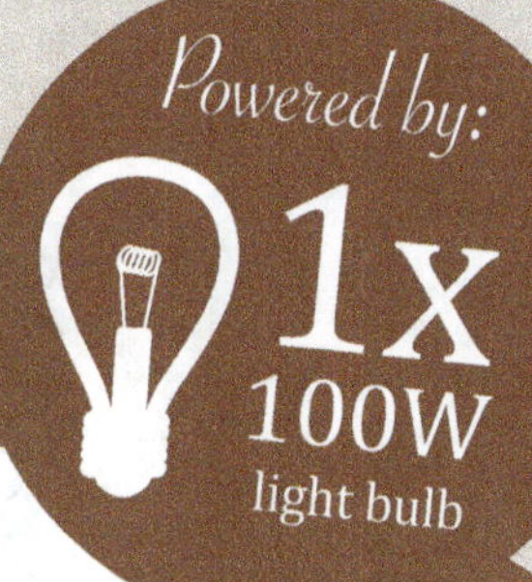

Powered by:

1x
100W
light bulb

In the box:

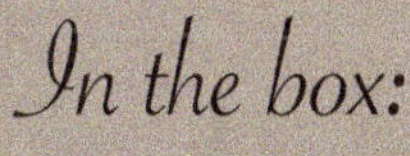

- 2 baking pans
- 3 Betty Crocker mixes
- Pan pusher
- Cookbook

Available in
White

Accent
Brown

Accent
Orange

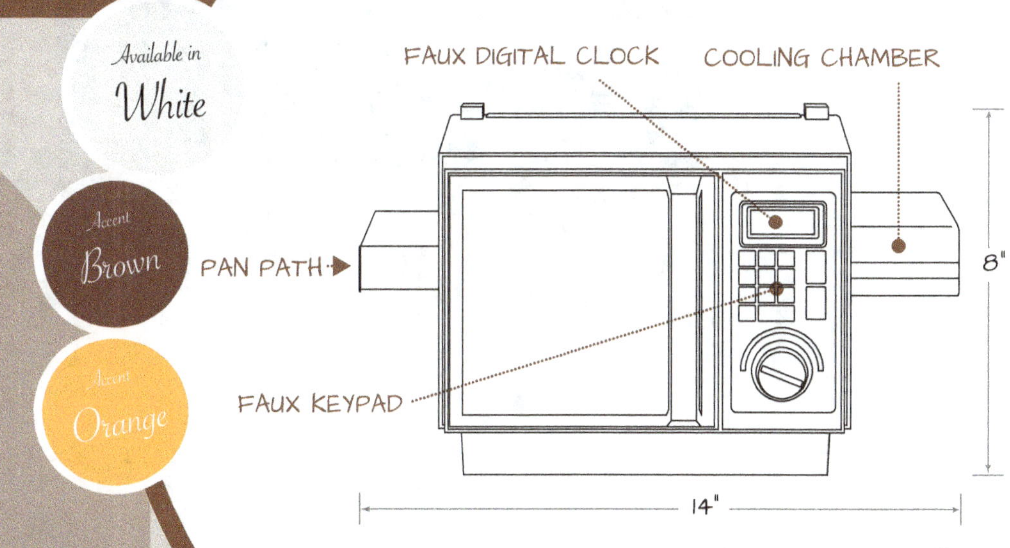

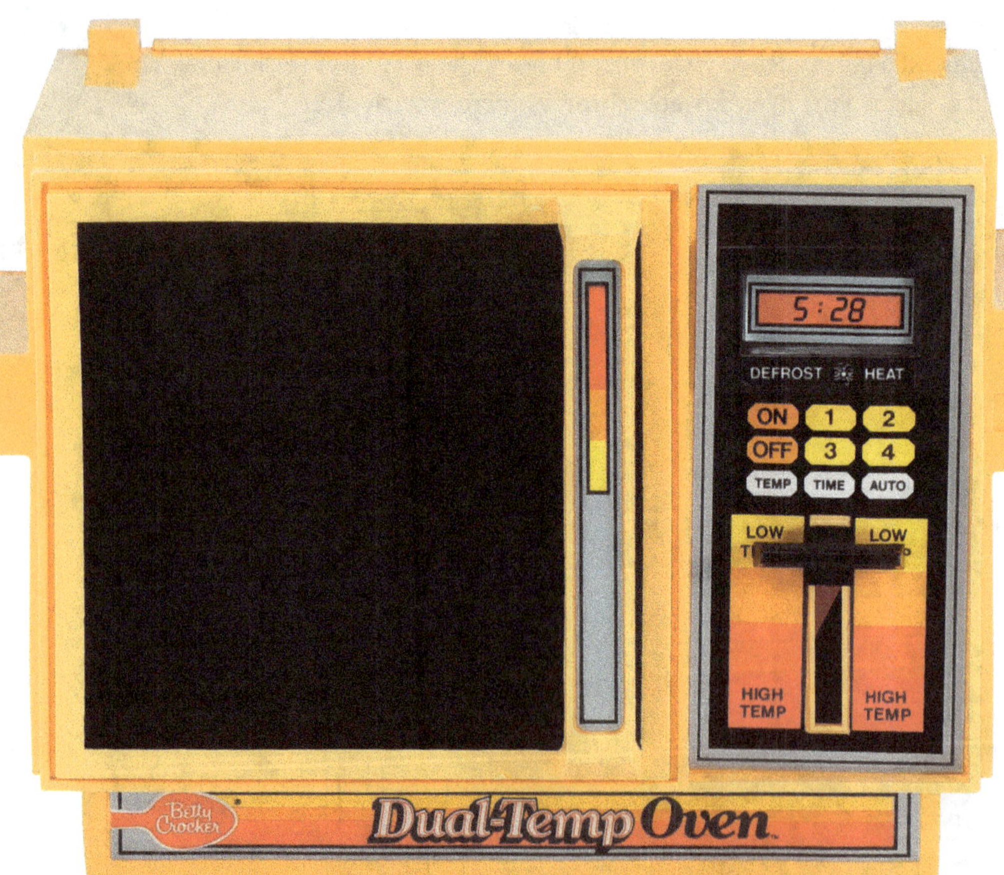

5:28
DEFROST HEAT
ON 1 2
OFF 3 4
TEMP TIME AUTO
LOW LOW
HIGH HIGH
TEMP TEMP
Betty Crocker
Dual-Temp Oven

Betty Crocker Dual-Temp Oven

For the 20th anniversary of the Easy-Bake Oven, Kenner rolled out a new model that provided young bakers with two temperature options. A lever on the oven allowed the internal temperature to be set to high (for cakes, brownies & cookies) or low (for fudge).

Kenner added this feature by updating the internal "oven-in-oven" construction to include a simple venting system. When set on low, the vent narrowed, allowing less heat to enter the enclosed baking chamber.

For clock-watchers, a new faux digital clock was added to the design, permanently set to 5:28.

Did you know?

At the time of its release, the Dual-Temp oven was the only toy oven on the market that provided two different temperature settings.

Original retail price:
$**19**.99

Powered by:
1x
100W
light bulb

In the box:

- 2 baking pans
- 4 Betty Crocker mixes
- Pan pusher
- Cookbook

Available in
Orange

Accent
Red

Accent
Silver

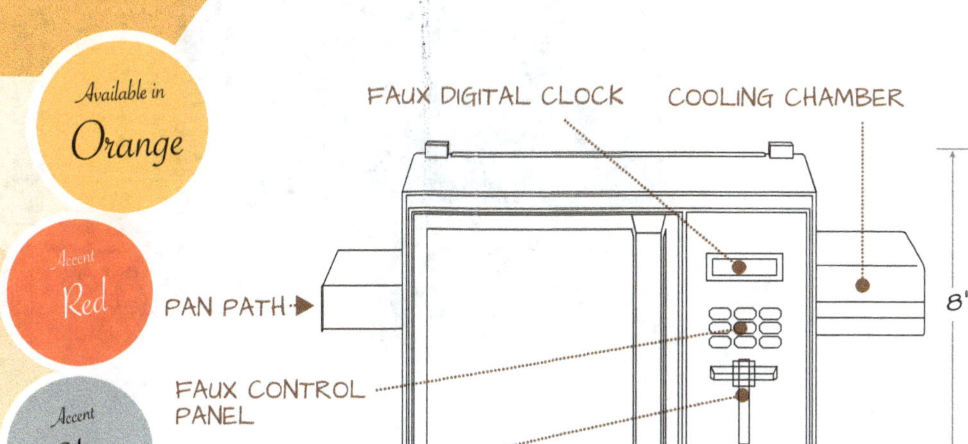

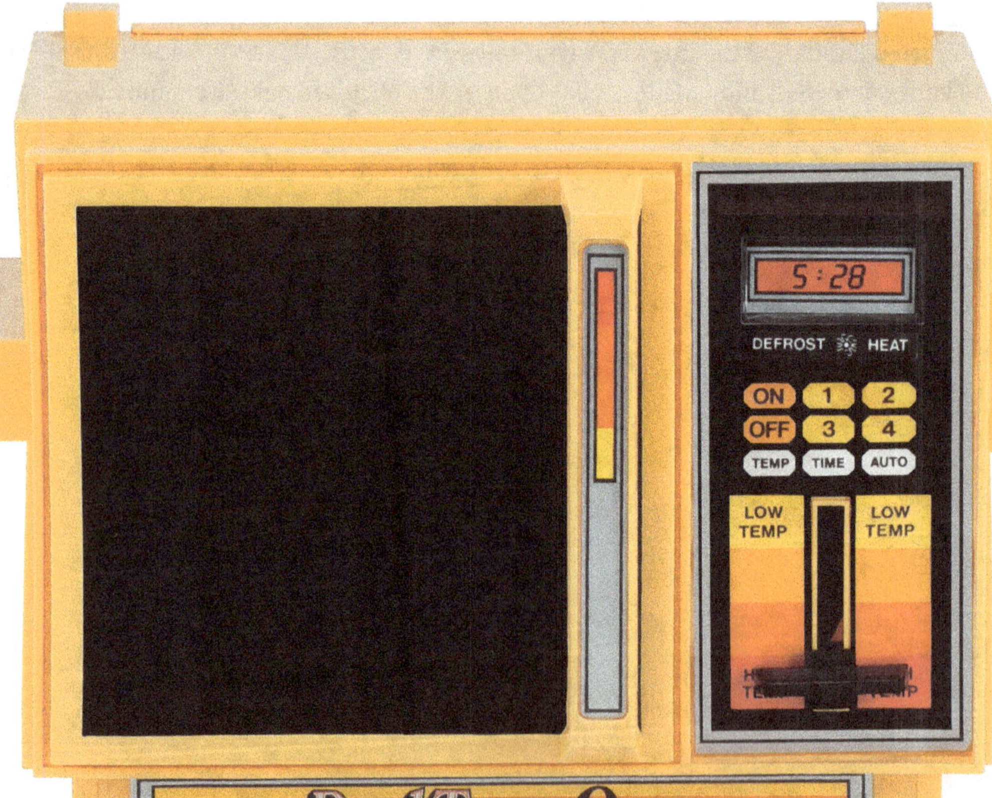

5:28
DEFROST HEAT
ON 1 2
OFF 3 4
TEMP TIME AUTO
LOW TEMP
LOW TEMP
Dual-Temp Oven

Easy-Bake Dual-Temp Oven

Tonka Corporation acquired Kenner Parker Toys Inc. from General Mills in 1987, effectively ending an era of Betty Crocker brand association with the oven.

The new model was functionally equivalent to the 20th-anniversary model, save for the lack of Betty Crocker branding.

Did you know?

The Easy-Bake Oven was co-branded with the Betty Crocker brand for 18 years.

Original retail price:
$**19**.99

Powered by:
1x
100W
light bulb

Available in
Orange

Accent
Red

Accent
Silver

In the box:

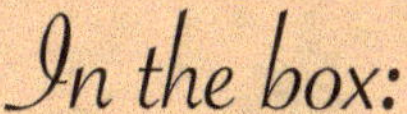

- 2 baking pans
- 4 mixes
- Pan pusher
- Cookbook

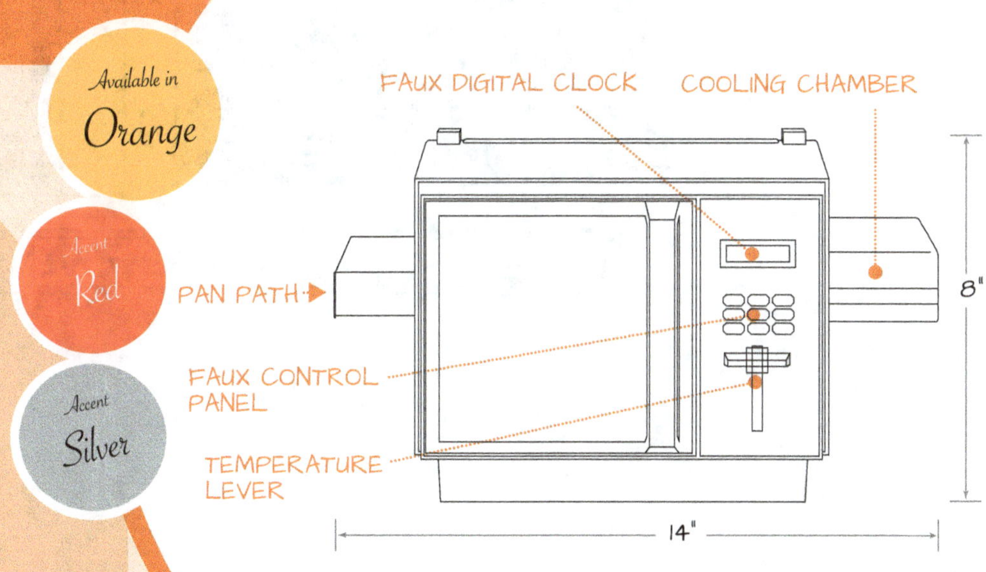

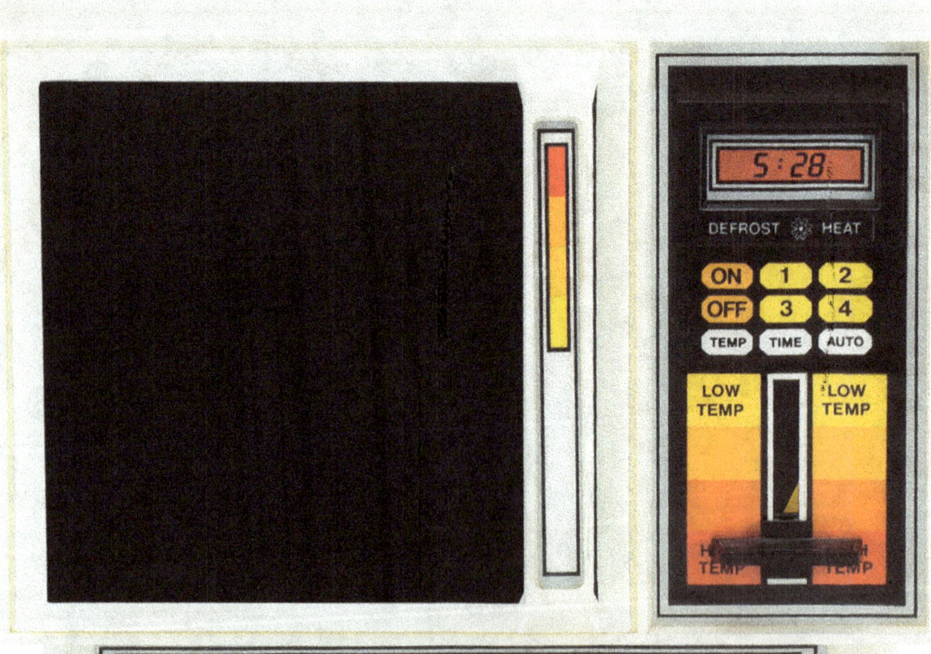
5:28
DEFROST HEAT
ON 1 2
OFF 3 4
TEMP TIME AUTO
LOW TEMP
LOW TEMP
HIGH TEMP
HIGH TEMP
EASY-BAKE OVEN

Easy-Bake Oven

Just in time for its 25th anniversary, the first Easy-Bake Oven to emerge after the Tonka Corporation acquisition was an updated version of the Dual-Temp model of 1987.

The changes were all cosmetic as Kenner returned to a base color palette of white (last seen in 1982). A new Easy-Bake Oven word mark was also introduced as part of a revitalized sticker package.

Did you know?

The 25th anniversary edition of the Easy-Bake Oven was the only toy oven on the market with Underwriters Laboratories (UL) approval.

Original retail price:
$19.99

Powered by:
1x
100W
light bulb

In the box:

- 2 baking pans
- 4 mixes
- Pan pusher
- Cookbook

Available in
White

Accent
Red

Accent
Orange

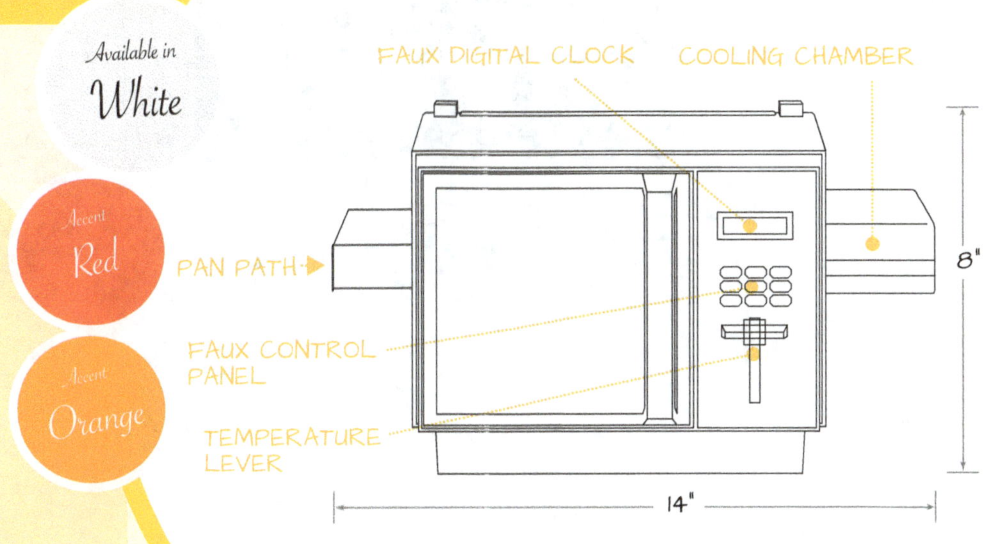

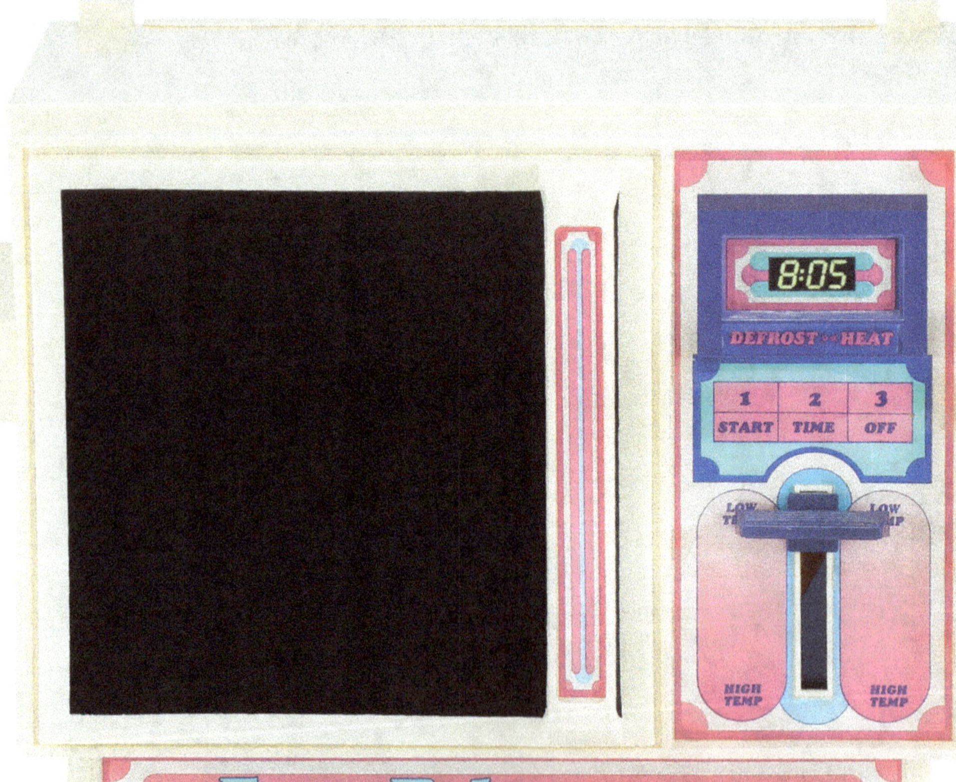
8:05
DEFROST HEAT
1 2 3
START TIME OFF
LOW TEMP
LOW TEMP
HIGH TEMP
HIGH TEMP
Easy-Bake

Easy-Bake Oven

Kenner went back to basics with the release of the 27th anniversary edition of the Easy-Bake Oven.

The dual-temp baking chamber of recent models was replaced with the earlier version used 12 years before. The temperature lever was replaced with a mock facsimile. For clock-watchers, the faux digital clock was revamped and permanently set to 8:05.

During this period, Kenner began to introduce tie-ins to other snack food brands aimed at children. The first example was the Easy-Bake Pizza Hut Bake Set, released in 1991. The set included everything needed to make a variety of pizzas, including pizza pans, a pizza cutter, and mixes for sauce, cheese, and crust.

Original retail price:

$24.⁹⁹

Powered by:

1x
100W
light bulb

Did you know?

The Easy-Bake Pizza Hut Bake Set was a portent of future cross-promotions between the Easy-Bake Oven and other kids' snack brands.

Available in
White

Accent
Pink

Accent
Blue

Accent
Turquoise

In the box:

- 2 baking pans
- 4 mixes
- Pan pusher
- Cookbook

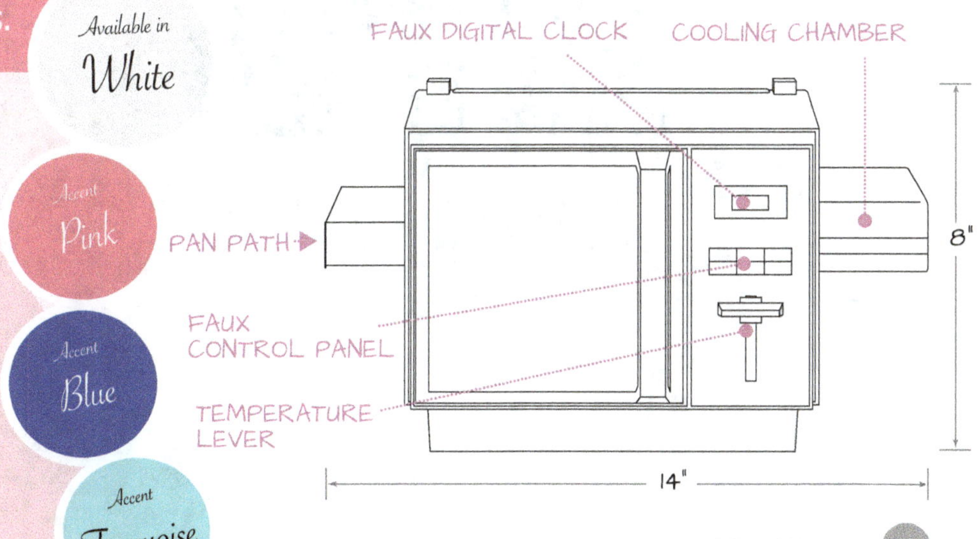

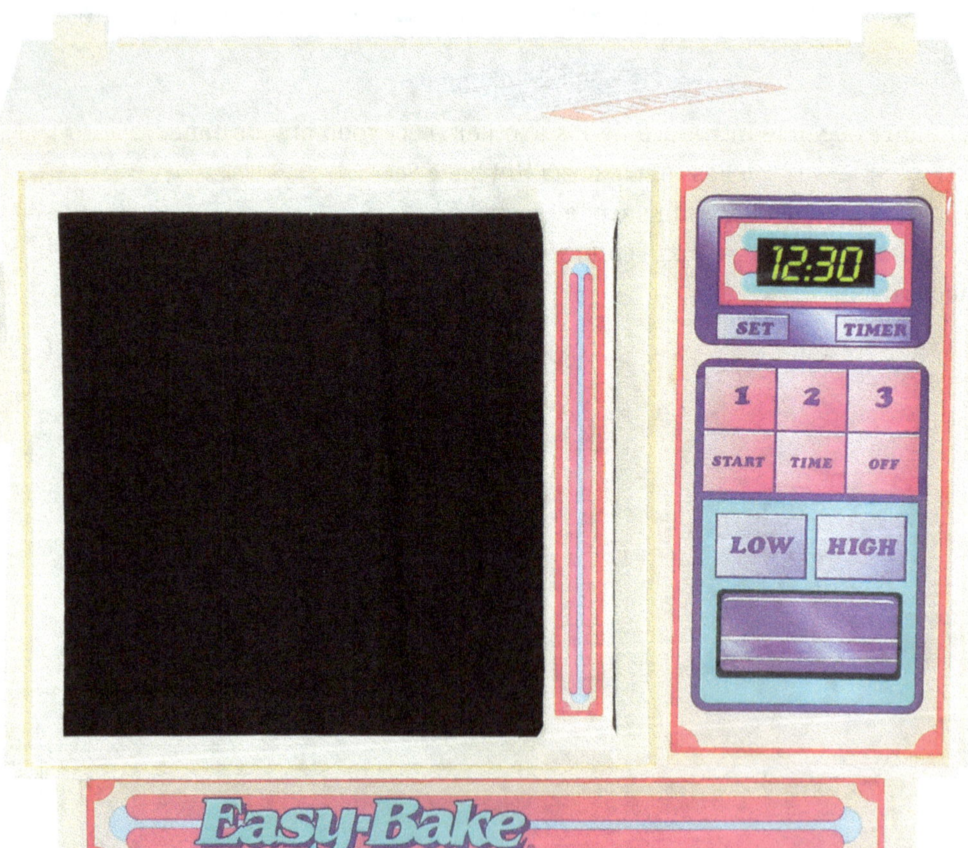

12:30
SET
TIMER
1
2
3
START
TIME
OFF
LOW
HIGH
Easy-Bake

Easy-Bake Oven

1992

Hasbro purchased Tonka Corporation in 1991 and Kenner became a division of one of the largest toy companies in the world.

The first Easy-Bake Oven produced by Hasbro was slightly smaller than previous versions and featured a new sticker set with over-sized buttons and a new faux digital clock set to 12:30. The mock temperature lever from the previous model was removed.

Did you know?

Since the introduction of the non-working digital clock, Easy-Bake Ovens have shown times of 5:28, 8:05, 11:47, and 12:30.

Original retail price:
$24.⁹⁹

Powered by:
1x
100W
light bulb

In the box:

- 2 baking pans
- 4 mixes
- Pan pusher
- Cookbook

Available in
White

Accent
Pink

Accent
Purple

Accent
Turquoise

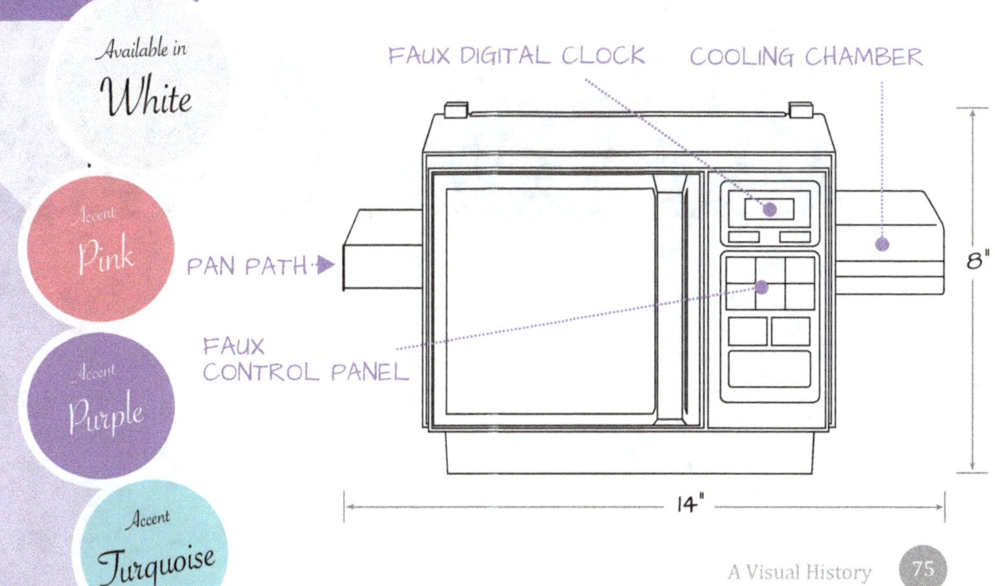

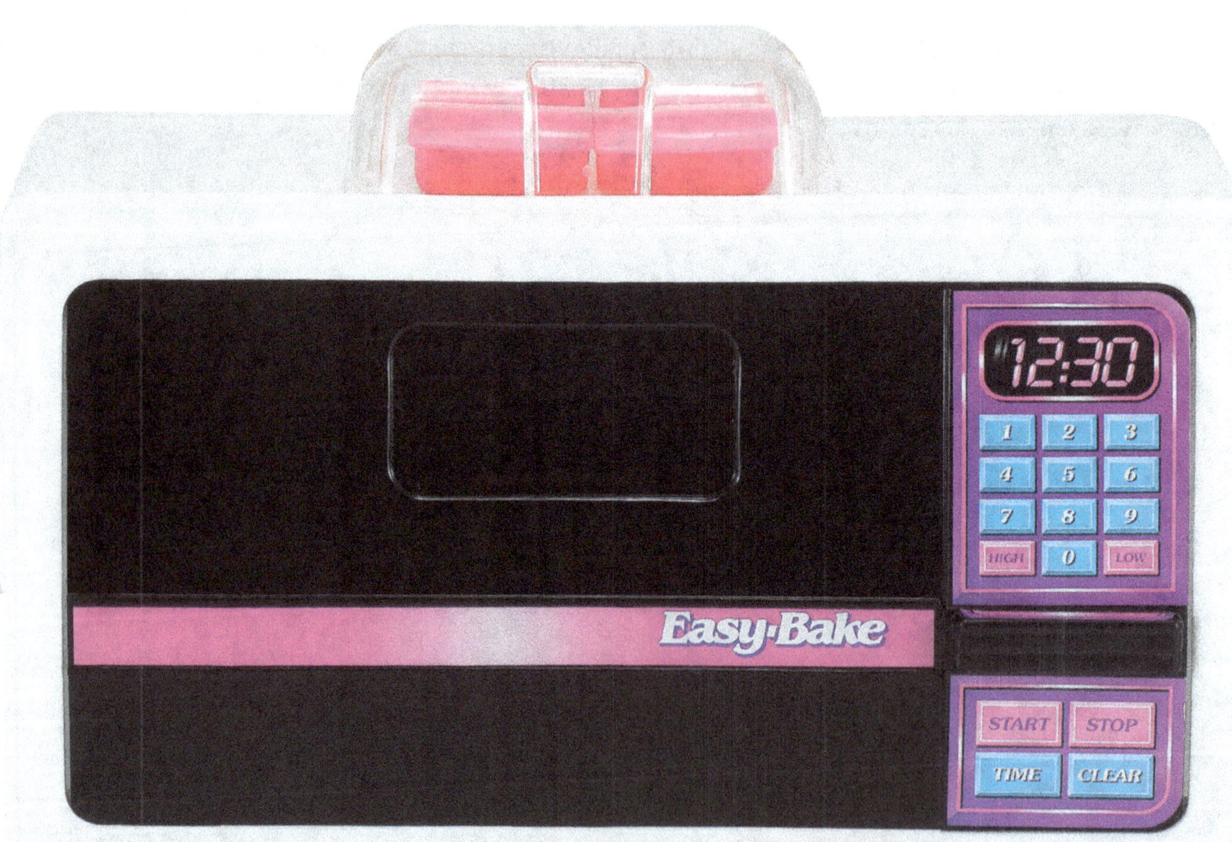
12:30
1 2 3
4 5 6
7 8 9
HIGH 0 LOW
Easy-Bake
START STOP
TIME CLEAR

Easy-Bake Oven & Snack Center

To celebrate the 30th anniversary of the Easy-Bake Oven, Kenner released an all-new model. The Mini-Wave form factor was super-sized into a more modern format that resembled the tabletop microwaves of its day.

The new design included a simulated touch-pad and LED display. A warming chamber and warming trays atop the oven allowed amateur bakers to create sauces and melted toppings using the oven's heat.

Original retail price:

$16.⁹⁹

Powered by:

1x
100W
light bulb

Did you know?

By 1993, more than 11 million Easy-Bake Ovens had been sold.

In the box:

- 4 mixes
- 2 baking pans
- 2 warming trays
- Warming cover
- Pan pusher
- Cooking utensils
- Cookbook

Available in
White

Accent
Pink

Accent
Purple

Accent
Turquoise

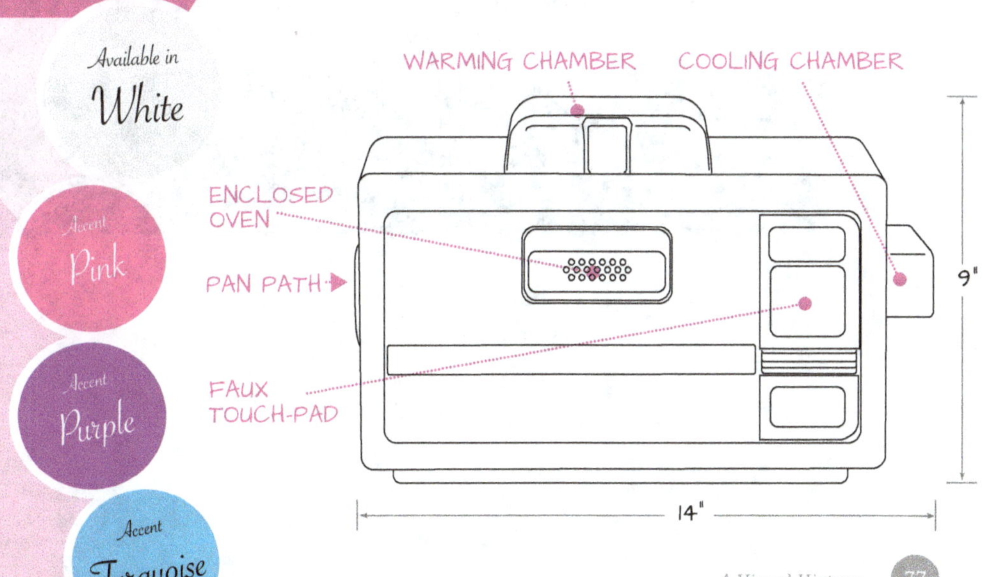

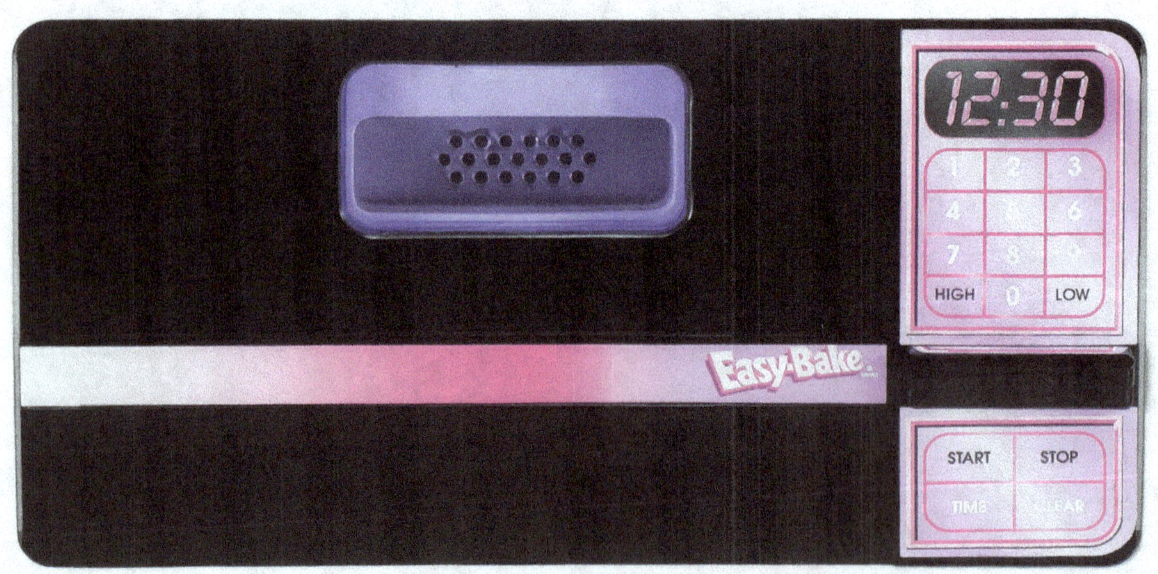

12:30
1 2 3
4 5 6
7 8 9
HIGH 0 LOW
Easy-Bake
START STOP
TIME CLEAR

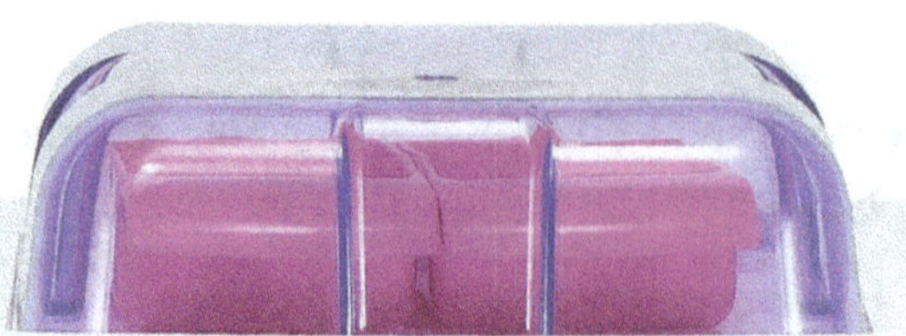

Easy-Bake Oven & Snack Center

In 1996, a cosmetic refresh to the Easy-Bake Oven yielded a new a sticker set and updated Easy-Bake logo.

To celebrate the 40th anniversary of the toy oven in 2003, Hasbro shipped this model with a limited-edition heart-shaped pan.

Did you know?

By 2002, more than 130 million Easy-Bake Mix Sets had been sold.

Original retail price:
$16.99

Powered by:
1x
100W
light bulb

Available in
White

Accent
Pink

Accent
Purple

Accent
Lavender

In the box:

- 4 mixes
- 2 baking pans
- 2 warming trays
- Warming cover
- Pan pusher
- Cooking utensils
- Cookbook

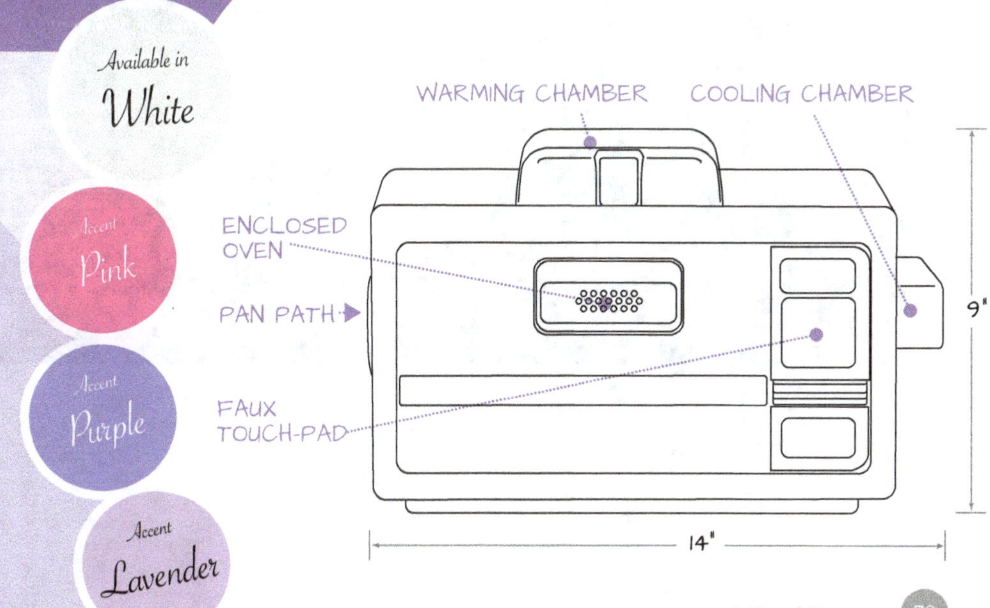

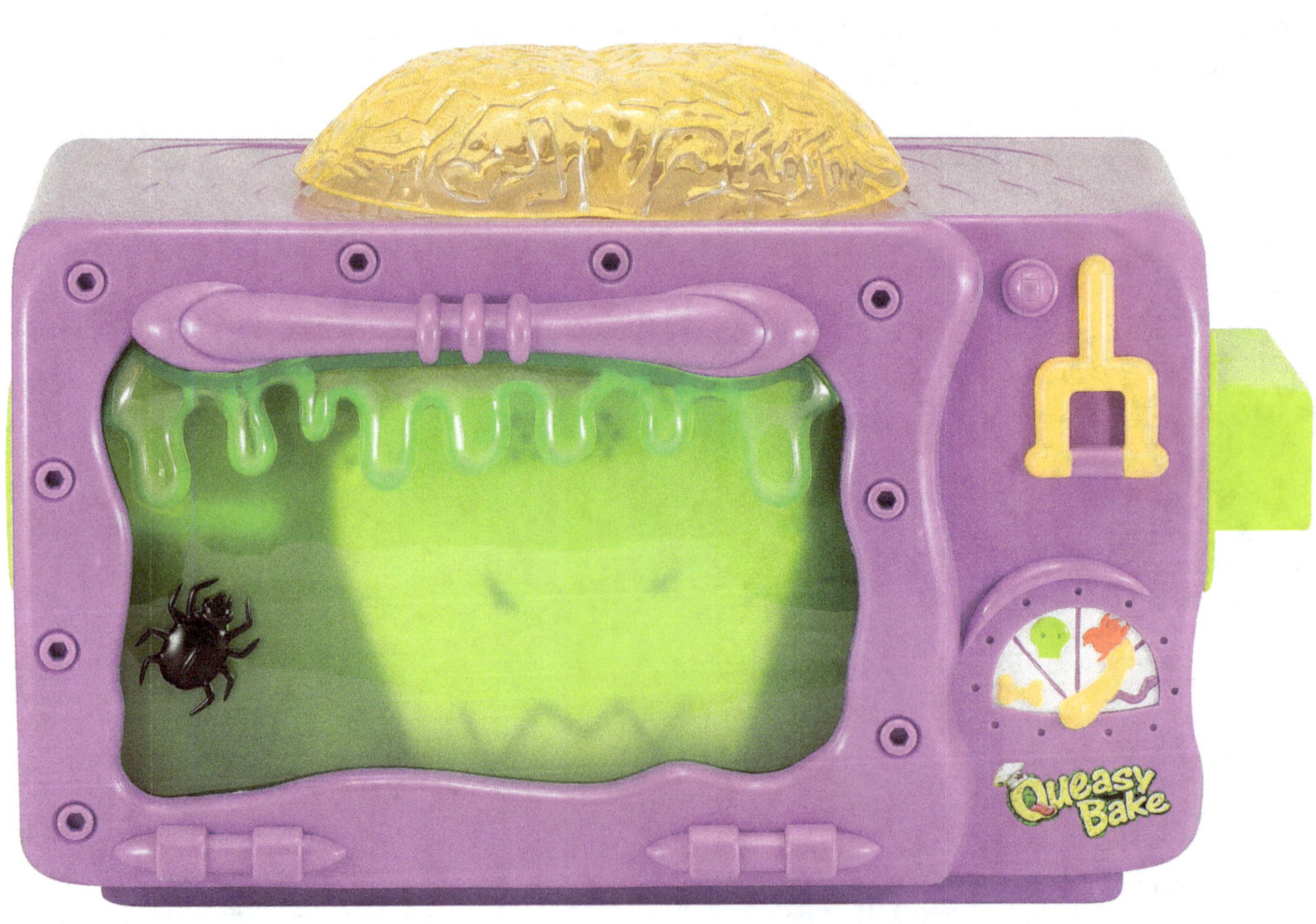
Queasy Bake

Queasy Bake Cookerator

2002

With the Queasy Bake Cookerator, Hasbro tried to tempt boys aged eight and older to get in on the fun. While the form factor of the toy remained similar to the Easy-Bake Oven & Snack Center, the color palette was darker with neon accents. The oven was also tricked out with spiders, skulls, and bones.

The food mixes for the Queasy Bake were also aimed at boys: *Chocolate Crud Cake, Mucky Mud, Delicious Dirt, Bugs 'n Worms Mix, Crunchy Dog Bones, Magic Surprise Gravel, Cool Drool*, and *Foaming Drool*.

In 2003, the mixes were expanded to include *Toe Dough Cookies, Black Widow Spider Cake, Martian Invasion Cookies, Bed Bug Cakes*, and *Awful Waffles*. Despite these efforts, the Queasy Bake never enjoyed the sales success of its predecessors.

Original retail price:
$19.⁹⁹

Powered by:
1x
100W
light bulb

Did you know?

This oven was marketed as "providing everything boys need to make ooey, gooey, gross-looking treats – that taste great!"

Available in
Purple

Accent
Green

Accent
Yellow

In the box:

- 8 mixes
- Baking pan
- 2 cooking utensils
- Cookie cutter
- Mixing bowl
- Warming tray cover
- Pan pusher
- Bug/worm mold
- Cookbook

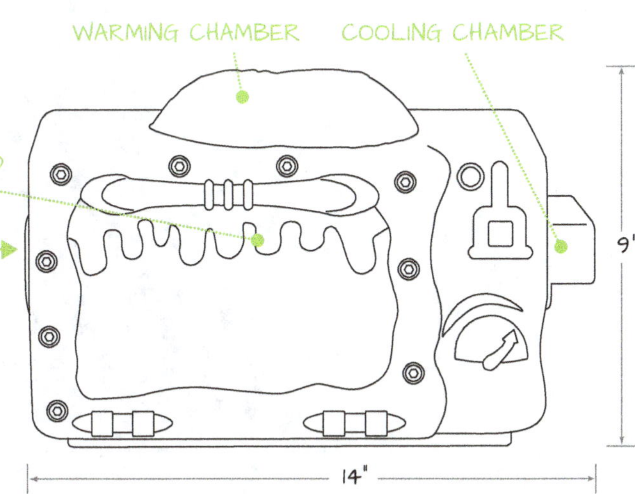

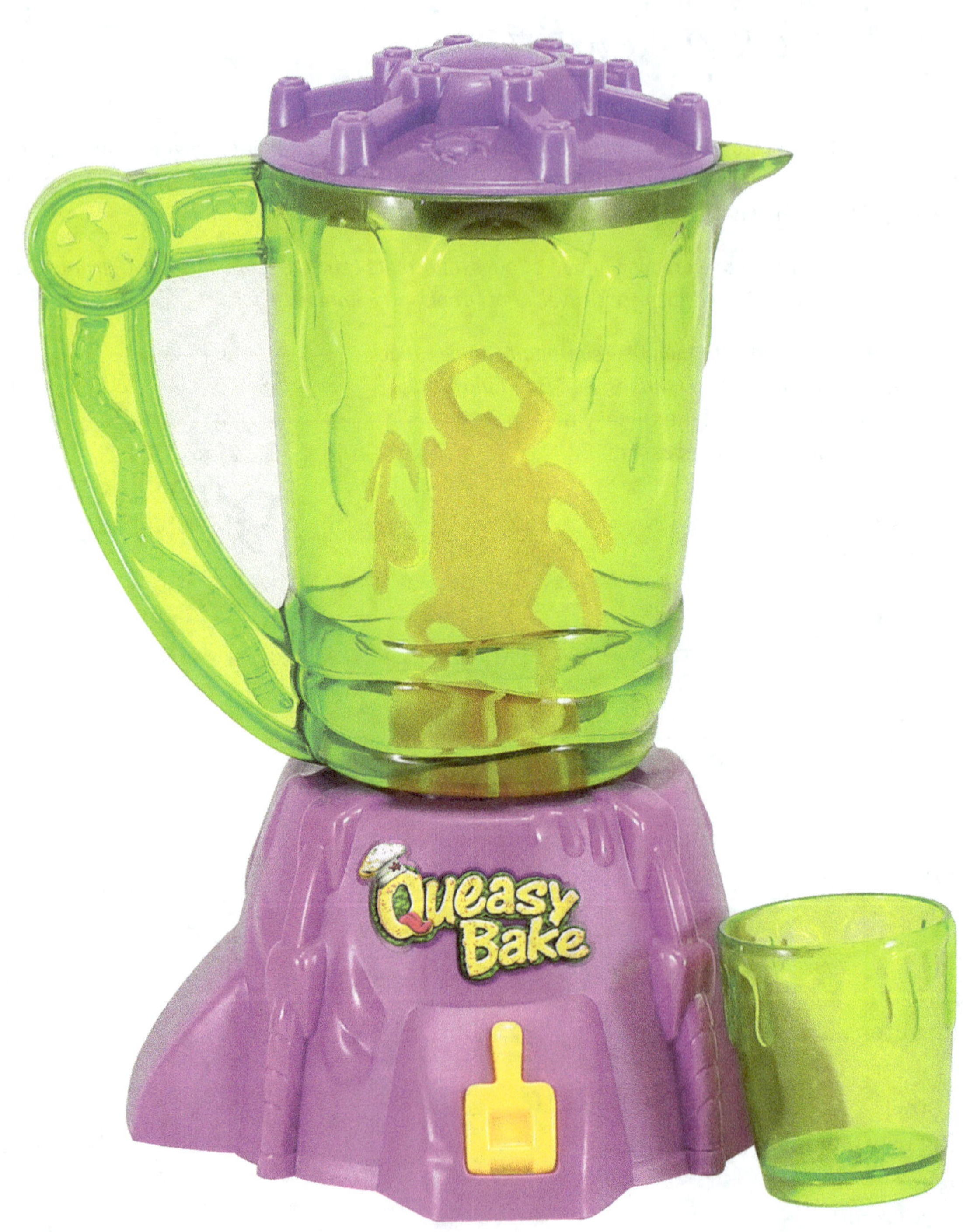

Queasy
Bake

Queasy Bake Mixerator

The Queasy Bake Mixerator was a blender designed to complement the Queasy Bake Cookerator. The color scheme and ornamentation matched the oven and the drink mixes were equally creative.

By adding milk to the mixes, kids could make such disgusting-sounding, yet edible, concoctions as: *Sewer Sludge* shakes, *Blend-a-Booger* & *Fizz 'n Foam Alien* drinks, and *Swamp* snacks.

In 2003, the Mixerator was replaced with pre-packaged drinks called *Queasy Bake Queasy Shakers* that came in two flavors: *Rusty Drain Pipe Drink Mix* and *Black Hole Vaporizer Drink Mix*.

Original retail price:

$14.⁹⁹

Powered by:

2x
C-batteries

Did you know?

The Queasy Bake Mixerator was advertised as a way for kids to "make goopy, gooey, nasty looking drinks that taste great!"

Available in
Purple

Accent
Green

Accent
Yellow

In the box:

- Drinking cup
- 1 mix
- 2 color change packets

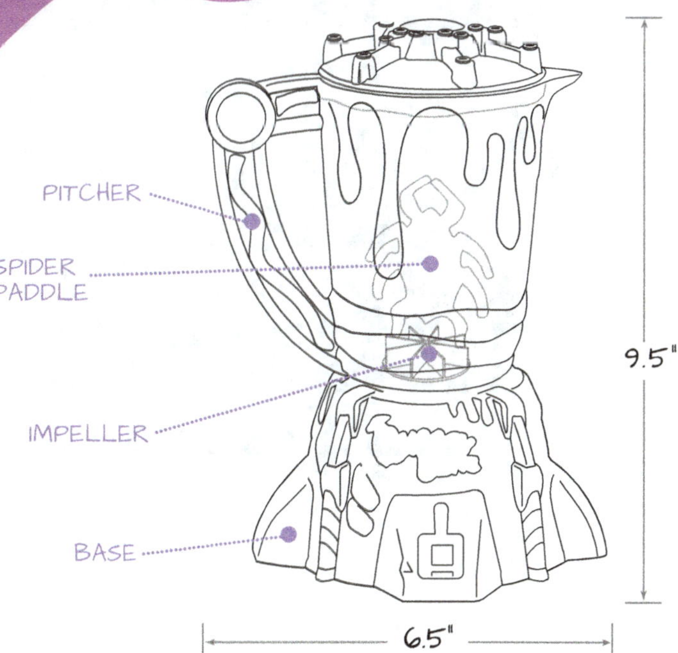

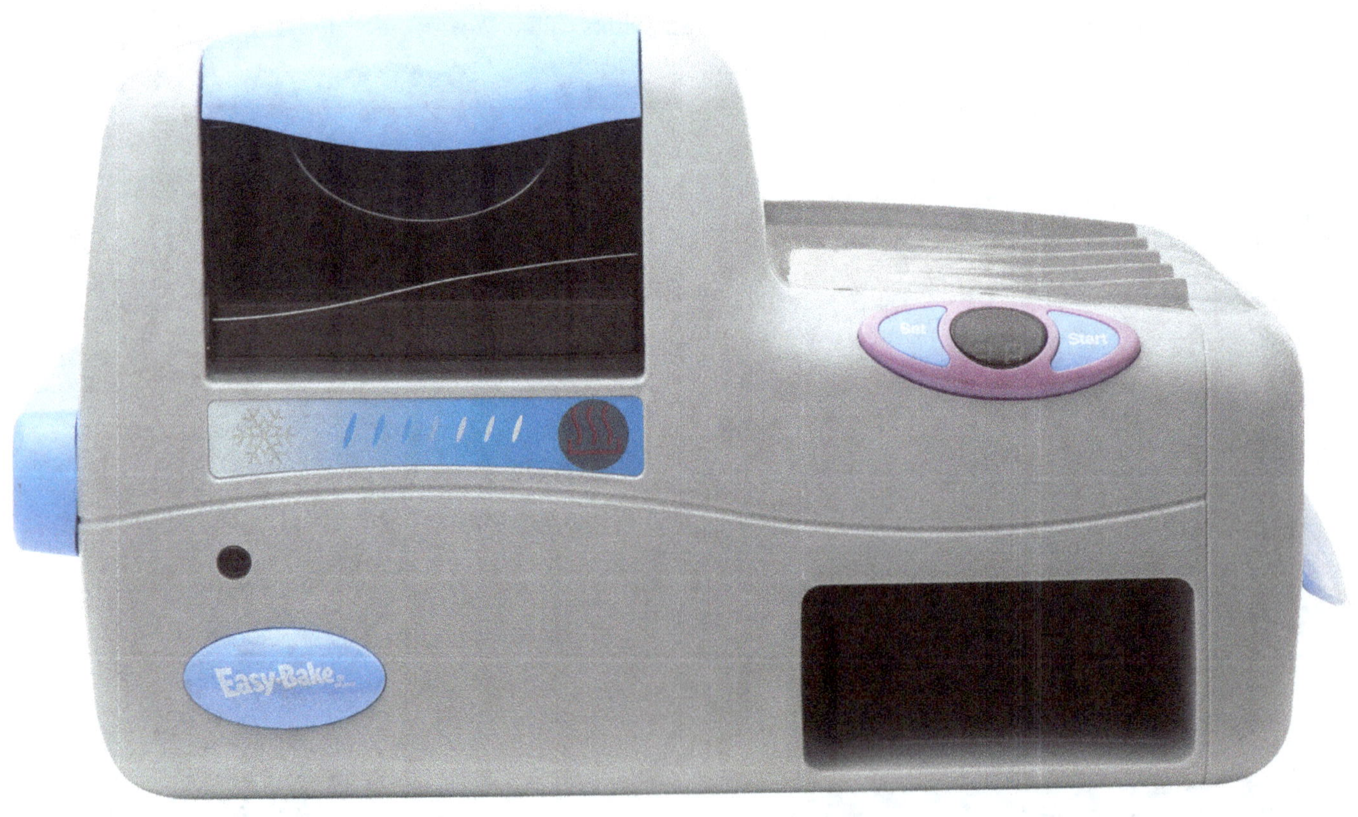

Set
Start
Easy-Bake

Easy-Bake Real Meal Oven

For the Easy-Bake Oven's 40th anniversary, Hasbro released the first model that featured a heating element instead of a light bulb as a heat source. Originally called the Master-Chef Oven (but never released under this name), the Real Meal Oven was the largest Easy-Bake Oven to date.

It came equipped with a working battery-powered timer, a temperature strip that would change color to indicate when the oven was pre-heated, an enclosed warming chamber, and the first working digital timer ever featured in an Easy-Bake.

With no light bulb to house, Hasbro was able to enlarge the cooking chamber to accommodate larger pans. This allowed for a wider variety of cooking options, such as macaroni and cheese, pizza, and pretzels.

Did you know?

The Easy-Bake Real Meal Oven was *Parenting Magazine's* 2003 Toy of the Year.

Original retail price:

$29.99

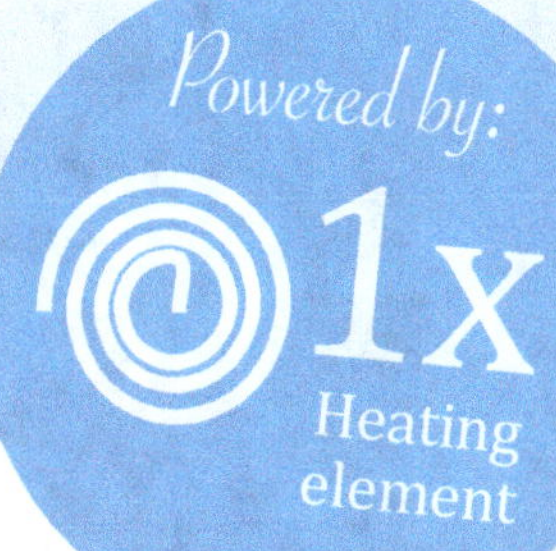

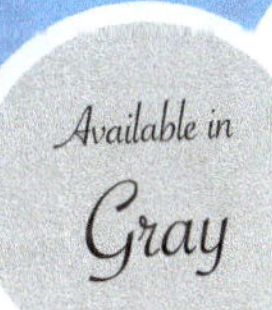

In the box:

- 6 mixes
- 2 cooking pans
- Spoon/spatula
- Mixing bowl
- Pan pusher

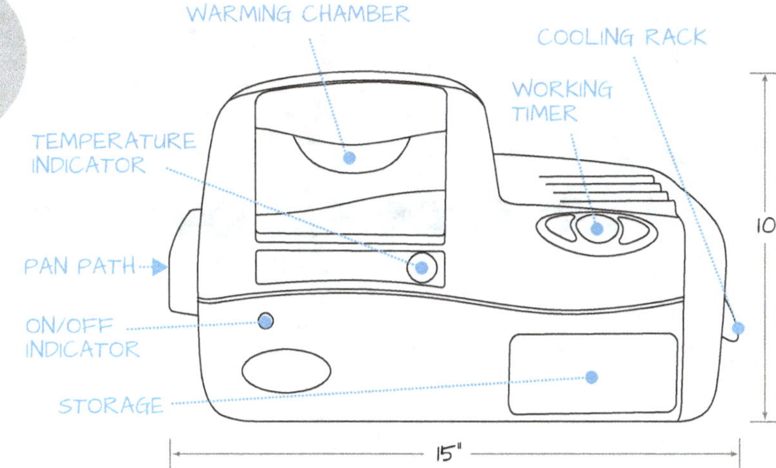

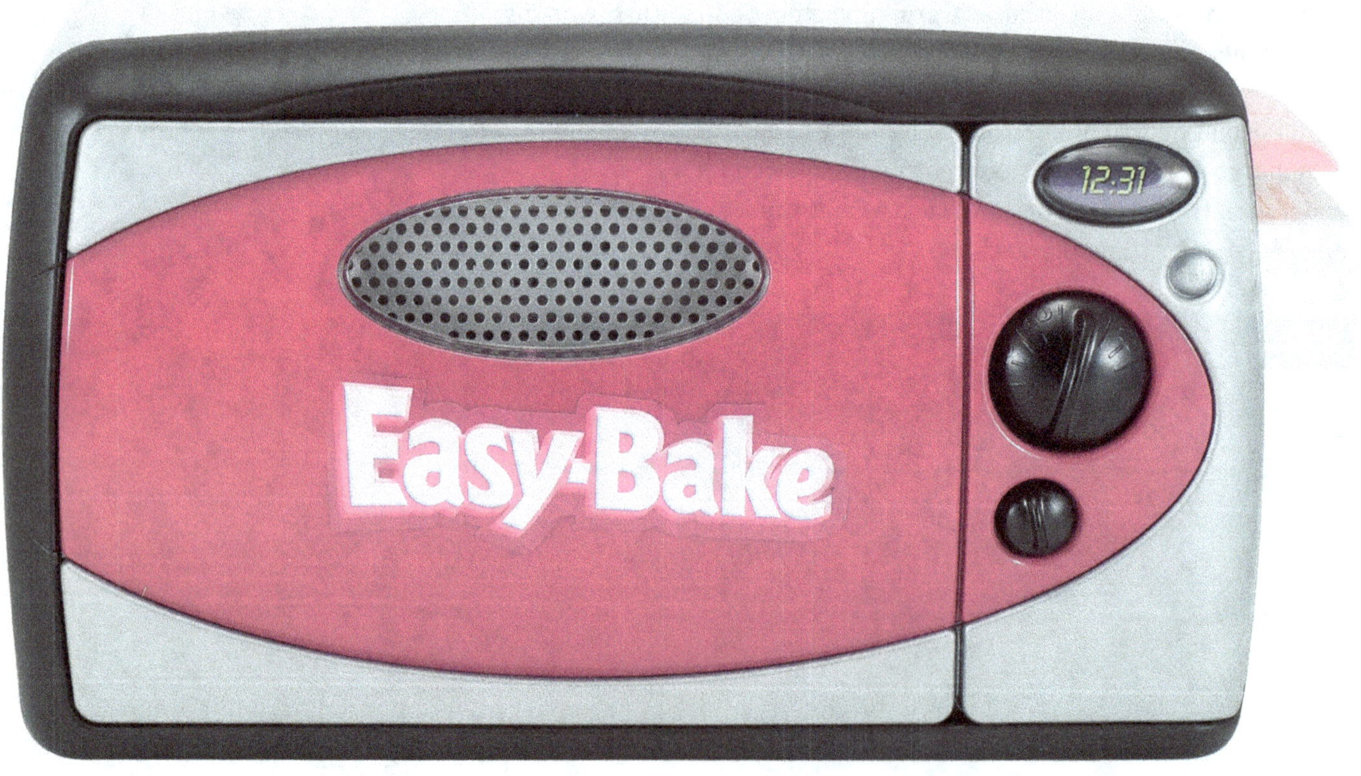

12:31
Easy-Bake

Easy-Bake Oven & Snack Center

In the mid-2000s deep hues dominated color palettes in both the fashion and automotive industries. Hasbro followed suit in 2004 with a new Easy-Bake Oven that was black, silver, and magenta.

The faux control panel was modernized with a series of dials replacing the numeric keypad and buttons of previous models. The time on the faux digital clock was advanced by a minute to 12:31.

Did you know?

This Easy-Bake was marketed as a "classic oven with all-new contemporary styling."

Original retail price:

$19.⁹⁹

Powered by:

1x
100W
light bulb

Available in
Magenta

Accent
Silver

Accent
Black

In the box:

- 3 mixes
- 2 baking pans
- Spoon
- Spatula
- 2 warming cups
- Pan pusher

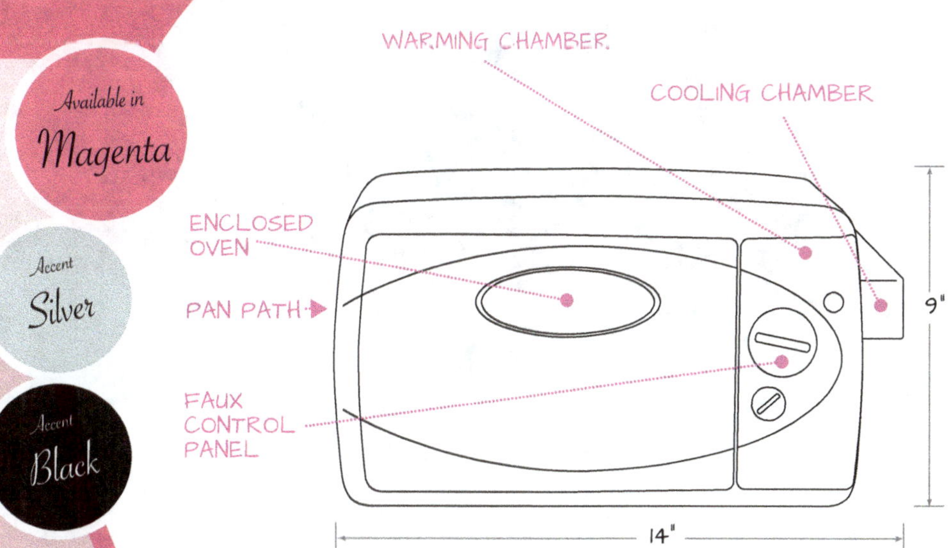

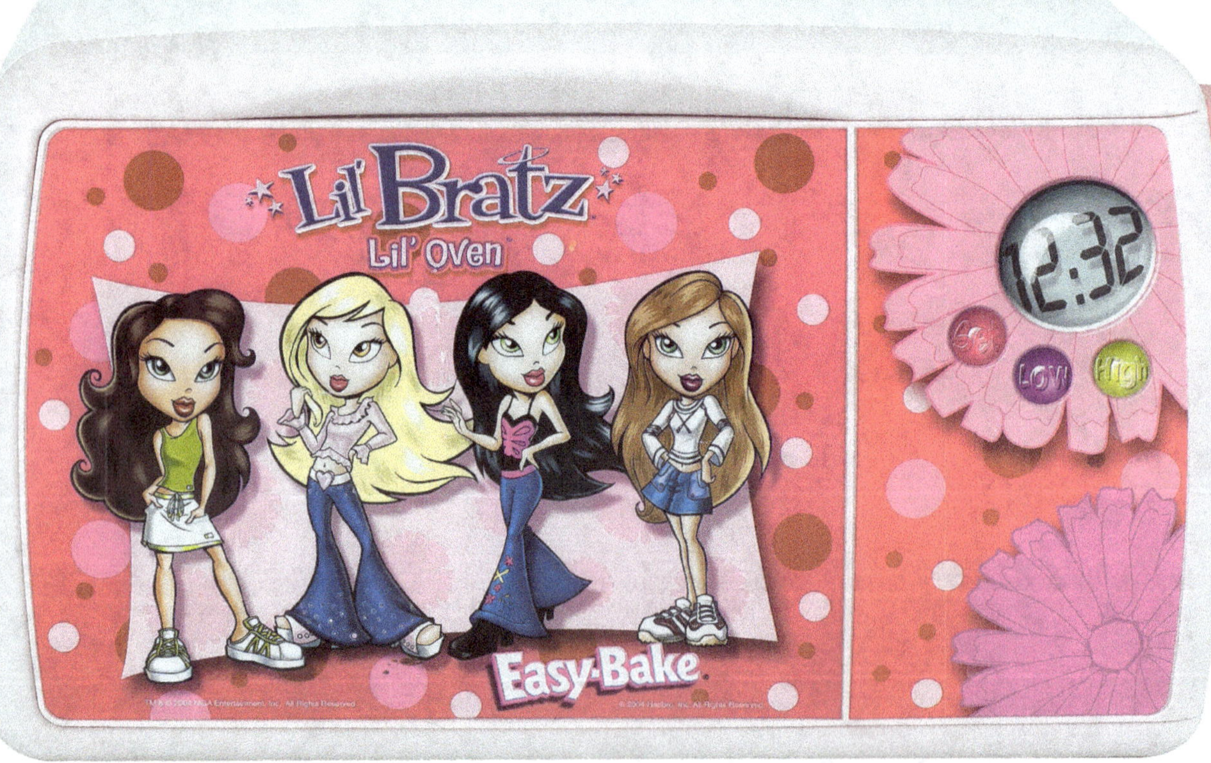

Li'l Bratz
Lil' Oven
Easy-Bake
12:32
LOW
High

Lil' Bratz Lil' Oven

2004

Hasbro capitalized on the popularity of Bratz—a fashion doll line from MGA Entertainment—with the 2004 release of the Lil' Bratz Lil' Oven.

The oven was pink and white and emblazoned with a large sticker of the Lil' Bratz foursome (Sasha, Chloe, Jade, and Yasmin) that covered the front of the oven.

On the sticker, plastic dials of earlier models were replaced with three buttons and an over-sized faux digital clock reading 12:32.

Did you know?

During the height of the Bratz craze, the doll was #2 in worldwide sales, outsold only by Barbie.

Original retail price:
$19.⁹⁹

Powered by:
1x
100W
light bulb

Available in
Pink

In the box:

- 3 mixes
- 2 baking pans
- Spoon
- Spatula
- 2 warming cups
- Pan pusher

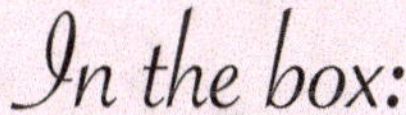

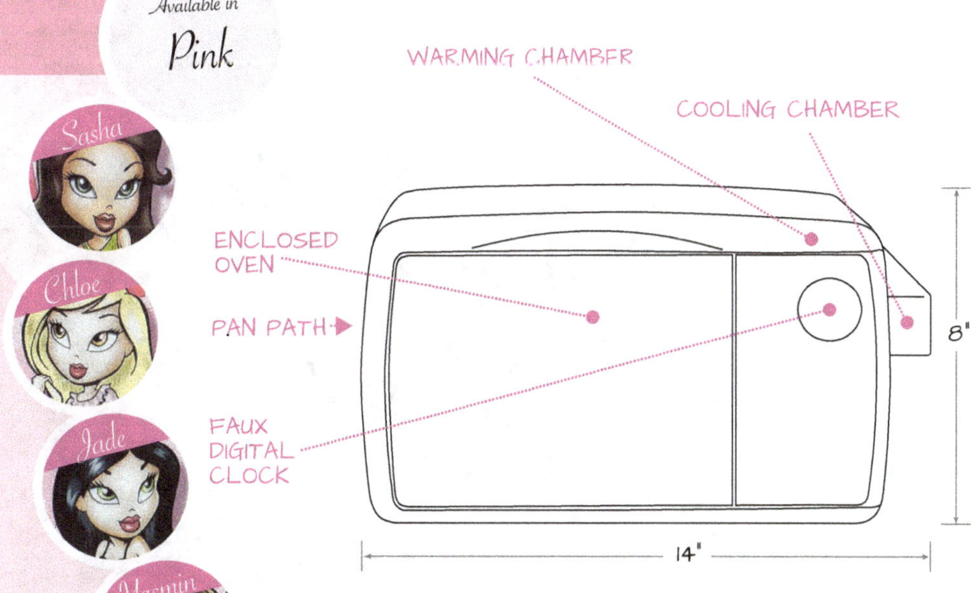

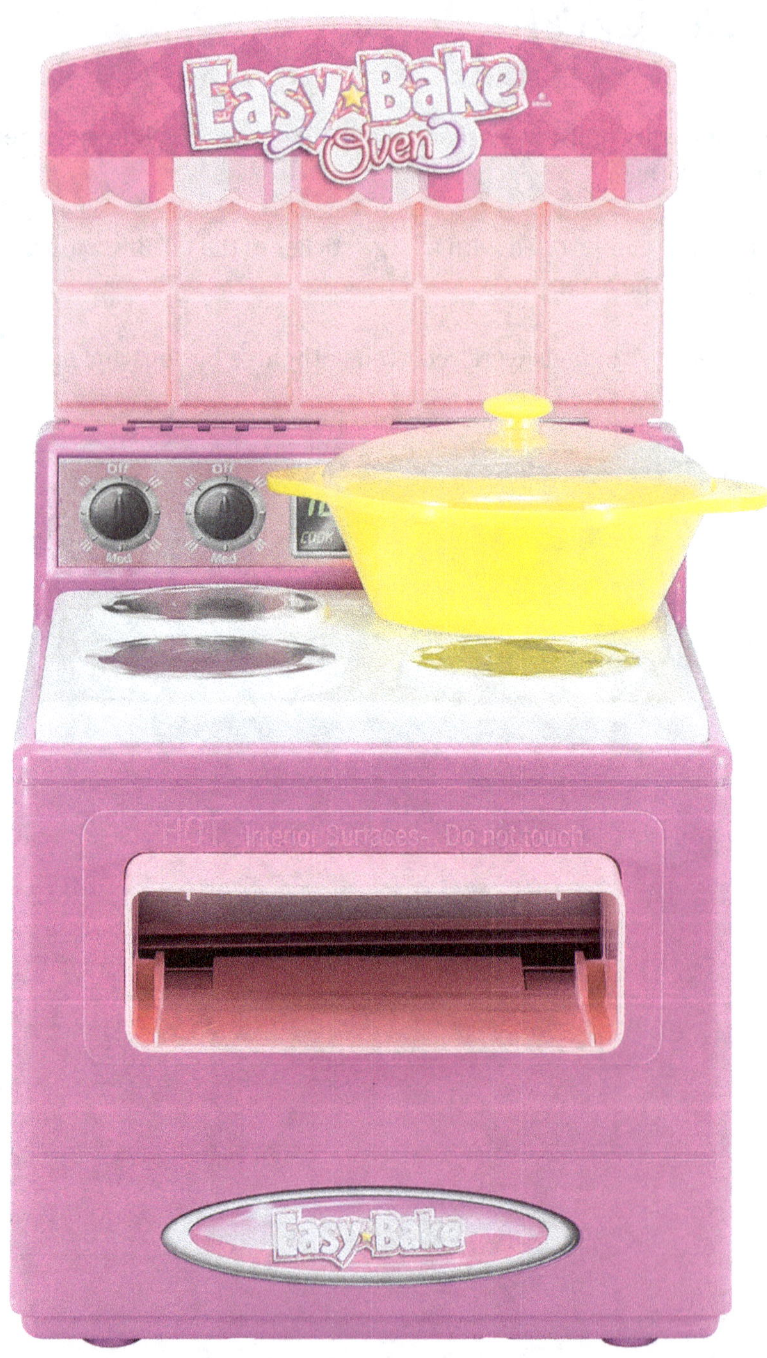

Easy Bake
Oven
Off
Med
Off
Med
HOT Interior Surfaces - Do not touch
Easy Bake

Easy-Bake Classic Oven

After releasing the first light-bulb-free Easy-Bake Real-Meal Oven in 2003, Hasbro officially retired the light bulb from the product line and released the Easy-Bake Classic Oven in 2006. Using a heating element instead of a light bulb, the new oven resembled a contemporary kitchen range, albeit in dark lavender.

Pans now entered the oven through the front using the patented MagiCool Pan Grabber. A heat sensor changed color to indicate when the pan was cool enough to touch. A stove-top warmer allowed toppings to be heated in a new mixing bowl with lid.

Original retail price:
$24.⁹⁹

Powered by:
1x
Heating element

Did you know?

Hasbro publicly retired the light bulb from the Easy-Bake Oven line at the 103ʳᵈ American International Toy Fair in 2006.

Available in
Dark Lavender

Accent
White

Accent
Pink

In the box:

- 3 mixes
- 2 baking pans
- 4-way measuring spoon
- Pan pusher
- Mixing bowl with lid
- MagiCool Pan Grabber

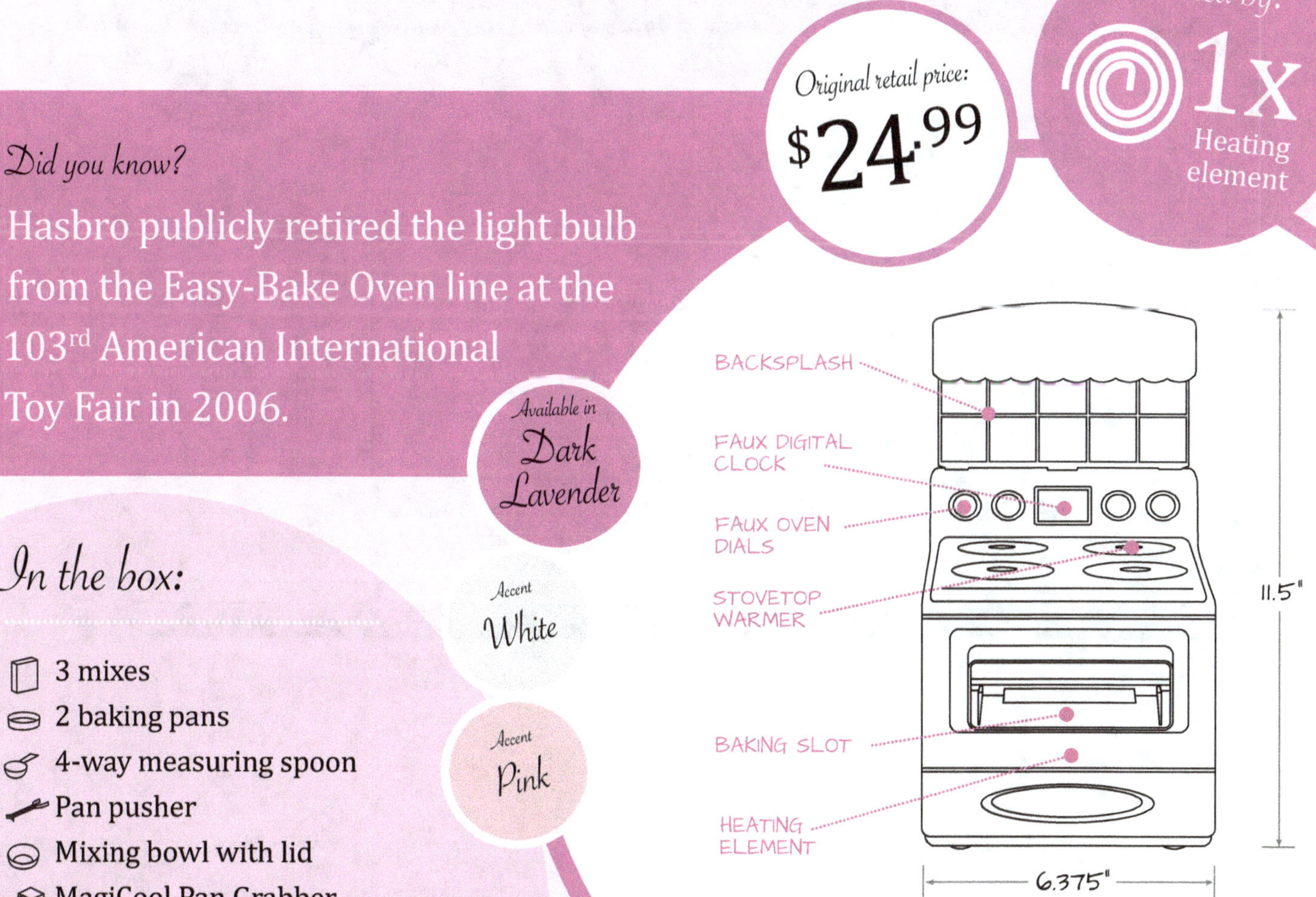

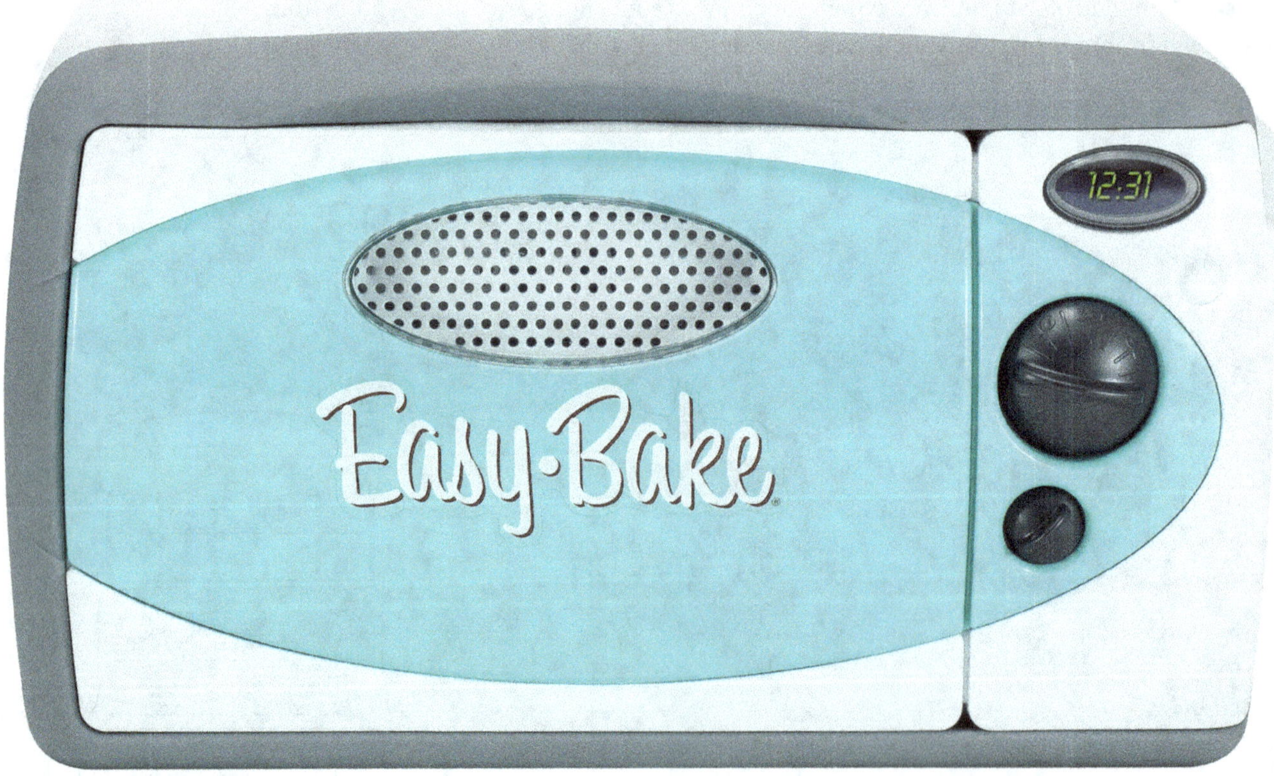

Easy-Bake
12:31

Easy-Bake Oven & Snack Center 2008

After the recall of the Easy-Bake Classic Oven (page 18), Hasbro returned to basics with the release of the Easy-Bake Oven & Snack Center in 2008. Essentially a re-packaged 2004 model, the new oven brought the light bulb back as a power source.

The color scheme was updated to white, teal, and gray, giving the oven a decidedly retro feel that was reflective of the burgeoning vintage trend of the day.

The faux clock was reset to 12:31 (the same time displayed by the 2004 model's clock).

Original retail price:

$24.⁹⁹

Powered by:

1x
100W
light bulb

Did you know?

In the Fox television show Fringe, Dr. Walter Bishop used this model to help unravel a mystery. (See page 136)

Available in
Teal

Accent
White

Accent
Gray

In the box:

- 3 mixes
- 2 baking pans
- Spoon
- Spatula
- 2 warming cups
- Pan pusher

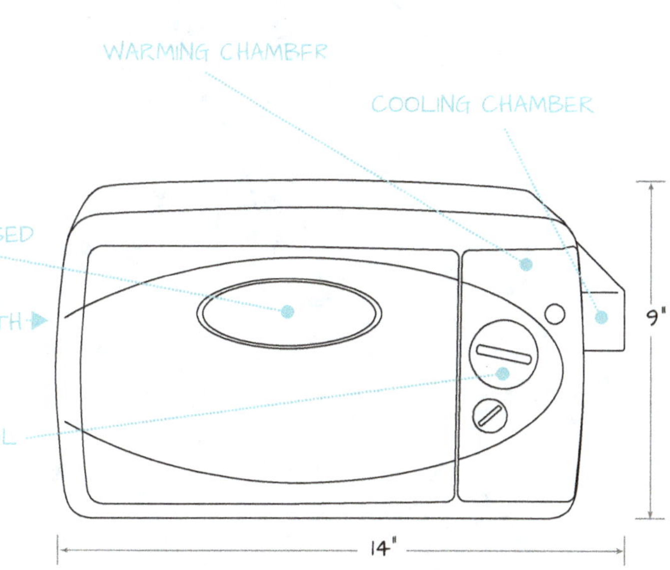

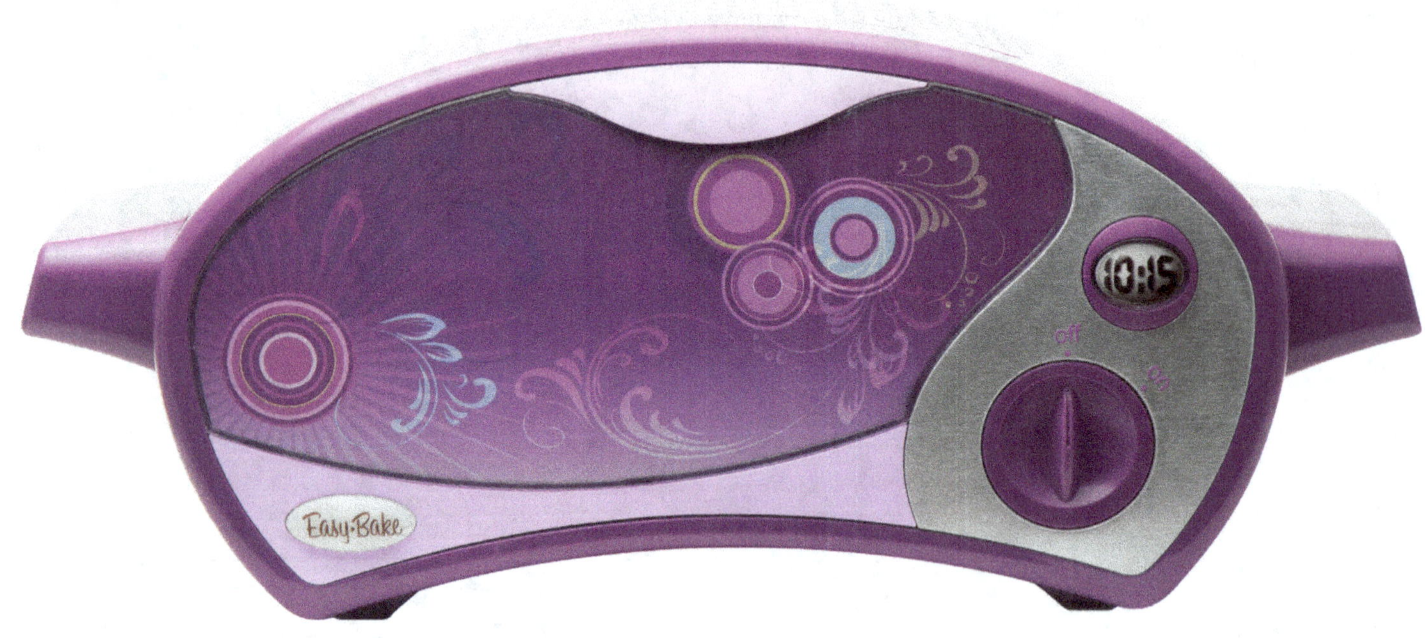
Easy-Bake
10:15
off
on

Easy-Bake Ultimate Oven

On the eve of the Easy-Bake Oven's 50th anniversary, its primary power source, the 100-Watt incandescent light bulb, was becoming extinct. The 2007 *Energy Independence and Security Act* required the incandescent to be phased out by 2012 (page 16). Rather than kill the toy, Hasbro opted instead to reboot it.

The light bulb was once again replaced with a heating element. The boxy design of the Easy-Bake Oven & Snack Center was radically retooled and modernized. Dubbed the Easy-Bake Ultimate Oven, the new model was equipped with a larger baking chamber, an updated set of pans and utensils, an on/off switch, and a storage chamber.

Options for aspiring bakers now included cakes, cookies, brownies, pizza, and pretzels. The faux digital clock was set to 10:15.

Original retail price:
$44.⁹⁹

Powered by:
1x Heating element

Did you know?

Joe Cacciola, now president of Fuzion Design Inc., the industrial design team behind the Easy-Bake Ultimate Oven, was also part of the design team at Hasbro that launched the Queasy Bake Cookerator.

Available in
Purple

Accent
Lavender

Accent
Silver

In the box:

- 4 mixes
- Baking pan
- Cupcake pan
- Pan pusher
- Cookbook

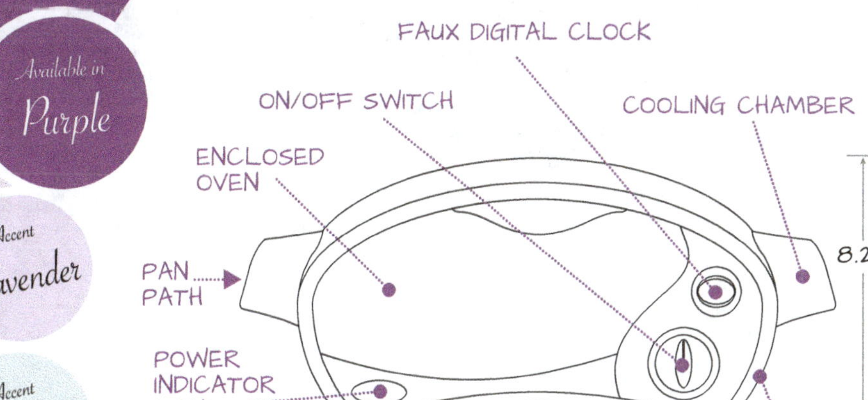

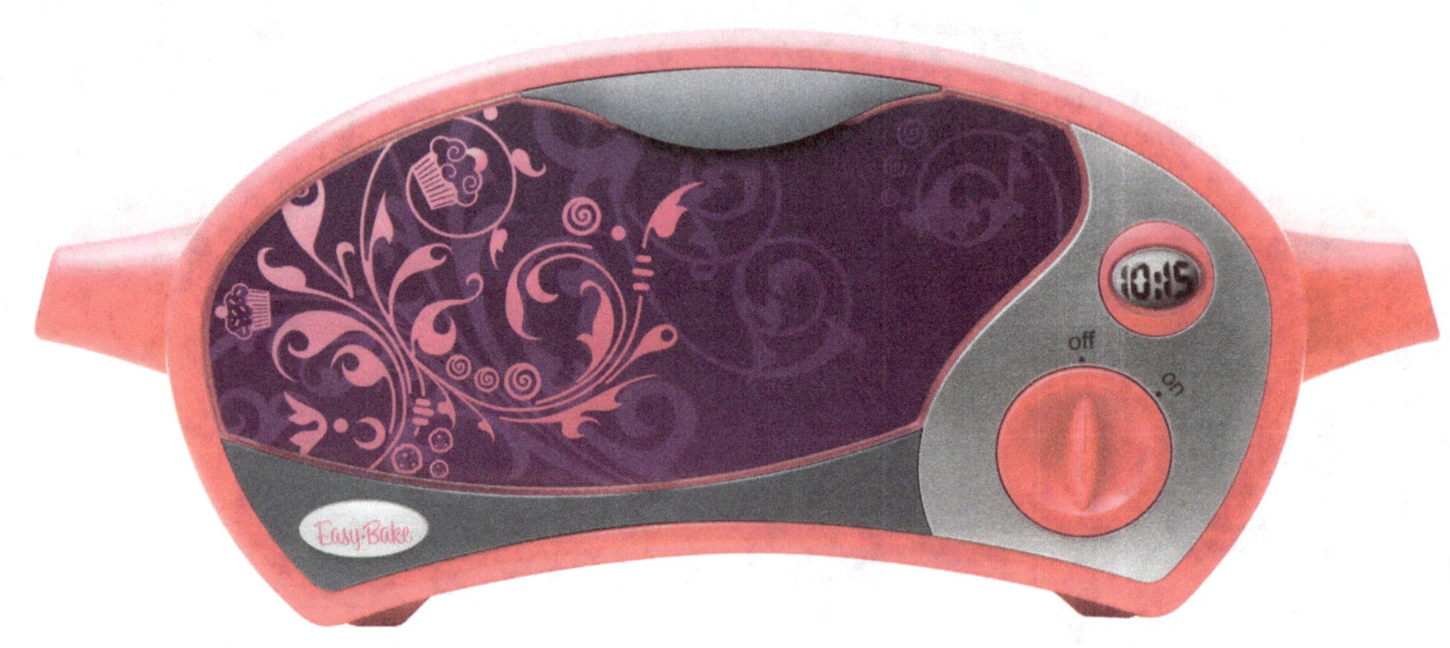

10:15
off
on
Easy-Bake

The "It's a cupcake party" edition of the Easy-Bake Ultimate Oven was available exclusively at Walmart stores. It contained four extra mixes and sprinkles, allowing young bakers to make 12 mini-cookies and 36 mini-cupcakes before needing refills.

The oven sported a unique color scheme and sticker set while retaining the same features as the purple model.

Did you know?

Once heated up, the Easy-Bake Ultimate Oven baked mini-cookies and cupcakes in 10 minutes.

Original retail price:

$44.⁹⁹

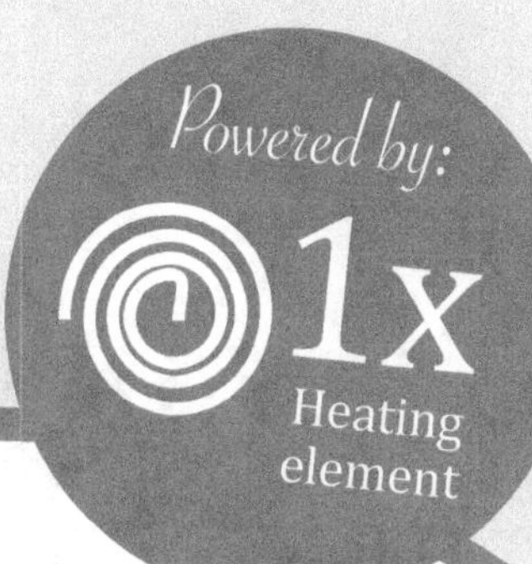

In the box:

- 8 mixes
- Baking pan
- Cupcake pan
- Pan pusher
- Cookbook

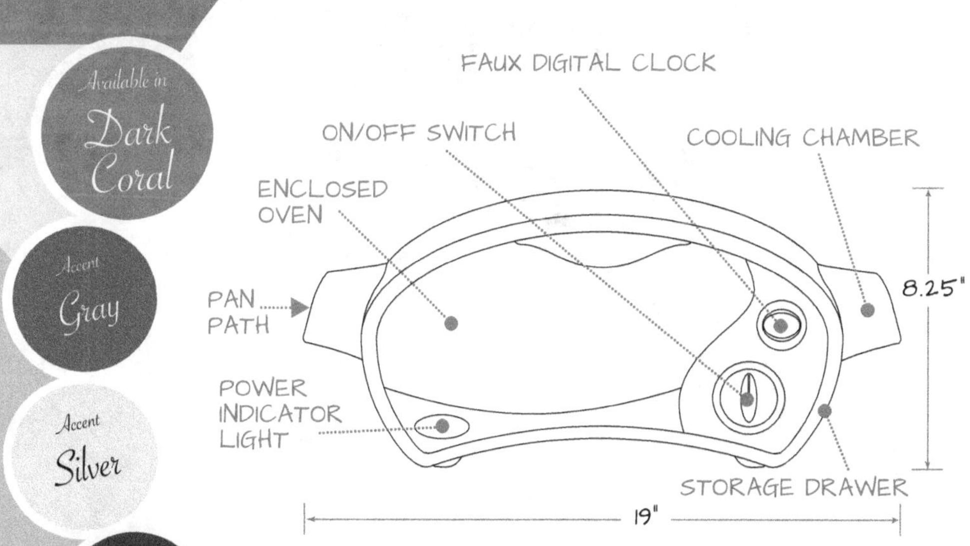

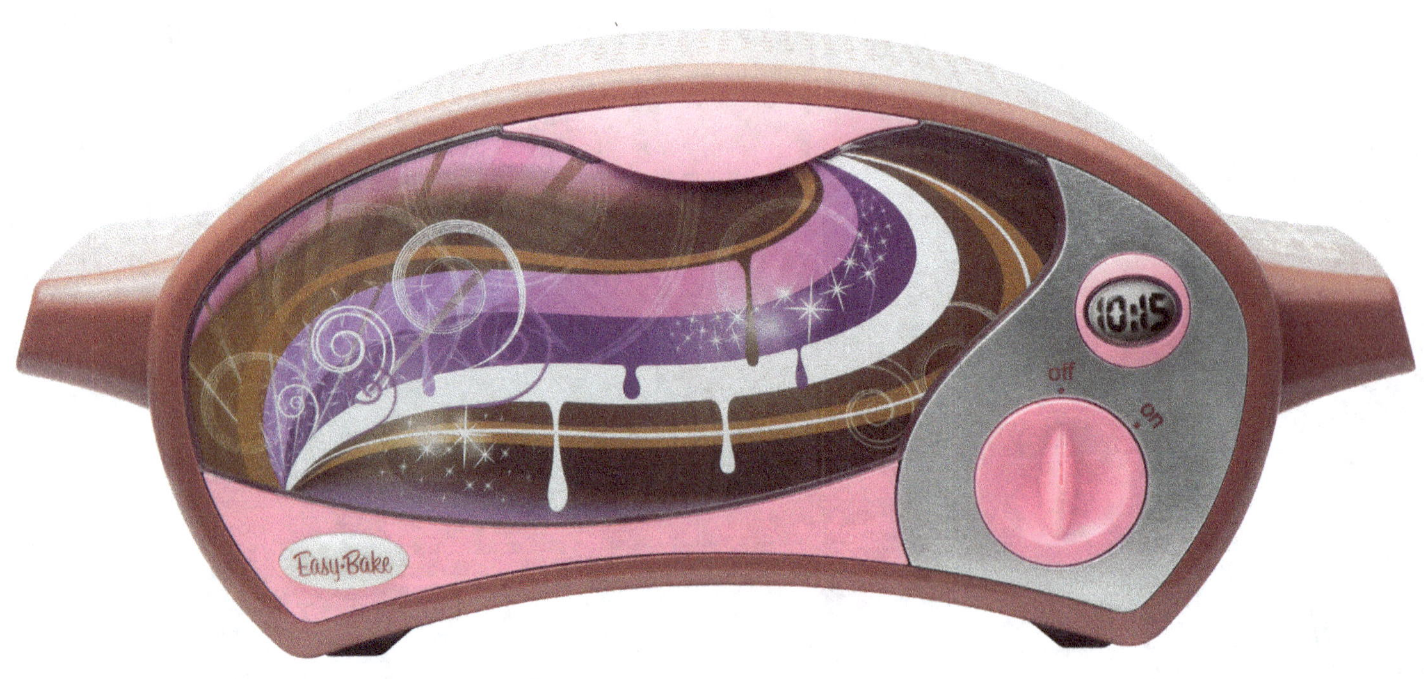
Easy-Bake
10:15
off
on

Easy-Bake Ultimate Oven – Target

The "Fun dipped in chocolate" edition of the Easy-Bake Ultimate Oven was available exclusively at Target stores. It contained four extra mixes and sprinkles, allowing young bakers to make cookies, cupcakes, brownies, and cinnamon twists.

The oven sported a unique color scheme and sticker set while retaining the same features as the purple model.

Did you know?

Cooking tips, instructions, and answers to frequently asked questions about the Ultimate Oven are available at easybake.com.

Original retail price: **$44.99**

Powered by: **1x** Heating element

Available in Chocolate

Accent Pink

Accent Silver

In the box:

- 7 mixes
- Baking pan
- Cupcake pan
- Pan pusher
- Cookbook

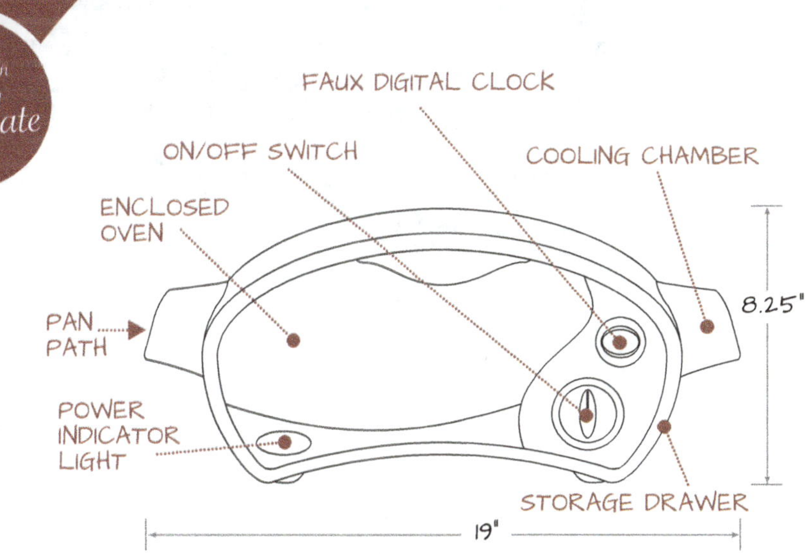

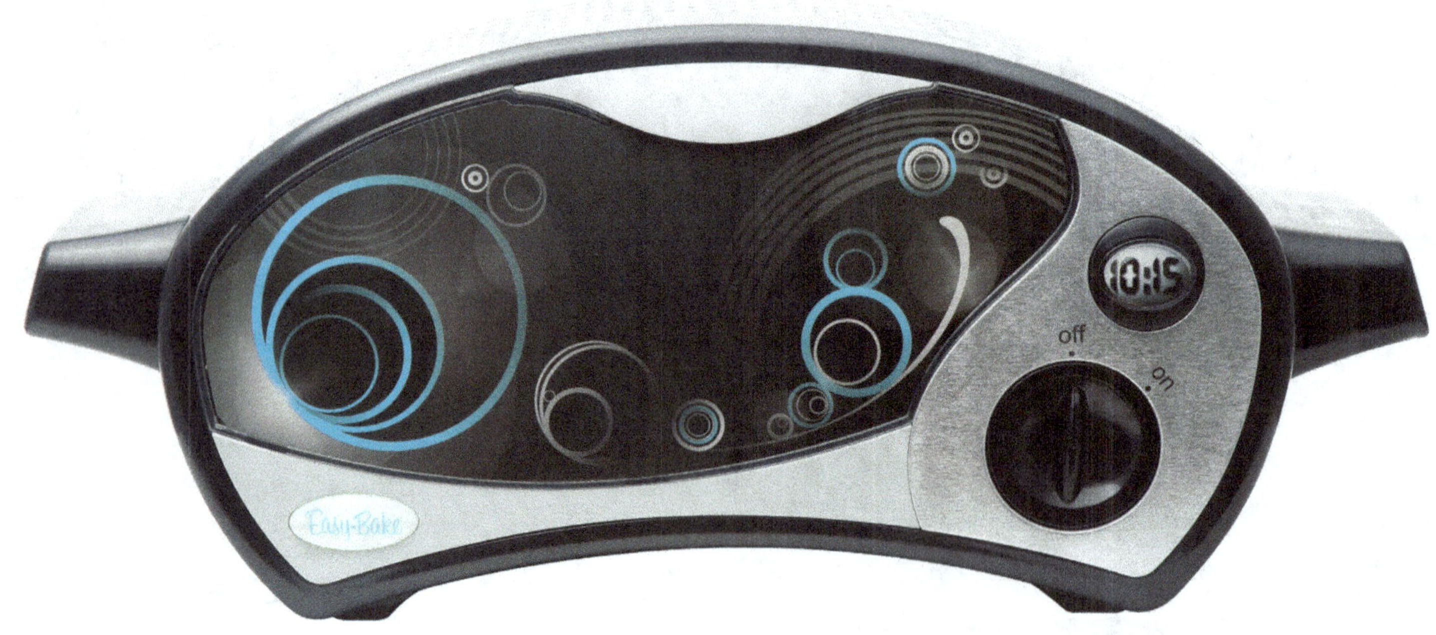

Easy-Bake
10:15
off
on

To commemorate the 50ᵗʰ anniversary of the Easy-Bake Oven, Hasbro unveiled a new color scheme. The traditional pink and purple of previous models was replaced with a more gender-neutral palette of black, silver, and blue.

These changes dovetailed with an online petition filed by 13-year old McKenna Pope asking Hasbro to make an oven that was more gender-neutral. That petition went viral and received more than 40,000 signatures.

Outside of the color change, this model retains all the features and functionality of its predecessor.

Original retail price:
$54.⁹⁹

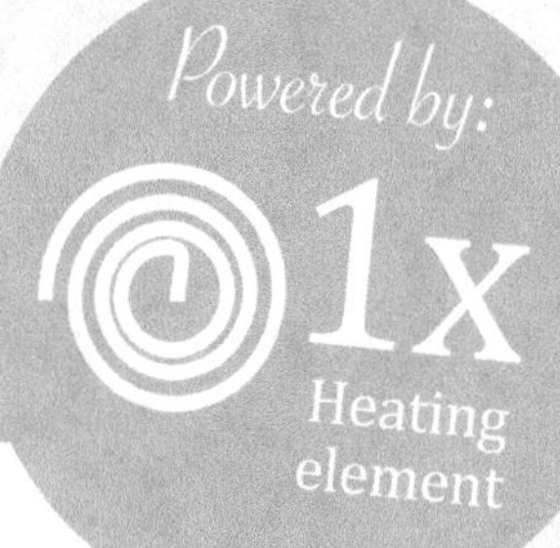

Did you know?

In 50 years, more than 30 million Easy-Bake Ovens and more than 150 million mix refills have been sold.

Available in
Black

Accent
Azure

Accent
Silver

In the box:

- 1 mix
- Baking pan
- Pan pusher
- Cookbook

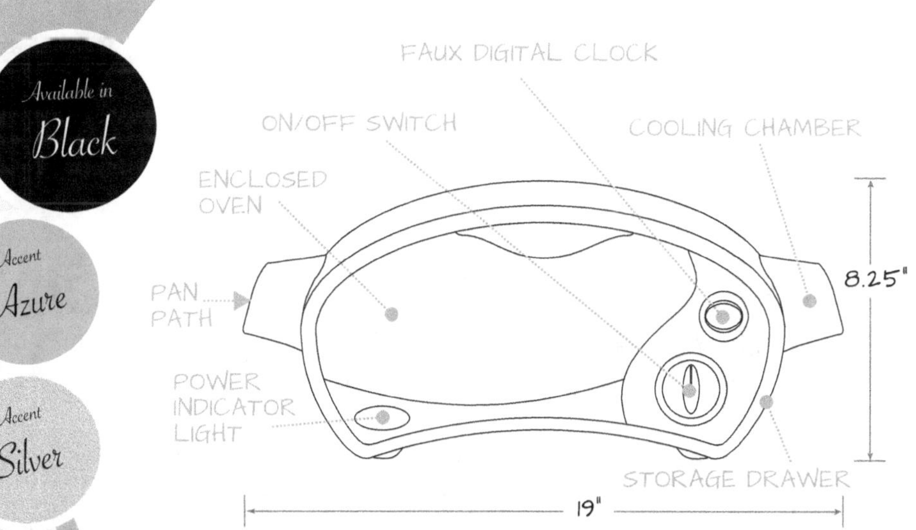

Pans & Pan pushers

Pans have always been important accessories to the Easy-Bake Oven, and an integral part of the toy's engineering. They need to fit safely into the oven while allowing mixes to bake properly in a reasonable amount of time. The size of Easy-Bake pans has changed over the years to match changes in the product's industrial design, updates to the internal baking chamber, and varying power requirements.

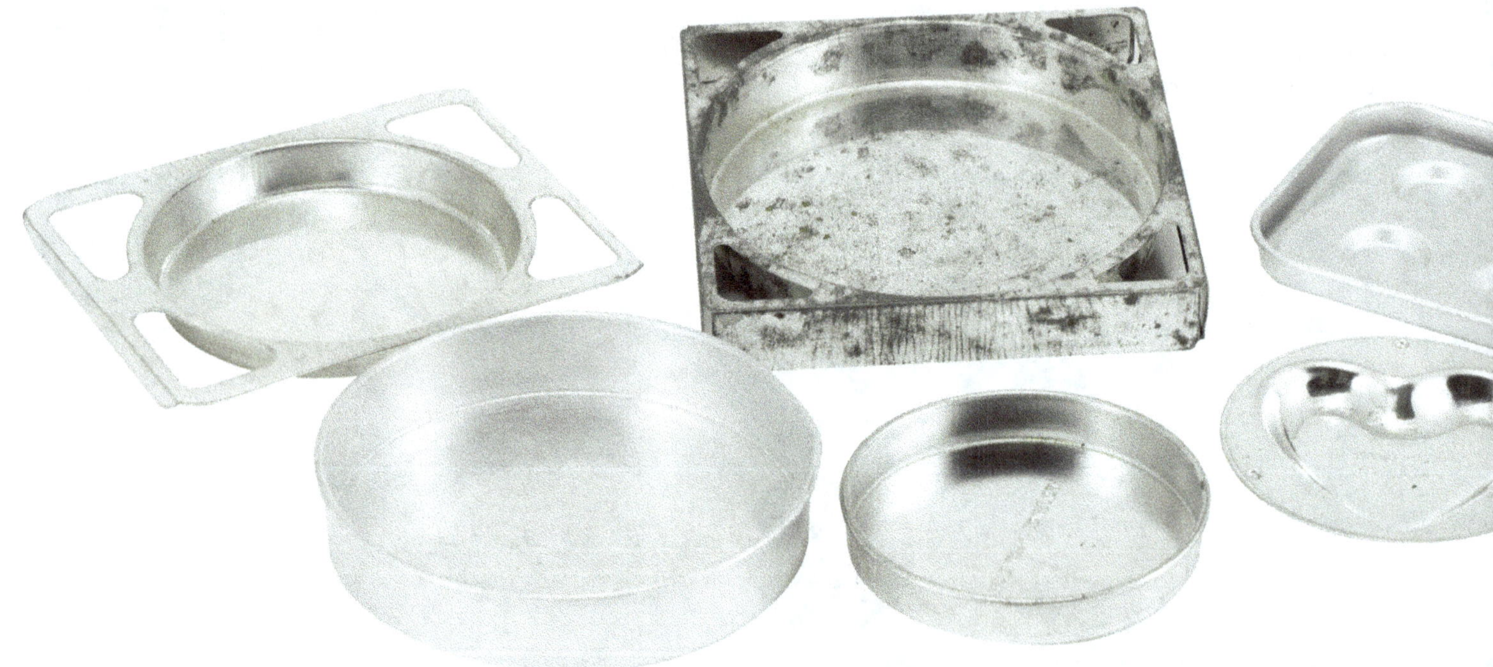

Did you know?

Baking pans included with early Easy-Bake Oven models were coated with non-toxic, food-grade vegetable oil to provide a barrier of protection during shipping and transit.

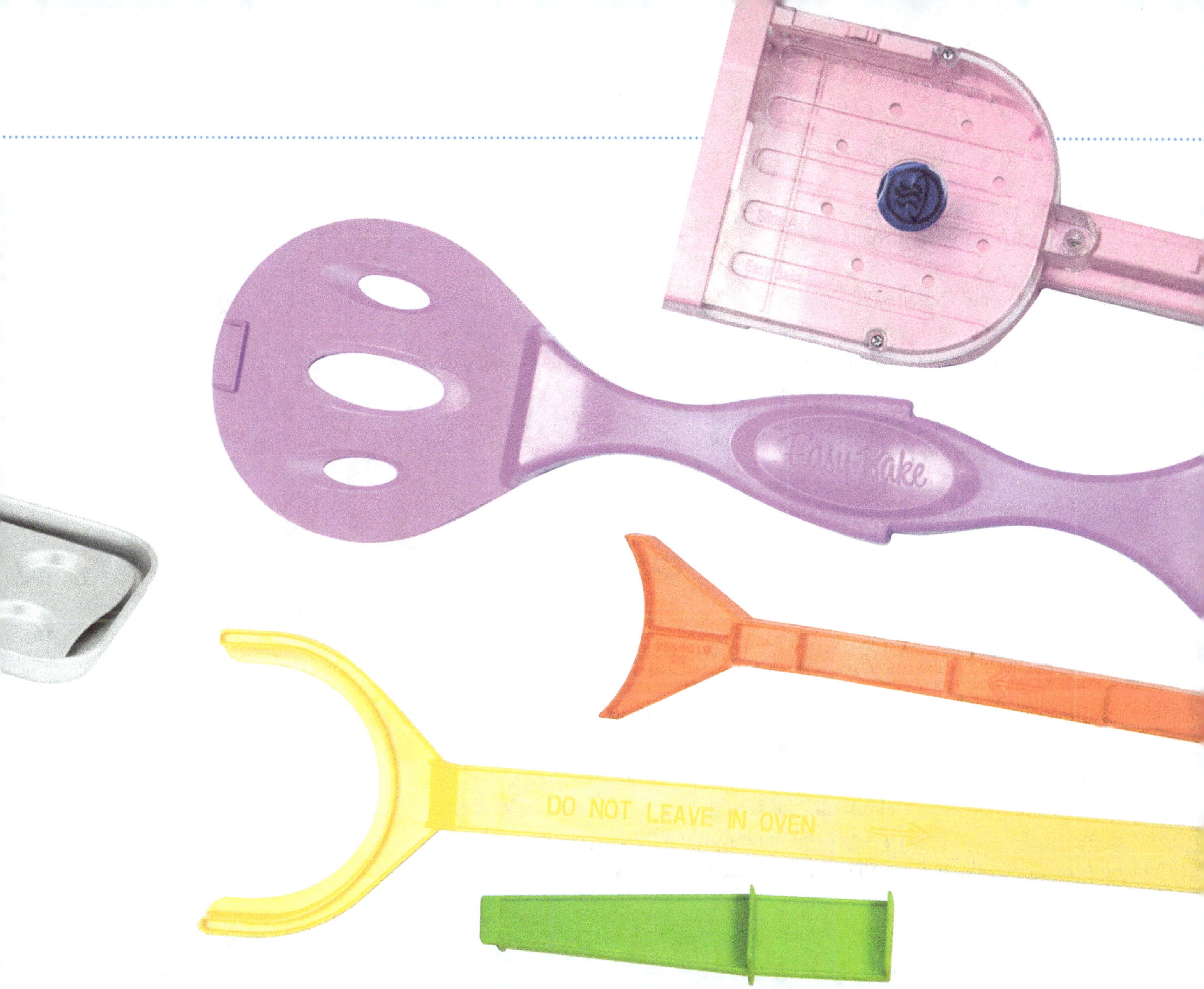

Working in concert with Easy-Bake pans is the pan pusher. First introduced in 1973 to accompany the Betty Crocker Easy-Bake Oven, the pan pusher utensil is used to move pans in and out of the oven. Made of heat-resistant plastic, it has also been redesigned several times to enhance safety and accommodate baking pans of various sizes. The latest version of the pan pusher is included with every Easy-Bake Oven sold today.

Refill Mixes & Bake Sets

Trying out new recipes is a natural progression for anyone developing a passion for baking. Thanks to the Easy-Bake Oven, generation after generation of kids have developed this curiosity from an early age. The release of every new model of the Easy-Bake Oven has typically been accompanied by a host of complementary refill mixes and bake sets. Since 1963, more than 150 million refill mixes and bake sets have been sold.

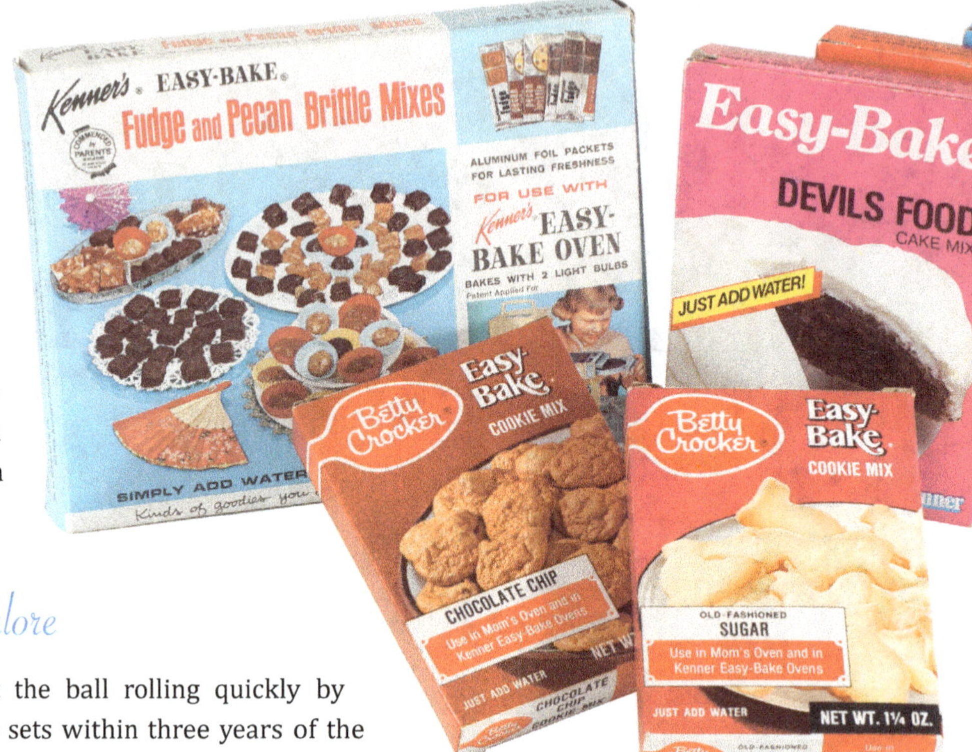

Kenner: Baking Options Galore

The creative minds at Kenner got the ball rolling quickly by releasing more than 25 different bake sets within three years of the toy's release. With prices ranging from $0.98 to $4.98 per mix, the possibilities for young bakers ran the gamut from cakes and cookies to fudge, pretzels, candy bars, and even bubble gum. While some of these yield better results than others, all could be baked in the Easy-Bake Oven.

Did You Know?

The first mixes for the Easy-Bake Oven had a two-year shelf life because they were packaged in polyethylene laminated to aluminum foil.

Hasbro: Brand & Character Cross-Promotion

When Hasbro acquired Kenner, a new strategy for refill mixes and bake sets emerged. Hasbro offered standard snacks and baked goods—like cakes and cookies—and focused on linking these to cross-licensed characters and well-known brands that appealed to children. Kids could now bake Pizza Hut pizza while also making cakes that looked like Oreo cookies and cookies shaped like M&Ms in their Easy-Bake Ovens. Hasbro's bake sets typically fell in the $5.00-$10.00 range.

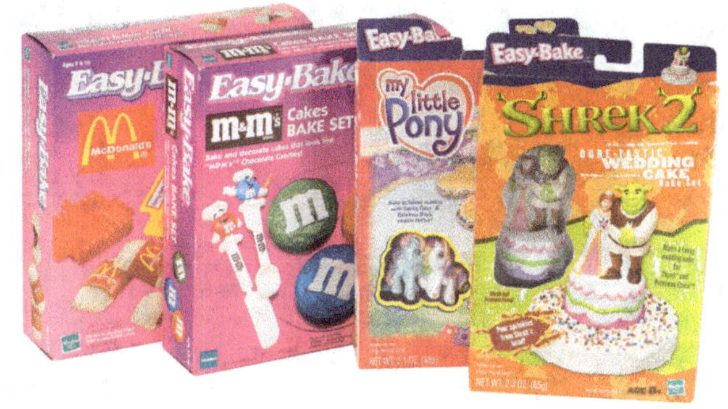

Snack Attack! Easy-Bake Oven menu items have included:

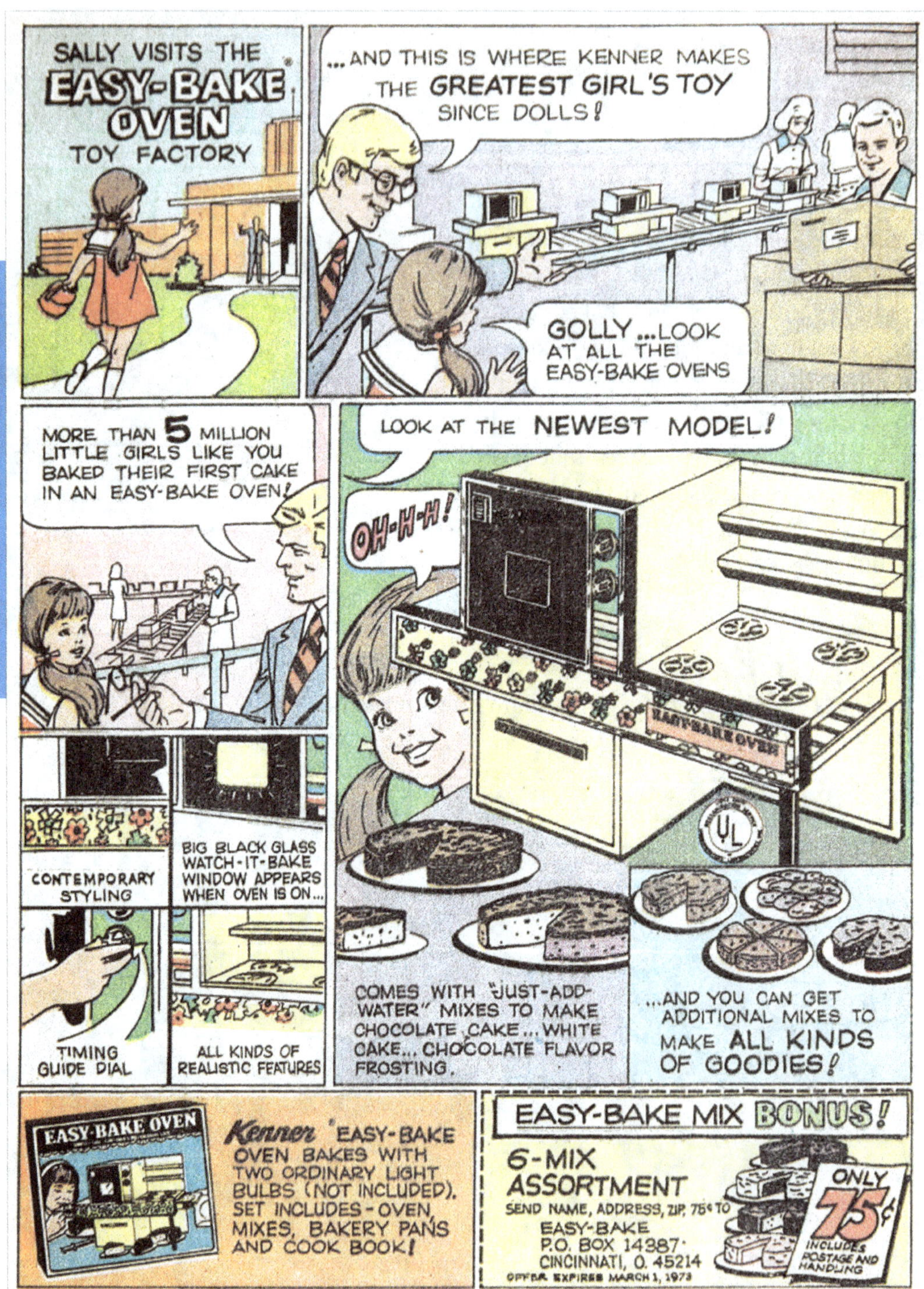

SALLY VISITS THE
EASY-BAKE OVEN
TOY FACTORY
...AND THIS IS WHERE KENNER MAKES THE GREATEST GIRL'S TOY SINCE DOLLS!
GOLLY...LOOK AT ALL THE EASY-BAKE OVENS
MORE THAN 5 MILLION LITTLE GIRLS LIKE YOU BAKED THEIR FIRST CAKE IN AN EASY-BAKE OVEN!
LOOK AT THE NEWEST MODEL!
OH-H-H!
EASY-BAKE OVEN
CONTEMPORARY STYLING
BIG BLACK GLASS WATCH-IT-BAKE WINDOW APPEARS WHEN OVEN IS ON...
TIMING GUIDE DIAL
ALL KINDS OF REALISTIC FEATURES
COMES WITH "JUST-ADD-WATER" MIXES TO MAKE CHOCOLATE CAKE...WHITE CAKE...CHOCOLATE FLAVOR FROSTING.
...AND YOU CAN GET ADDITIONAL MIXES TO MAKE ALL KINDS OF GOODIES!
EASY-BAKE OVEN
Kenner EASY-BAKE OVEN BAKES WITH TWO ORDINARY LIGHT BULBS (NOT INCLUDED). SET INCLUDES - OVEN, MIXES, BAKERY PANS AND COOK BOOK!
EASY-BAKE MIX BONUS!
6-MIX ASSORTMENT
SEND NAME, ADDRESS, ZIP, 75¢ TO
EASY-BAKE
P.O. BOX 14387
CINCINNATI, O. 45214
OFFER EXPIRES MARCH 1, 1973
ONLY 75¢
INCLUDES POSTAGE AND HANDLING

Chapter 5

Million-Dollar Baby

> "The most sophisticated people I know –
> inside they are all children."
>
> — *Jim Henson*

As any inventor or product manager will tell you, a new product launch is a lot like the birth of a child. And like a new child, the first years of a new product's life are critical to its longevity.

Kenner's careful and consistent investment in promoting the Easy-Bake Oven during its early years—along with the toy's inherent appeal to children and its attractive design—helped secure its place as one of the world's most popular and iconic toys.

A review of the Easy-Bake Oven's advertising mix during its formative years reveals a successful blueprint that Kenner repeatedly used to market and promote all of its top brands. Over time, this formula became a finely tuned mix of print and television advertising, sweepstakes, rebate programs, and product showcases. Along the way, Kenner took risks and pioneered ideas, as well as taking measured steps and monitoring what did and didn't work.

While the Easy-Bake Oven was only one of Kenner's many early hits, it can be argued that it was one of the most successful. In 1958, sales at Kenner hovered below $1 million a year. In 1966, fewer than five years after the toy oven was introduced, Kenner's net sales had sky rocketed to over $25 million fueled in part by Easy-Bake sales figures. By then, over 1 million ovens and 20 million mix sets had been sold.

Easy-Bake Milestones

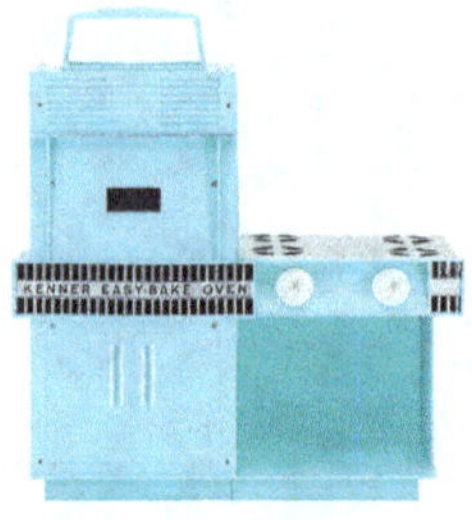

The Easy-Bake Oven is introduced. Kenner sells 500,000 units the first year.

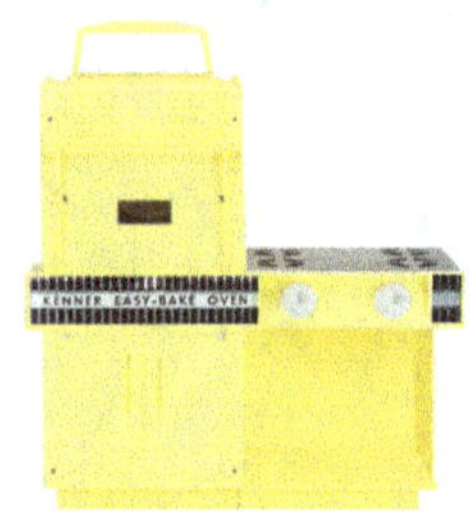

More than 2 million ovens and 28 million mixes sold.

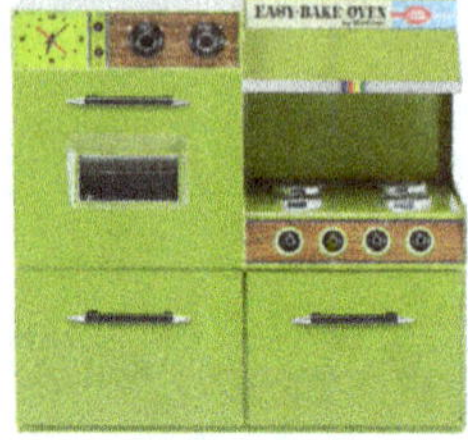

Betty Crocker-branded oven model released. Nearly 4 million ovens and more than 67 million mixes sold.

1963 **1966** **1967** **1968** **1969** **1971**

More than 1 million ovens and 20 million Easy-Bake mixes sold.

Easy-Bake Ovens begin to be sold with Betty Crocker mixes. More than 3 million ovens and 50 million mixes sold.

More than 5 million ovens and 80 million mixes sold.

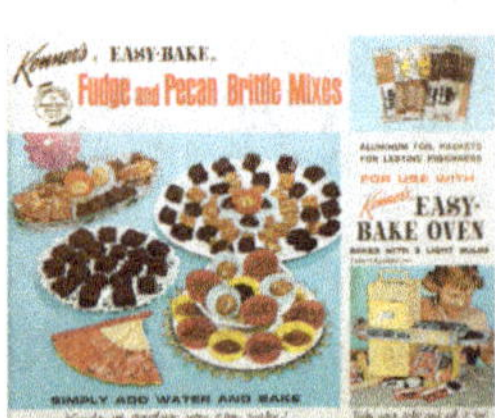

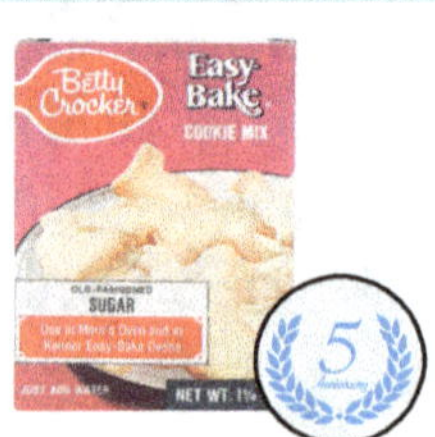

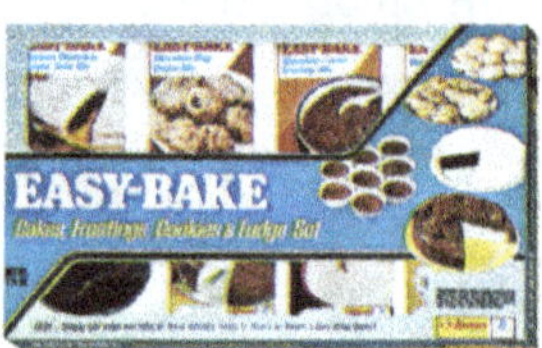

As the Easy-Bake line matured and Kenner was acquired, General Mills, Tonka, and now Hasbro remained committed to nurturing the oven's long-lasting appeal through traditional advertising programs that included cross-character promotion and more.

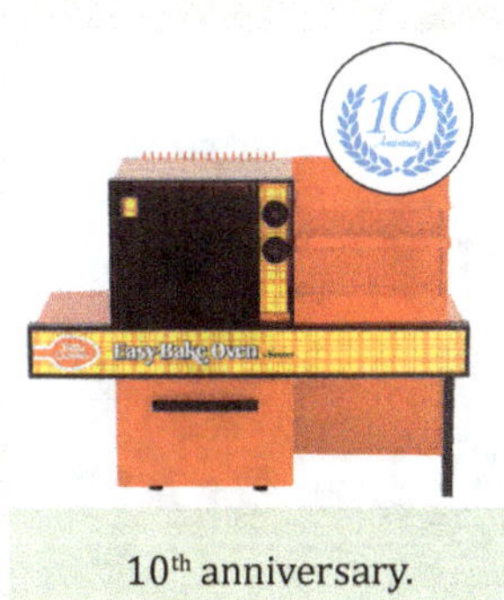

10th anniversary.

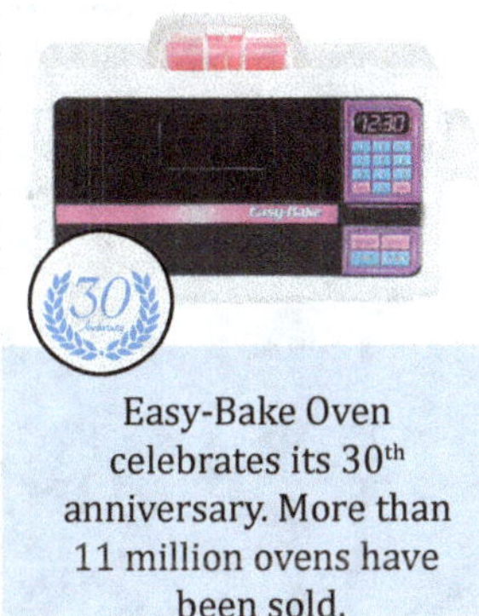

Easy-Bake Oven celebrates its 30th anniversary. More than 11 million ovens have been sold.

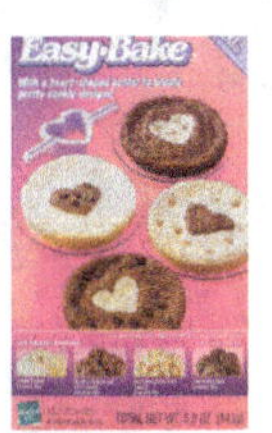

More than 19 million ovens and 130 million mix refills sold.

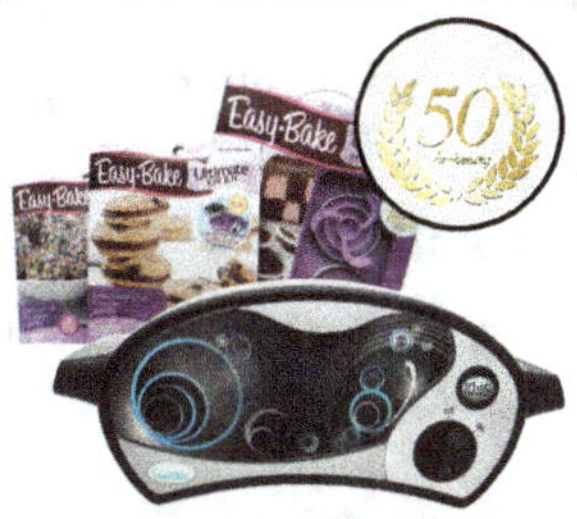

More than 30 million ovens and 150 million mix refills sold.

1973 **1978** **1993** **1997** **2000** **2006** **2013**

15th anniversary; Mini-Wave Oven introduced.

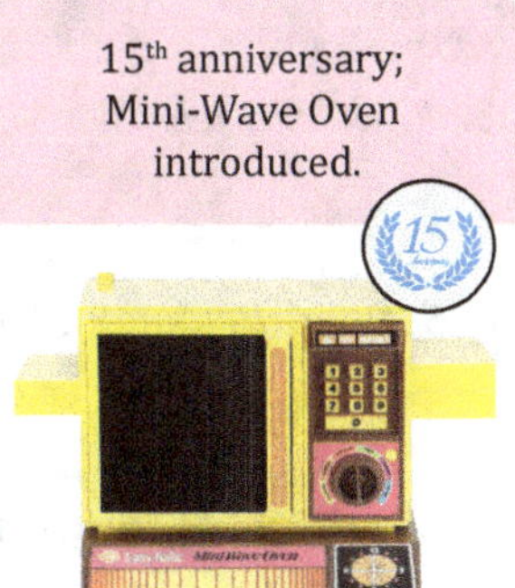

Easy-Bake Oven turns 35. More than 16 million Easy-Bake Ovens and 100 million baking sets sold.

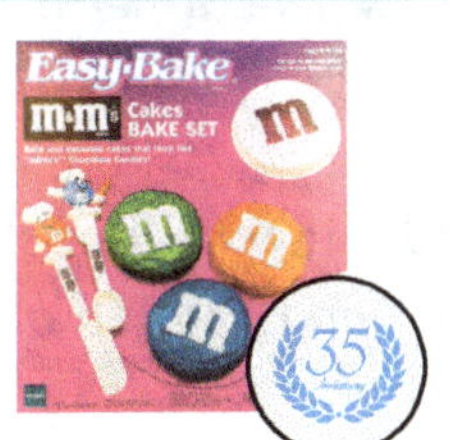

Easy-Bake Oven is elected to the National Toy Hall of Fame. More than 23 million ovens sold.

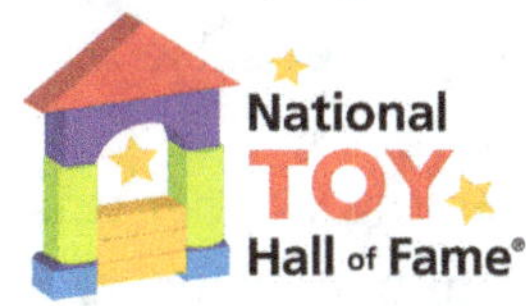

On T.V.

Like most toy companies that promoted their products in the 1950s, Kenner spent its advertising budgets primarily on print promotion in the form of catalogs and ads in periodicals and newspapers. In that decade, however, television became firmly established as a preferred form of communication and entertainment in the United States. Almost 75% of all American households had a television set, and Kenner recognized the enormous potential of the medium.

Humble Beginnings

Not everyone on the management team was convinced of the viability of creating on-air advertising focused on toys and aimed at children, so Kenner's first television campaign was a small one. In 1958 Robert Steiner, then a territory salesman in the mid-west (and son of one of the company's founders, Albert Steiner), got the ball rolling. He felt that two of the company's newly released products, *The Girder and Panel Building Set* and *Bridge and Turnpike Building Set* were very televisable[1].

A family watches television in the 1950s.

After a bit of cajoling, Steiner was given a $2,100 budget (almost $16,000 in today's dollars) to produce the company's first commercial, which was created by Bob Grannen of Leonard M. Sive and Associates—Kenner's

---

[1] During a telephone conversation, Bob Steiner referenced the two new toys as "very televisable."

advertising agency of record at the time. As the commercial aired locally in Cincinnati, sales of both building sets in the area picked up, requiring Kenner to make more inventory available to meet demand. Although the sample size was small, the positive reception by consumers to the commercial and the resulting up-tick in sales was enough for Kenner to begin to embrace television advertising to bolster its bottom line and increase the profile of popular brands and new-to-market toys.

— Headline from 1965 Kenner Toy Dealer Catalog

Toys and Television: A Potent Mix

Kenner quickly increased its advertising coverage to 10 local markets and established a four-point merchandising strategy in which television advertising was a cornerstone. With the new strategy in place, Kenner began advertising on CBS's *Captain Kangaroo Show*, becoming one of its first sponsors, and launched a series of ad campaigns that saw its products appearing on all three major networks (ABC, CBS, NBC) and in hundreds of local markets.

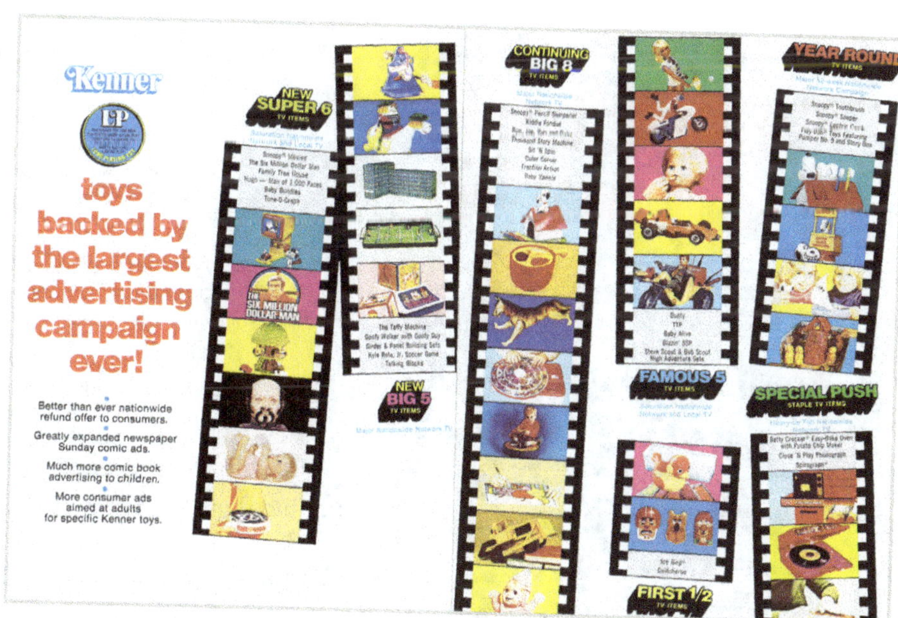

A spread from Kenner's 1975 dealer catalog, providing insight into its television ad campaign.

As Kenner began to invest more dollars into television advertising, a direct correlation between ad spend and net sales became apparent. According to Steiner, the formula was simple—the cost of television time was about 10% of net sales. A sampling of sales results from these years bears out this formula. In 1965, Kenner spent $1.9 million on television advertising and saw net sales of $18.2 million. In 1967, the ad spend almost doubled to $3.4 million, with net sales rising to $31 million.

Starring Role

Due to the toy's success, the Easy-Bake Oven was given a starring role in Kenner's on-air advertising plan. In 1966, the budget for the Kenner TV campaign had reached $2.4 million—more than four times the industry average at that time. The campaign was anchored by a 52-week promotion of the Easy-Bake Oven line, which saw the toy being advertised nationally on 10 top-rated shows for children and adults across all three networks.

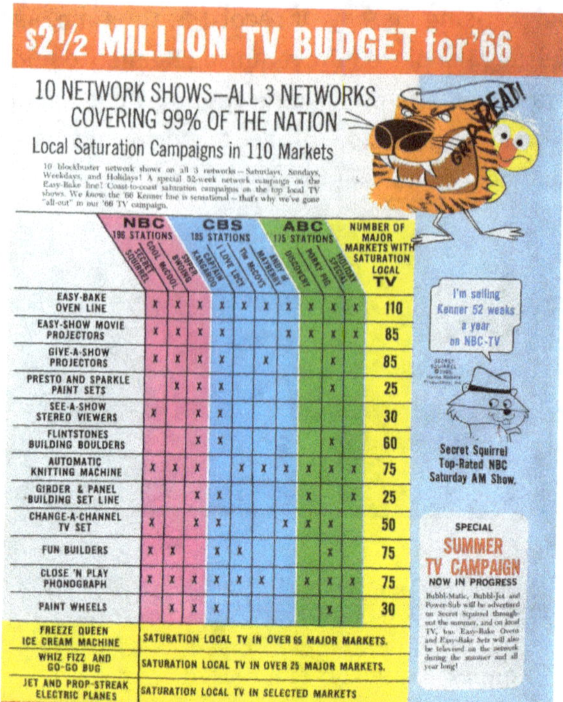

	NBC — 196 STATIONS			CBS — 185 STATIONS				ABC — 175 STATIONS			NUMBER OF MAJOR MARKETS WITH SATURATION LOCAL TV
	Secret Squirrel	Cool McCool	Super Swingin'	Captain Kangaroo	I Love Lucy	The McCoys	Andy & Mayberry	Discovery	Porky Pig	Holiday Special	
EASY-BAKE OVEN LINE	X	X	X	X	X	X	X	X	X	X	110
EASY-SHOW MOVIE PROJECTORS	X	X	X	X			X	X	X	X	85
GIVE-A-SHOW PROJECTORS	X	X	X	X		X			X		85
PRESTO AND SPARKLE PAINT SETS		X	X	X					X		25
SEE-A-SHOW STEREO VIEWERS	X		X	X							30
FLINTSTONES BUILDING BOULDERS			X	X					X		60
AUTOMATIC KNITTING MACHINE	X	X	X		X	X	X	X	X	X	75
GIRDER & PANEL BUILDING SET LINE			X	X				X		X	25
CHANGE-A-CHANNEL TV SET	X		X	X			X	X	X		50
FUN BUILDERS	X	X		X	X				X		75
CLOSE 'N PLAY PHONOGRAPH	X	X	X	X	X	X		X	X	X	75
PAINT WHEELS		X	X	X					X		30
FREEZE QUEEN ICE CREAM MACHINE	SATURATION LOCAL TV IN OVER 65 MAJOR MARKETS.										
WHIZ FIZZ AND GO-GO BUG	SATURATION LOCAL TV IN OVER 25 MAJOR MARKETS.										
JET AND PROP-STREAK ELECTRIC PLANES	SATURATION LOCAL TV IN SELECTED MARKETS										

Kenner's 1966 television advertising plan provided blanket coverage across all three major networks in the United States.

Highlights of Kenner's television advertising campaign from its 1966 dealer catalog.

The impact on sales of the toy was palpable as the Easy-Bake enjoyed double-digit sales growth during its formative years from 1966-1969.

This pattern repeated throughout the 1960s and 1970s. Children who watched Saturday- and Sunday-morning cartoons like *Road Runner*, *The Flintstones*, and *Bullwinkle* were exposed to Kenner's advertisements for popular toy lines such as Spirograph, Baby Alive,

Close 'n' Play Phonograph, The Six Million Dollar Man, and the Easy-Bake Oven. While the list of toys that received television exposure changed from year to year, the photogenic oven seemed to always make the cut.

Adult Appeal

Kenner also recognized the power of television not only to entice children but also to educate adults about the importance of play. Thus, Easy-Bake Oven ads were also seen during top-rated shows including *I Love Lucy, Donna Reed*, and *Father Knows Best;* and late-night television, including the *Tonight Show* and *CBS Evening News*.

To further influence adults, Kenner also incorporated known television personalities of the time into its ads. In 1970 the company commissioned famed television psychologist Dr. Joyce Brothers to participate in a series of six commercials discussing the psychological aspect of toys and children's play. Later, the company turned to comedian Paul Lynde and actor Geoffrey Holder (of the famous "un-cola" ad campaign for 7 Up) to promote the merits of fun and the overall quality of the Kenner product line.

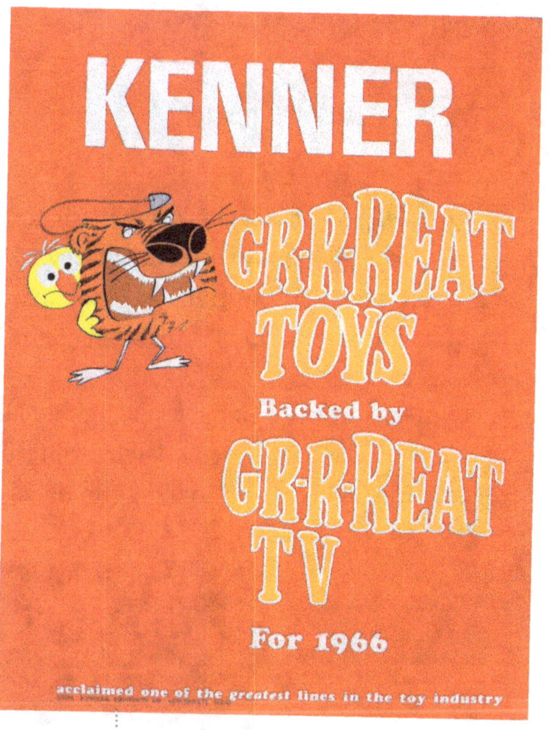

Cover of Kenner's 1966 dealer catalog.

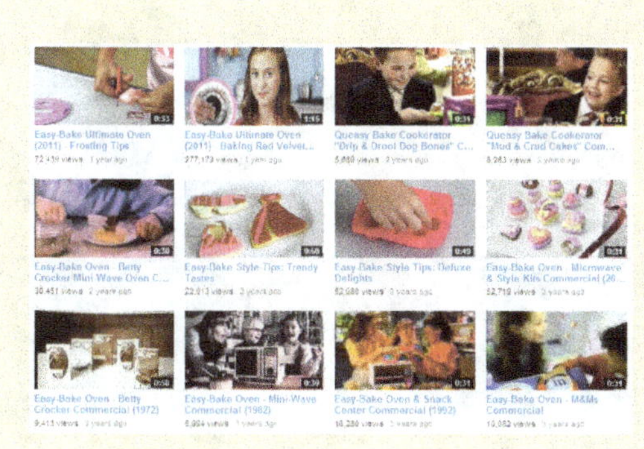

Did you know?

You can see a range of Easy-Bake Oven TV commercials at youtube.com/lightbulbbaking

A Star is Born

For well over a decade, the Easy-Bake Oven remained a staple in Kenner's television advertising campaigns. One of the most well-known television spots to feature the product was a commercial directed in 1968 by a then 31-year-old Jim Henson. Henson, who created The Muppets in 1955, had already made his mark mixing puppet characters into TV ads with commercials for *Linit Fabric Finish*, *La Choy Chow Mein*, and *Wilkins Coffee*.

Kenner contacted Henson through its ad agency, Leonard Sive and Associates, requesting his involvement in a new Easy-Bake commercial. Their primary request was for Henson to create a Muppet version of the company's Gooney Bird mascot and to integrate the character into the new television spot.

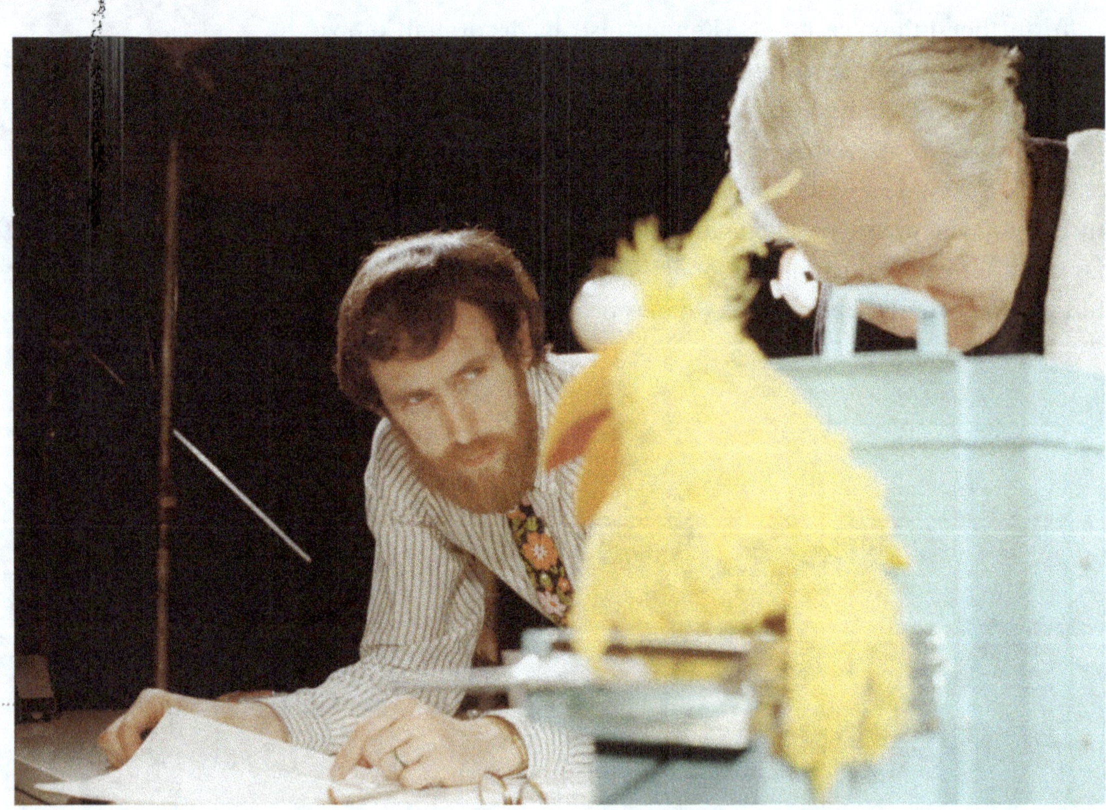

Jim Henson on the set of the 1968 Easy-Bake Oven commercial.

Henson proposed to "build a hand puppet bird and duplicate of it as a marionette." He believed that such a combination "would enable us to show it flying in mid-air, and then cutting in for a close-up of the hand puppet. I would prefer to use the puppet in connection with a real little girl. I think this makes both the puppet and the Easy-Bake Oven more real."

Once the basic idea was approved, the commercial was launched a month later. In it, the Gooney Bird interacted with child actress Barbara Price, pulling stunts like snacking on the sweets she baked, popping out of a pie, and flying into a wall of Easy-Bake products while squawking the company slogan.

Reaction to the Gooney Bird was so positive that Henson later refurbished the character as Little Bird, a sidekick to Big Bird in early seasons of the ground-breaking *Sesame Street* television show.

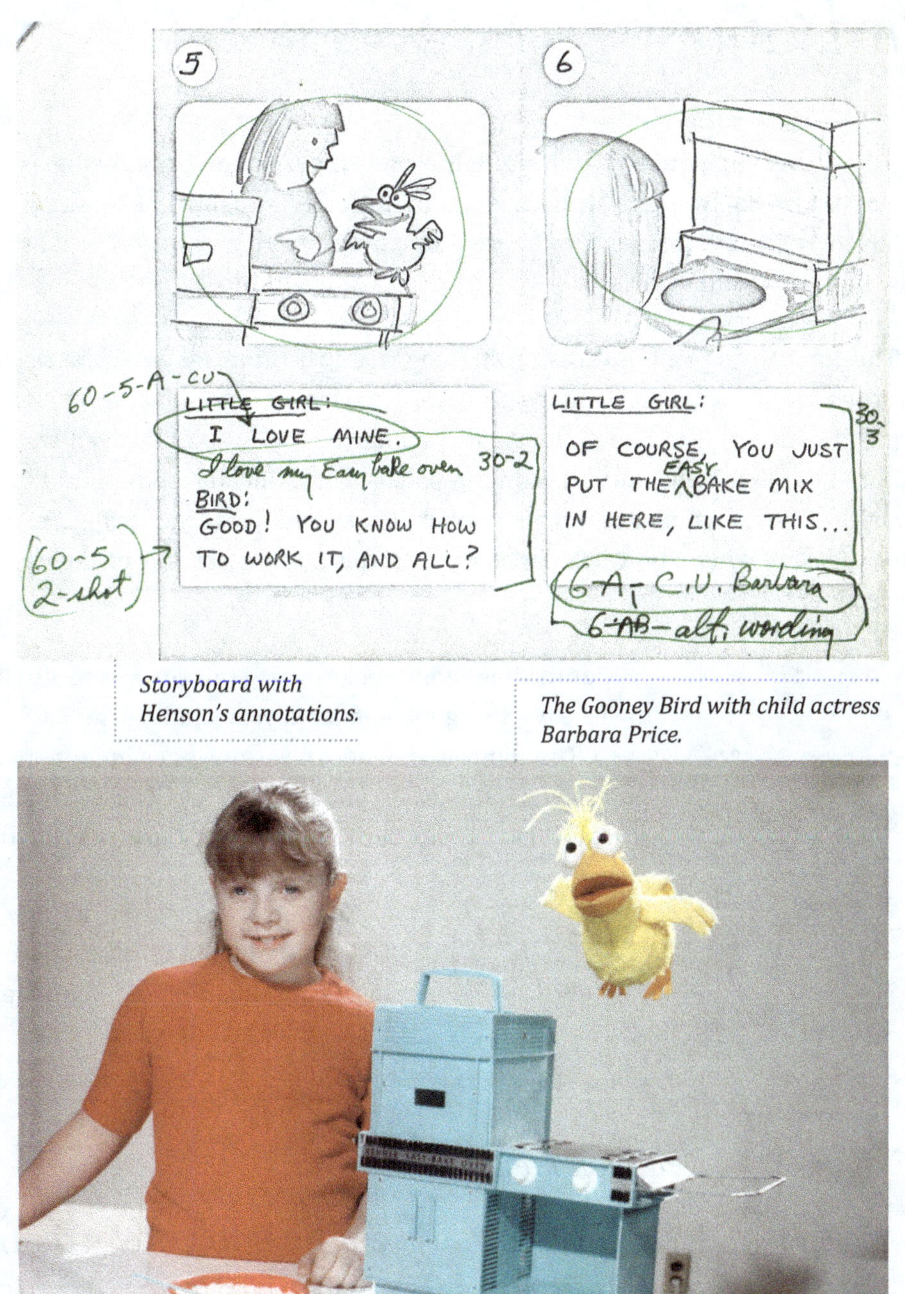

Storyboard with Henson's annotations.

The Gooney Bird with child actress Barbara Price.

In Print

*L*ike all toy companies of its time, Kenner relied heavily on print media to advertise its products. Its choice of publications through the 1960s and 1970s gives insight into who influenced toy-purchasing decisions, as well as how toys were sold to girls.

The company's print-advertising strategy was two-pronged: create desire for toys among children and heighten awareness of the same products among women and mothers. Due to its popularity, the Easy-Bake Oven was featured frequently in Kenner's print campaigns, which included ads placed in a variety of national magazines, like *Better Homes and Gardens, Family Circle, Good Housekeeping,* and *McCall's*; as well as the Comics section of Sunday newspapers.

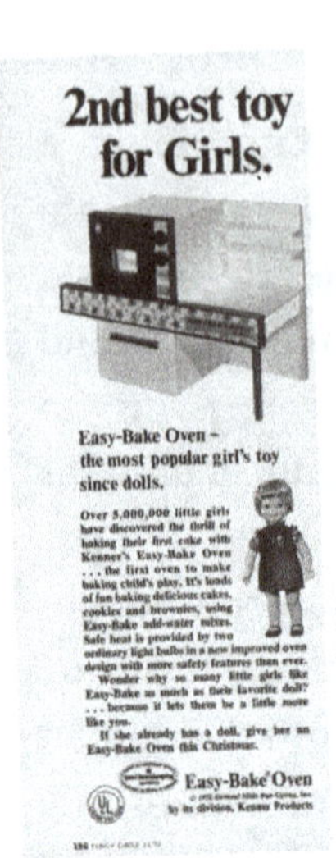

Easy-Bake ad, *McCall's,* November 1971.

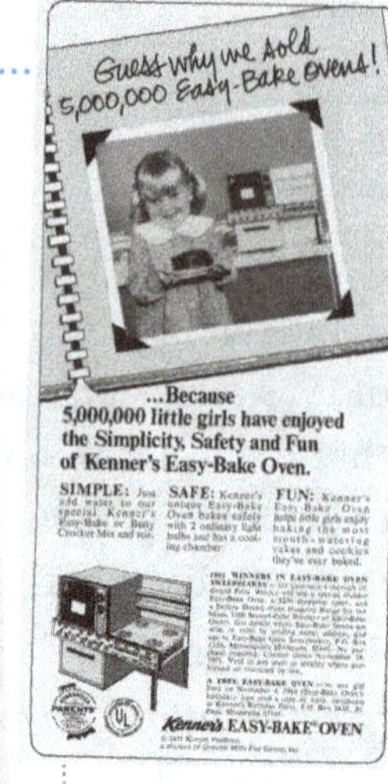

Easy-Bake ad, *Family Circle,* November 1972.

Kids reading comic books during this time were also likely to see advertising for Kenner toys, including the Easy-Bake Oven. The company ran ads of various sizes in more than 60 different comic books from three publishers: *National, Archie,* and *Gold Key*. These campaigns were typically launched leading up to peak buying times, such as before the Christmas holidays.

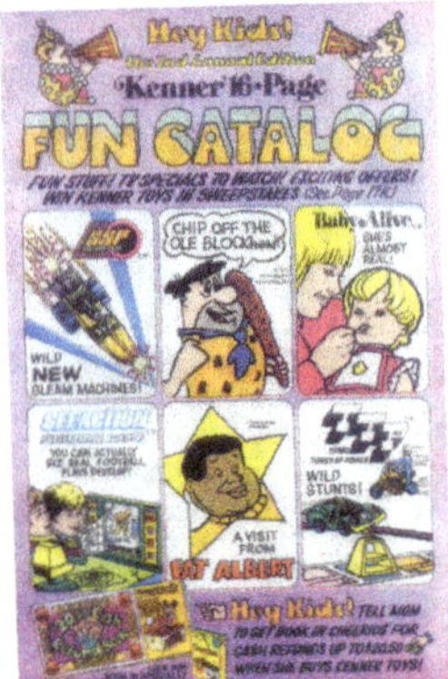

The Kenner Fun Catalog was attached as an insert in select comic books.

Kenner also inserted its *Fun Catalogs* into comic books. Typically 16 pages in length, these pull-out publications acted as comic books inside the main comic book, depicting Kenner's toy lines in a highly visual format that was familiar to comic book readers.

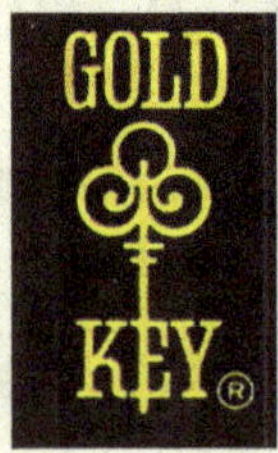

Did you know?

In 1972, Kenner's comic book advertising was expanded to a circulation of 82 million *National, Archie,* and *Gold Key* comics.

Cashing In

Advertisement for the 5,000,000th Easy-Bake Oven Sweepstakes.

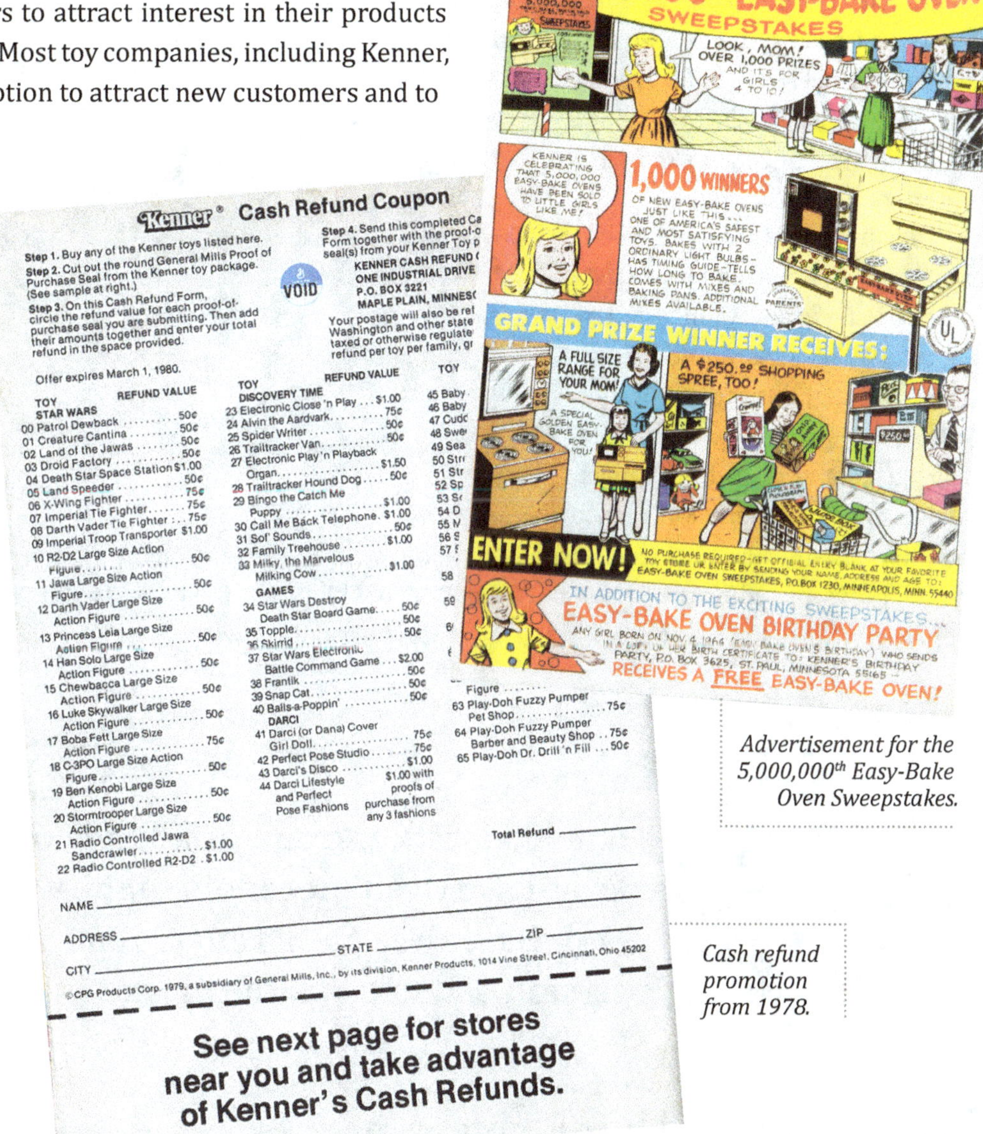

Kenner® Cash Refund Coupon

Step 1. Buy any of the Kenner toys listed here.
Step 2. Cut out the round General Mills Proof of Purchase Seal from the Kenner toy package. (See sample at right.)
Step 3. On this Cash Refund Form, circle the refund value for each proof-of-purchase seal you are submitting. Then add their amounts together and enter your total refund in the space provided.

VOID

Step 4. Send this completed Ca Form together with the proof-o seal(s) from your Kenner Toy p
KENNER CASH REFUND (
ONE INDUSTRIAL DRIVE
P.O. BOX 3221
MAPLE PLAIN, MINNES(

Your postage will also be ref Washington and other state taxed or otherwise regulate refund per toy per family, gr

Offer expires March 1, 1980.

TOY	REFUND VALUE
STAR WARS	
00 Patrol Dewback	50¢
01 Creature Cantina	50¢
02 Land of the Jawas	50¢
03 Droid Factory	50¢
04 Death Star Space Station	$1.00
05 Land Speeder	50¢
06 X-Wing Fighter	75¢
07 Imperial Tie Fighter	75¢
08 Darth Vader Tie Fighter	75¢
09 Imperial Troop Transporter	$1.00
10 R2-D2 Large Size Action Figure	50¢
11 Jawa Large Size Action Figure	50¢
12 Darth Vader Large Size Action Figure	50¢
13 Princess Leia Large Size Action Figure	50¢
14 Han Solo Large Size Action Figure	50¢
15 Chewbacca Large Size Action Figure	50¢
16 Luke Skywalker Large Size Action Figure	50¢
17 Boba Fett Large Size Action Figure	75¢
18 C-3PO Large Size Action Figure	50¢
19 Ben Kenobi Large Size Action Figure	50¢
20 Stormtrooper Large Size Action Figure	50¢
21 Radio Controlled Jawa Sandcrawler	$1.00
22 Radio Controlled R2-D2	$1.00

TOY	REFUND VALUE
DISCOVERY TIME	
23 Electronic Close 'n Play	$1.00
24 Alvin the Aardvark	75¢
25 Spider Writer	50¢
26 Trailtracker Van	50¢
27 Electronic Play 'n Playback Organ	$1.50
28 Trailtracker Hound Dog	50¢
29 Bingo the Catch Me Puppy	$1.00
30 Call Me Back Telephone	$1.00
31 Sof' Sounds	50¢
32 Family Treehouse	$1.00
33 Milky, the Marvelous Milking Cow	$1.00
GAMES	
34 Star Wars Destroy Death Star Board Game	50¢
35 Topple	50¢
36 Skirrid	50¢
37 Star Wars Electronic Battle Command Game	$2.00
38 Frantik	50¢
39 Snap Cat	50¢
40 Balls-a-Poppin'	50¢
DARCI	
41 Darci (or Dana) Cover Girl Doll	75¢
42 Perfect Pose Studio	75¢
43 Darci's Disco	$1.00
44 Darci Lifestyle and Perfect Pose Fashions	$1.00 with proofs of purchase from any 3 fashions

TOY	REFUND VALUE
45 Baby	
46 Baby	
47 Cudd	
48 Swe	
49 Sea	
50 Str	
51 Str	
52 Sp	
53 S	
54 D	
55 M	
56 S	
57 F	
58	
59	
6	
Figure	
63 Play-Doh Fuzzy Pumper Pet Shop	75¢
64 Play-Doh Fuzzy Pumper Barber and Beauty Shop	75¢
65 Play-Doh Dr. Drill 'n Fill	50¢

Total Refund ___________

NAME ________________

ADDRESS ________________ STATE ________ ZIP ________

CITY ________________

©CPG Products Corp. 1979, a subsidiary of General Mills, Inc., by its division, Kenner Products, 1014 Vine Street, Cincinnati, Ohio 45202

See next page for stores near you and take advantage of Kenner's Cash Refunds.

Cash refund promotion from 1978.

Sweepstakes and rebate programs are popular marketing promotions for manufacturers and retailers to attract interest in their products and drive sales through incentives. Most toy companies, including Kenner, used both of these modes of promotion to attract new customers and to reward customer loyalty.

During the first 15 years that the Easy-Bake Oven was on the market, the toy was routinely part of the various cash-back promotions that Kenner offered. The first of these was the *$150,000 Kenner Toy Sweepstakes*, which was advertised on more than 90 million Post cereal boxes in 1964. According to *Playthings* magazine, it was at the time the largest promotion of its kind in toy history.

The Easy-Bake Oven took center stage in 1972's *5,000,000th Easy-Bake Oven Sweepstakes*, which celebrated the toy's milestone achievement of five million units sold. Free to enter, it offered 1,000 chances to win. The grand-prize package included something for kids and parents alike: a full-size kitchen range, a special golden-colored Easy-Bake Oven, and a $250.00 shopping spree at a local toy store.

Running concurrently to the sweepstakes, the *Easy-Bake Oven Birthday Party* promotion offered a free Easy-Bake Oven to "any girl born on Nov. 4, 1964 (Easy-Bake Oven's Birthday) who sends in a copy of her birth certificate" to Kenner[1].

The natural tie-in between kids' toys and morning breakfast cereal was again tapped after General Mills acquired Kenner in 1967. Throughout the 1970s and '80s, the company routinely advertised and placed premiums inside some of General Mills most popular cereals, like Cheerios. Usually in booklet form, these promotions offered cash refunds on all of Kenner's popular toys, including the Easy-Bake Oven. Each booklet contained a rebate form which, when sent to Kenner with an appropriate proof of purchase, would trigger the cash-back reward.

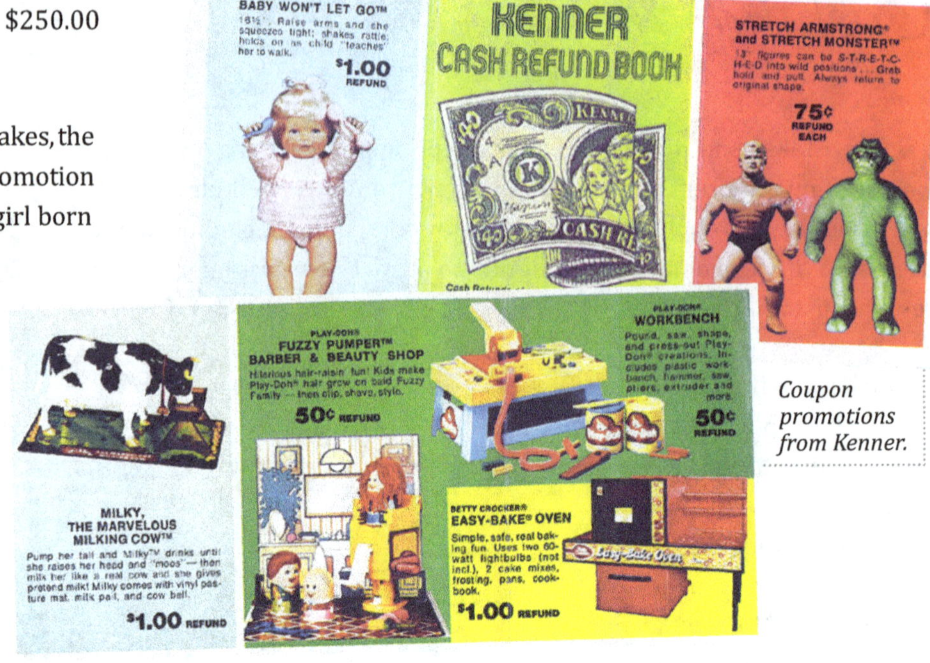

Coupon promotions from Kenner.

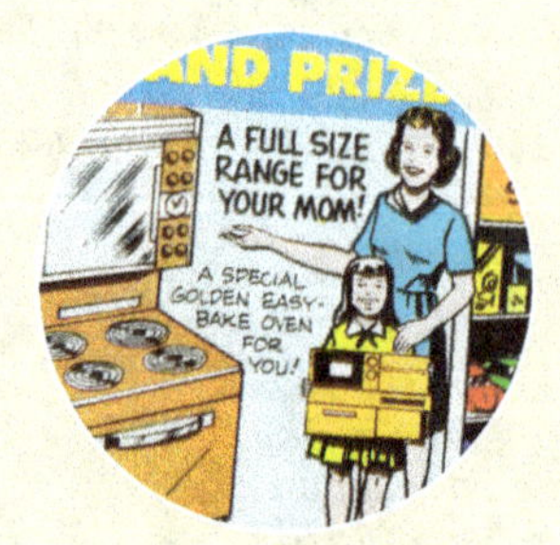

Did you know?

If it still exists, the one-of-a-kind golden-colored Easy-Bake Oven presented to the winner of the *5,000,000th Easy-Bake Oven Sweepstakes* remains the most collectable version of the toy on the market.

---

[1] Research revealed that the actual birthday of the Easy-Bake Oven is a year earlier — November 4, 1963.

On Display

By definition, toys are meant for play, and play is interactive. It's not surprising, then, that toy demonstrations and showcases have been a cornerstone of toy marketing since the 1960s.

Show and Tell

Kenner was one of the pioneers of embedding toy demonstrators into established retails stores—especially during the peak buying season leading up to Christmas. According to Corky Steiner, who had a 20+ year career in sales at Kenner, in-store toy demonstrations were "one of the smartest and easiest ways to have a toy seen by the most potential customers."

In the 1950s and 60s, the company primarily focused its demonstration efforts in department stores like Macy's and Marshall Field's. Demonstrators would spend the day showcasing a toy or toys to gathered crowds and passers-by, proving the toy worked as advertised and answering questions along the way. In the 1970s, the demo program migrated to discount stores, like Kmart.

When the Easy-Bake Oven was part of the demo circuit, it was often used in a "dry demo" format, where the demonstrator would display the oven, use the provided utensils to mix the just-add-water mixes, slide the pan into

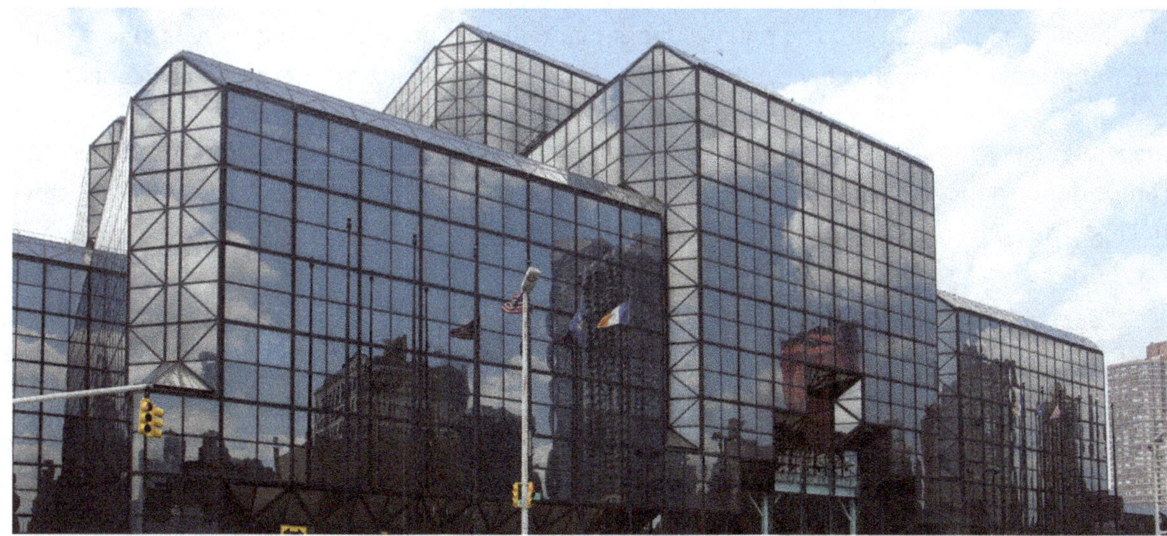

The Jacob Javits Convention Center in New York City hosts the American International Toy Fair each year.

the oven and then show a final result—very similar to what occurs on television cooking shows today.

Cornerstone of the Toy Market

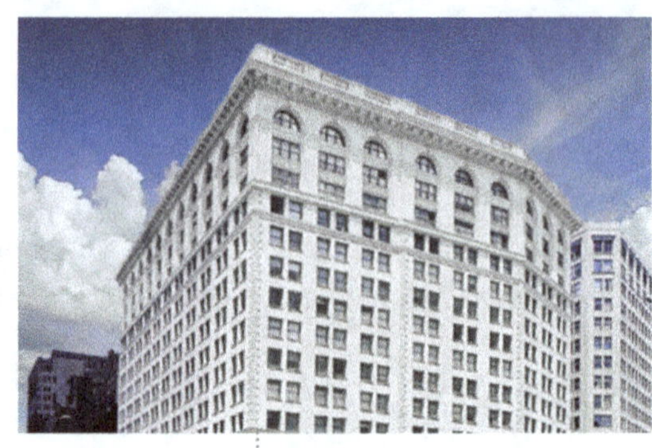
The International Toy Center in New York City.

Located in the Flatiron district of New York City's Manhattan borough, The International Toy Center at 200 Fifth Avenue had a tremendous impact on the sales and marketing of toys in the United States. Spanning an entire city block, this landmark structure became a hub for the American toy industry during World War I. By the late 1960s, it had expanded to two buildings connected by a glass pedestrian bridge.

The center housed showrooms for every major toy company in the United States, including all of the major players in the Easy-Bake Oven's history: Kenner Products, General Mills, Tonka and Hasbro. The building (in partnership with the Jacob Javits Convention Center) also co-hosted The American International Toy Fair every February. During the show, sales agents, importers, and distributors from around the country descended on the Toy Center to assess new toy lines and do their buying and selling.

A Victim of the Times

Over time, economic realities began to take a toll on The International Toy Center. Rival developers started to lure away tenants into other buildings in Manhattan. The entry of mass-market merchandisers into the toy business, such as Target and Walmart, put pressure on smaller toy companies that resulted in downsizing, mergers, and acquisitions.

In 2005, with vacancy rates hovering around 60%, The Toy Center was sold to a luxury condominium developer. The industry's symbolic epicenter disappeared, and the annual Toy Fair became the primary venue for toy buyers—now compressed into a much shorter time period of four days.

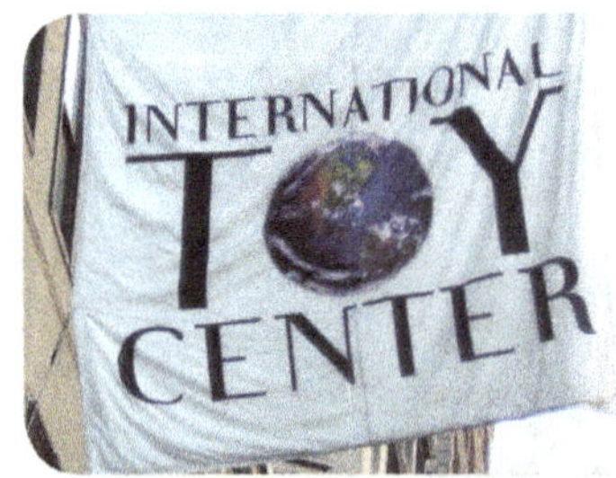

Did you know?
In its heyday, the International Toy Center facilitated more than 95% of all toy-buyer transactions in the United States.

Popular By Association

Being the number-two toy maker in the world has its advantages. It has given Hasbro the clout to negotiate licensing deals and merchandising relationships with other recognizable brands in the food and toy industries. After acquiring Tonka (and its subsidiary, Kenner) in 1991, the company began to weave characters from recognizable brands into its collection of just-add-water mixes for the Easy-Bake Oven.

The infographic below shows which mixes have been paired with which brands

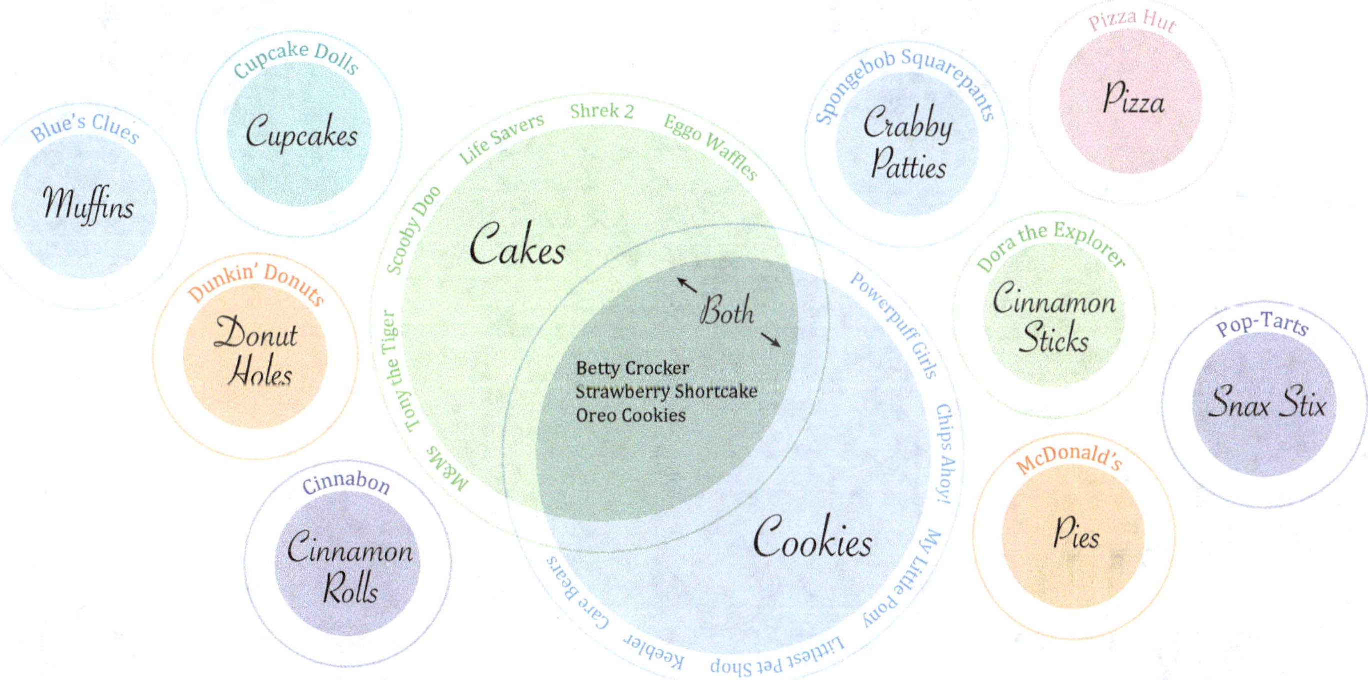

Character cross-promotion slowly faded and, by 2008, the only third-party brand still used was Betty Crocker, until 2009. Since the release of the Ultimate Oven series in 2011, Hasbro has shipped only Easy-Bake branded mixes.

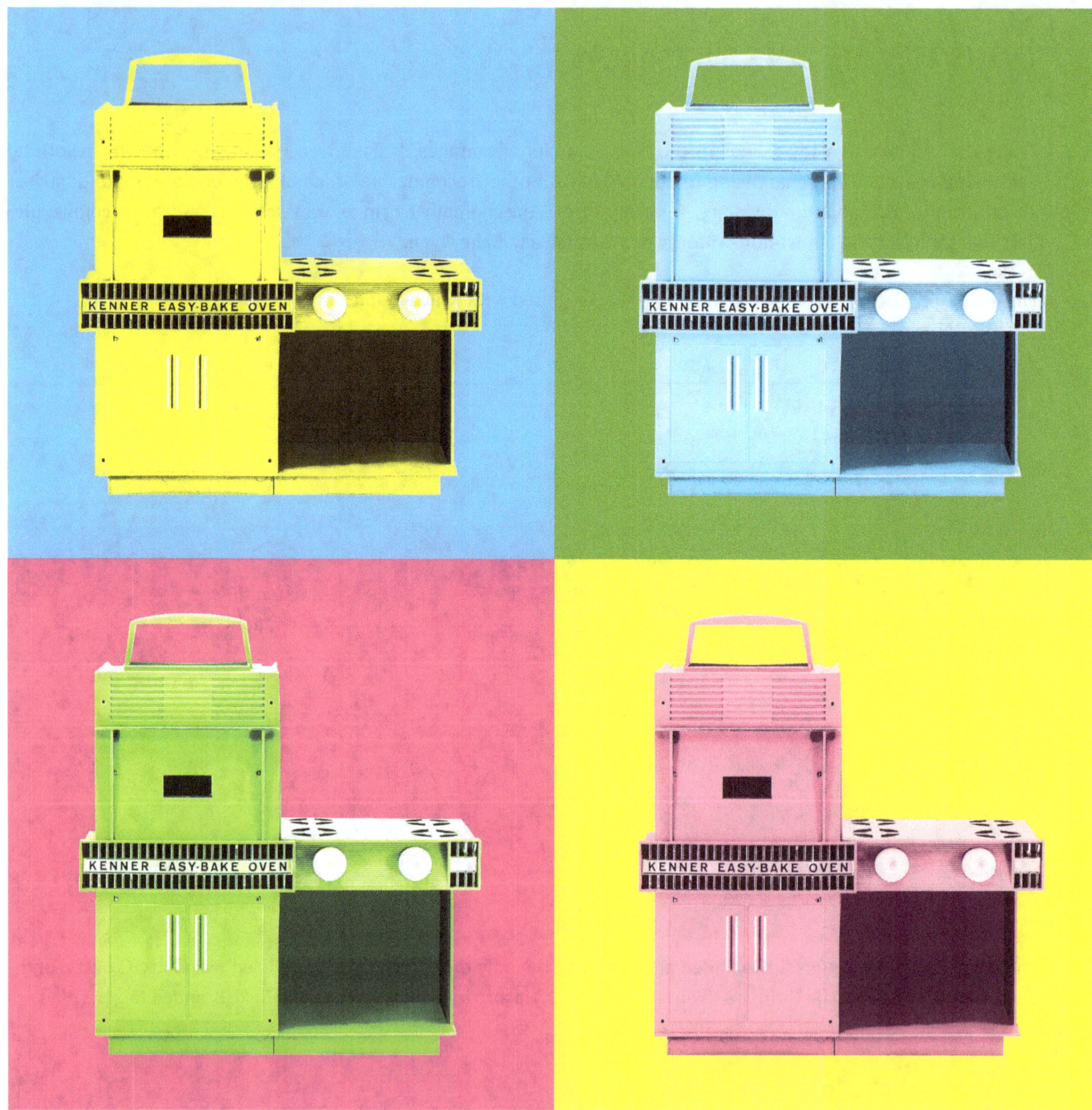
KENNER EASY-BAKE OVEN
KENNER EASY-BAKE OVEN
KENNER EASY-BAKE OVEN
KENNER EASY-BAKE OVEN

Chapter 6

Pop Culture Icon

The Easy-Bake Oven has been a staple of popular culture since its debut in 1963. Over a span of 50 years, more than 30 million Easy-Bake Ovens have been sold. Hasbro calls the toy "a rite of passage" that has stood the test of time.

Nearly anyone born since 1955 has some memory of baking with—or eating from—an Easy-Bake Oven. For generations, this toy has taken and continues to take "playing house" to a level of realism that is nearly impossible for a child to hope for. It is arguably the most successful effort by Kenner to produce a small, realistic, working version of something that kids saw done at home—such as baking in an oven.

From its many color schemes—always sporting the *de rigueur* palette of its time—to the language and focus of its marketing, to its forays into interactive games and mobile apps, the Easy-Bake Oven is symbolic of the decades through which it has lived. Its 2006 induction into the National Toy Hall of Fame is certainly well deserved.

Sweet Talker

*B*etty Crocker was a fictional character created by The Washburn Crosby Company in 1921 and continued by General Mills, which grew out of Washburn Crosby in 1928. By the 1930s, Betty Crocker—who dispensed recipes and down-to-Earth domestic advice—was widely known as "The First Lady of Food". Her radio show ran for more than 25 years and her 1950 cookbook—dubbed "Big Red"—became one of the best-selling books in the country. At the height of her popularity, this brilliantly developed character received thousands of letters each day.

Women in the United States connected to Betty Crocker, who was given a face by an artist in 1936 and then began to appear on product packaging. In 1945, *Fortune* magazine named her America's second most popular woman after Eleanor Roosevelt.

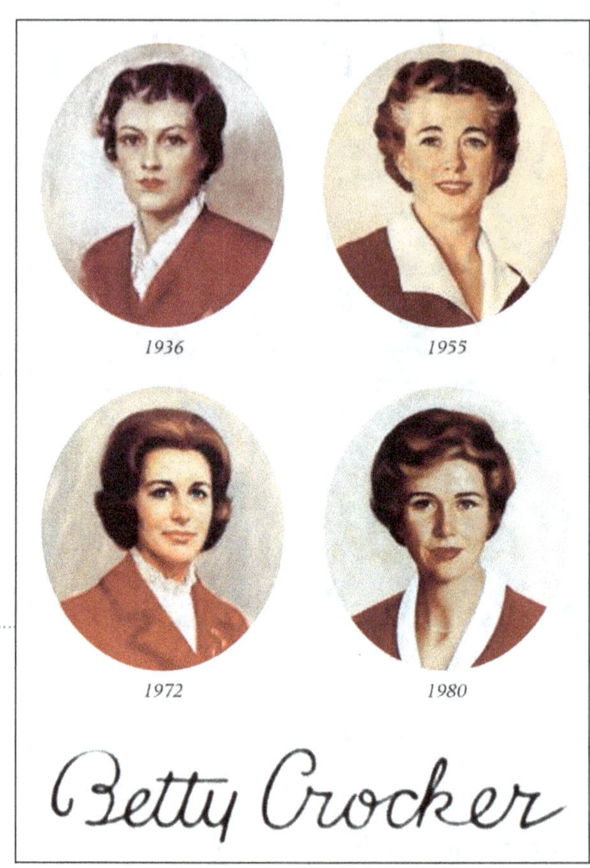

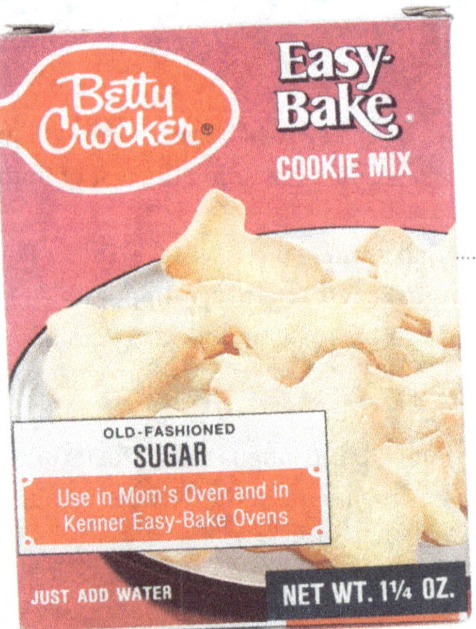

General Mills has updated Betty Crocker's image through the years to remain contemporary with consumers.

Betty Crocker Easy-Bake Oven box mixes and designs matched their larger counterparts.

When General Mills acquired Kenner Products in 1967, the company saw an ideal fit between the Betty Crocker and Easy-Bake Oven brands.

General Mills repackaged Easy-Bake box mixes in replicas of Betty Crocker packaging that children recognized from their parents' kitchens. Betty Crocker-branded baking kits soon followed, and in 1969 a new Betty

Crocker model of the Easy-Bake Oven was released. Children also got to experience promotional marketing like their parents did, as Betty Crocker coupons were included across the entire Easy-Bake Oven line, allowing kids to shop the coupon catalog with Mom and Dad.

"Be a Betty Crocker baker,

make a Betty Crocker Cake,

in your Betty Crocker Easy-Bake Oven"

Betty Crocker Easy-Bake Oven jingle from the 1970s.

Betty Crocker remained a staple in Easy-Bake Oven branding until 1987, when Tonka Corporation acquired what was then called Kenner-Parker Toys from General Mills. More than 20 years later, Hasbro briefly re-introduced Betty Crocker in several mix sets in 2008 and 2009.

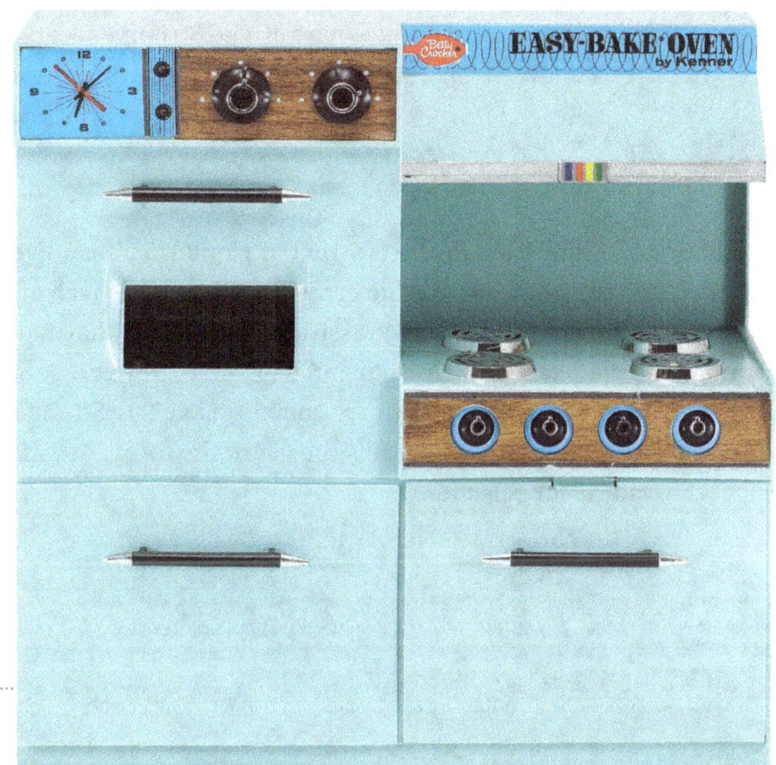

In 1969, Kenner introduced the co-branded Betty Crocker Easy-Bake Oven.

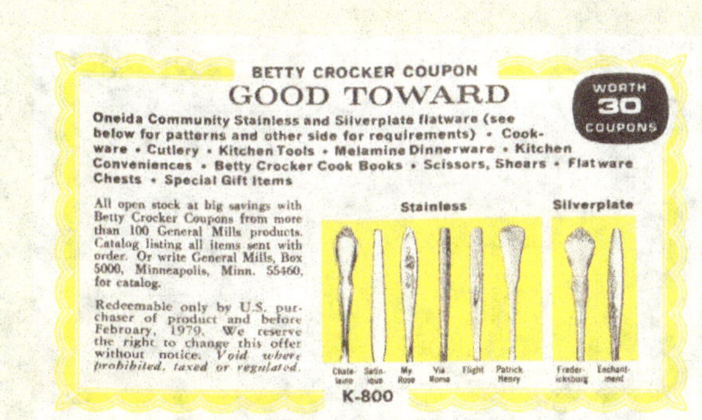

Did you know?

Between 1965-1970, American women redeemed $30,000,000 worth of Betty Crocker premiums—a 50 percent increase over the previous five years.

Hall-of-Famer

The National Toy Hall of Fame—part of The Strong educational institution in Rochester, New York—honors toys that have achieved iconic status and longevity or which have "profoundly changed play or toy design."

Measuring Up

The road to induction in the Toy Hall of Fame isn't easy. Every year, nominations are solicited from the general public via the web or regular mail. Impassioned pleas and grassroots campaigns have occurred throughout the years to help spur public support for the nomination of a specific toy. An internal advisory committee at The Strong reviews all submitted nominations and culls the list to the top 12 toys that best meet the criteria for selection.

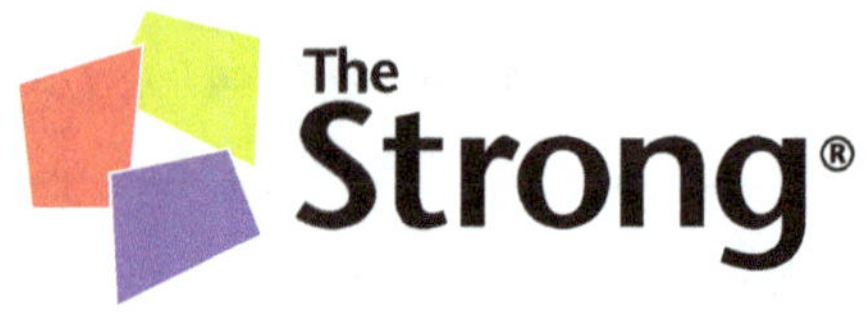

The Strong educational institution in Rochester, New York.

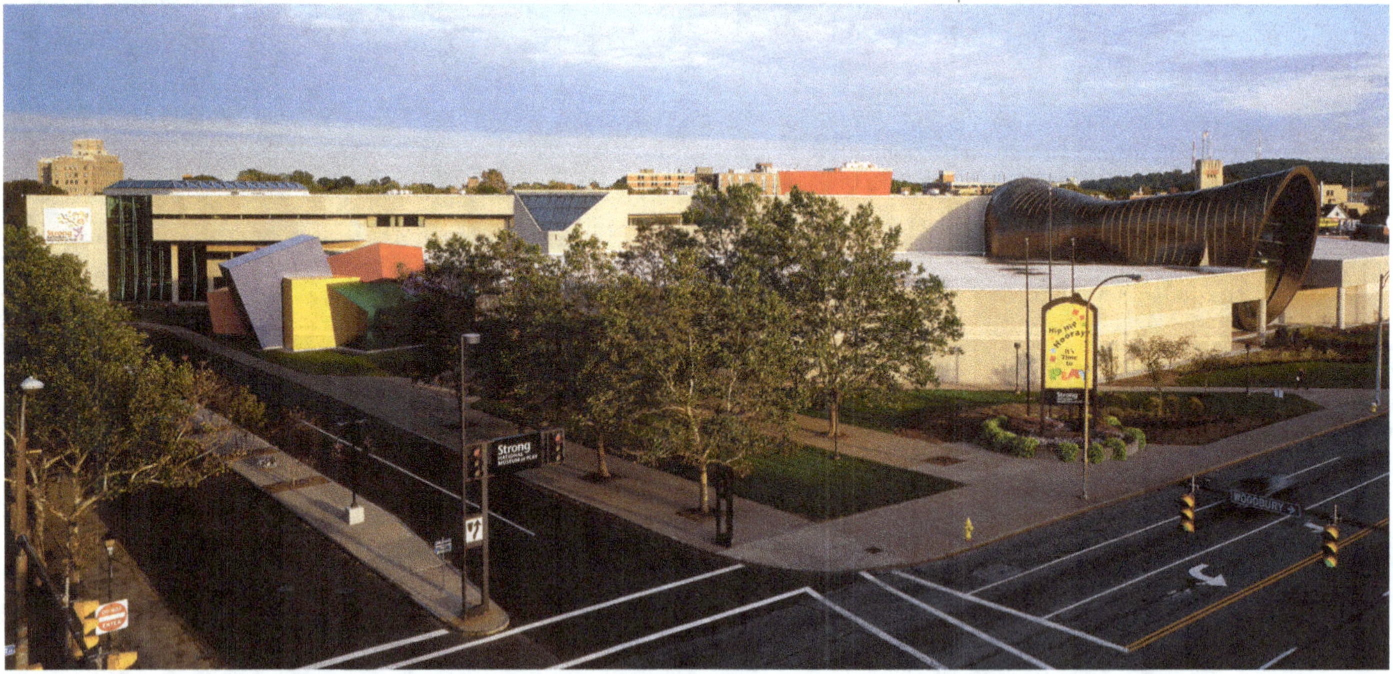

A National Selection Committee then reviews and critiques the top 12 nominees. Each committee member must choose two of the toys and craft an essay that supports their choices. Finally, the two toys receiving the most committee votes are announced in November for induction into the Hall of Fame.

Authors, educators, inventors, historians, scholars, and others who focus on the areas of play, child development, and innovation comprise the selection committee. Past members have included Michael Berenstain of the *Berenstain Bears* books; Cheryl Henson, daughter of the late Jim Henson and an advocate of puppet theatre; renowned play theorist Brian Sutton-Smith; and, the chair persons of the toy design program at the Fashion Institute of Technology (FIT) in New York City and the Otis College of Art & Design in Los Angeles, California.

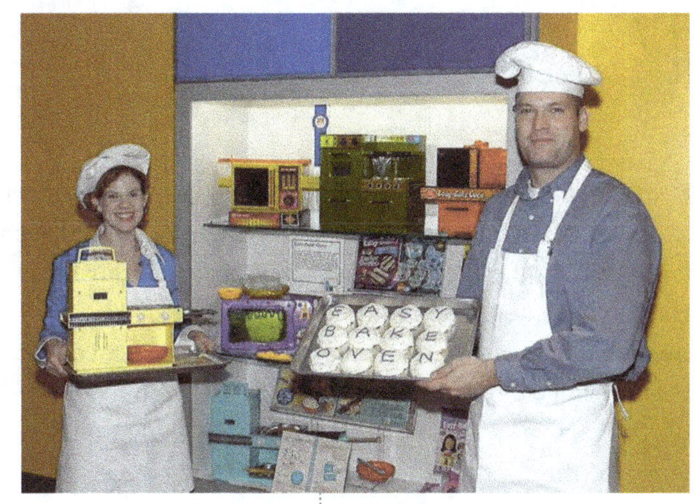

Staff members of the Strong induct the Easy-Bake Oven into the National Toy Hall of Fame in 2006.

Baking the Grade

The Easy-Bake Oven was a finalist for the National Toy Hall of Fame for three years (2003-2005) before finally breaking through in 2006, when it was inducted along with Lionel Trains. Both entrants were the first plug-in toys to be included in the hall, paving the way for other electricity-dependent inductees in future years.

The oven was lauded as a toy that both educated and rewarded the kids who played with it.

Did you know?

The first class of toys to be inducted to the Hall of Fame in 1998 included Barbie, Etch A Sketch, Lego, and Play-Doh.

Virtual Baker

In the early to mid-'90s, before the age of the internet, CD-ROMs became a cultural phenomenon as vehicles for gaming and reference information. To leverage this trend, Hasbro launched Hasbro Interactive in 1995. A wholly owned subsidiary of the company, its primary focus was on video game development and the production of interactive versions of existing Hasbro brands. Some of the first products produced by the company included the Easy-Bake Kitchen CD-ROM Playset, along with releases of Monopoly, Scrabble, and Frogger.

The Easy-Bake Kitchen CD-ROM playset and kitchen controller.

Aimed at children ages three and up, the virtual play set ran on Windows 95/98 and allowed children to explore the basics of baking in a virtual kitchen that was free of real hazards such as a heating element. A key feature of the game was a kitchen controller that was made of molded plastic and rested on top of a standard PC keyboard. The controller provided access to a kitchen counter full of tools and appliances, including a bowl, mixing cup, mixer, rolling pin, oven dial, cookie cutter, cake decorator, and mini-oven. By using and moving the appliances on the controller, kids managed the action in the virtual kitchen.

The Playset also included four additional virtual games that allowed kids to host tea parties and interact with on-screen characters named Billy Batter and Sally Sprinkles.

Did you know?

In 1999, Hasbro allocated $60 million and a three-year plan to develop the online games portal games.com.

Video Star

U ntil the 1990s, television programming for children was limited to Saturday-morning cartoons on the "Big Three" networks. But this changed as basic cable became prominent in households, and kid-focused channels—like Nickelodeon, Cartoon Network, and The Disney Channel—made their way into popular culture.

At the same time, VCRs had become popular sources of home entertainment. Seeing an opportunity to extend its brands using this dominant, rich medium, Hasbro released a series of videos starring some of its top brands, including the Easy-Bake Oven.

The Easy-Bake Club videos chronicled the "real life cooking adventures" of three friends. Two Episodes, "The Bake Sale" and "Dinner with Doris", were promoted in 30-second national TV ads and on Radio Aahs—a radio network managed in the 1990s by the Children's Broadcasting Corporation.

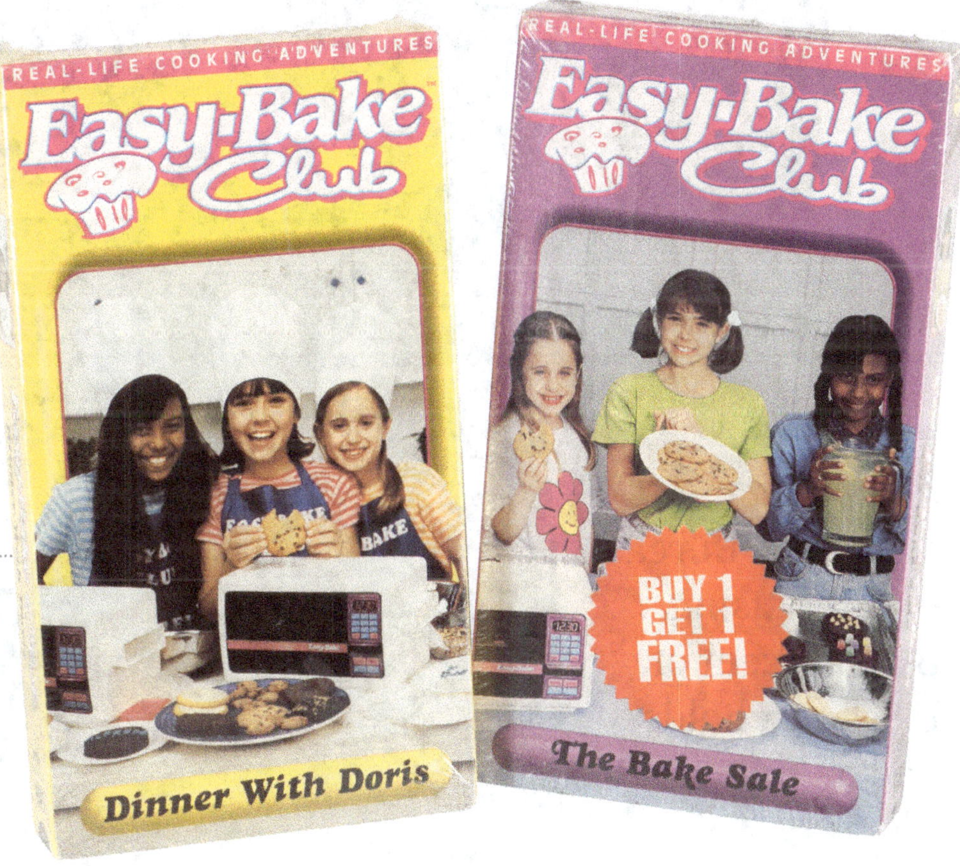

The Easy-Bake Oven starred in two "Easy-Bake Club" videos in the 1990s.

These plot synopses give insight into the early days of Hasbro's video marketing:

The Bake Sale

For Jennifer Bates, being the new girl on the block isn't easy. But when she discovers an irresistible stray puppy and names her Cookie, they swiftly become the center of attention. Mrs. Bates tells Jennifer that she can keep the puppy if she takes responsibility for some expenses. That's when she has a great idea for the first annual "Easy-Bake Oven" bake sale!

Dinner with Doris

Jennifer, Alex, and Carey are big fans of the TV cooking show, "Dinner with Doris." They love to watch and cook along with Doris using their Easy-Bake Oven and when the three win a competition to bake on the show they can't wait to appear! Jennifer even invites her Dad to show how easy it is to bake yummy treats. Will the girls' plans go perfectly? Will Jennifer's dad be a great baker? It's all in the timing and the Easy-Bake Oven!

Did you know?

According to the Television Bureau of Advertising, 88.6 percent of U.S. households had a VCR in 1996.

Mobile Gamer

*I*n the 2000s, as the internet and home computers became ubiquitous and children became even more skilled at using these tools than their parents, CD-ROM-based games fell by the wayside. Internet gaming grew in popularity, and more recently with the rise of mobile technology (smart phones and tablets), a new industry was born: applications (apps).

Essentially small, self-contained, focused software programs designed for mobile devices, apps now pervade nearly every imaginable facet of life—giving rise to the "There's an app for that!" meme. Hasbro jumped on the trend in 2011 to help promote the new light-bulb-free Easy-Bake Ultimate Oven.

The Easy-Bake Cupcakes! mobile app allowed Easy-Bake Oven fans to download a virtual Easy-Bake Ultimate Oven to their iOS devices and virtually bake, decorate, and share cupcake creations via email or Facebook.

Incremental updates to the app saw a name change to Easy-Bake Treats!, expanding the variety of virtual treats to better match the actual items that could be prepared in an Ultimate Oven. This included cakes, cookies, cake pops, and pizza.

Newer releases of the app now leverage the accelerometer built into iOS devices for greater interactivity. Treats can be "shaken" from the pan and lit candles can be placed on treats and "blown out."

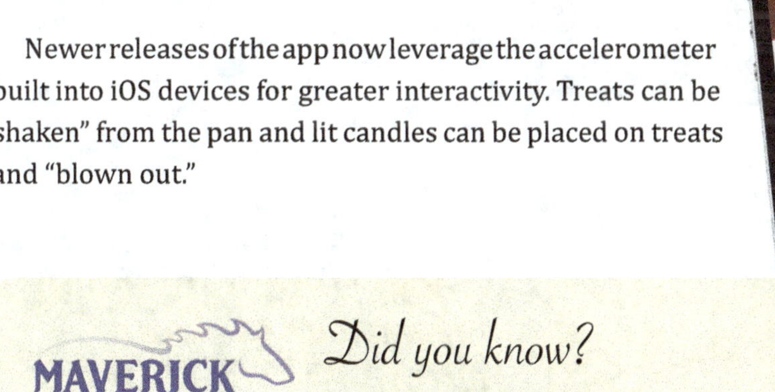

MAVERICK SOFTWARE

Did you know?

Easy-Bake Cupcakes! was developed by Maverick Software, an original developer of shareware for the Macintosh.

Gender Politician

*T*he gender stereotyping of toys—and the question of which comes first, the stereotype or the child's preference—is a topic of academic study as well as popular debate. A discussion about the Easy-Bake Oven's gender politics is unavoidable given the era in which the toy was introduced and the nature of the marketing mix that surrounded it.

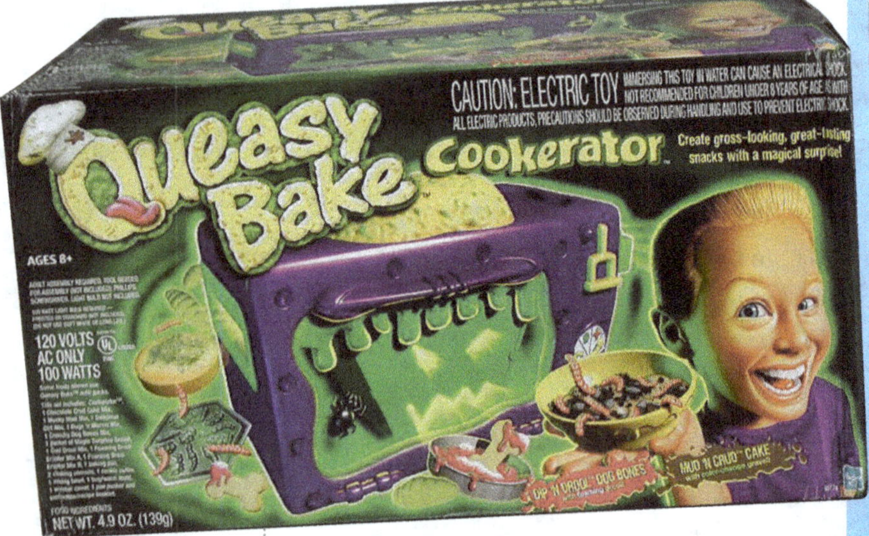

The Queasy Bake Cookerator was designed to appeal to boys' natural affinity for disgusting things.

The toy has always been marketed primarily to girls and their mothers, and by Kenner's own claims it was the "most popular girl's toy since dolls" and, "a little girl's dream come true!" Nevertheless, over the years both Kenner and Hasbro have made attempts to expand the appeal of the Easy-Bake Oven to boys:

Marketing by Kenner to attract boys to use the Easy-Bake Oven with bubble gum mixes.

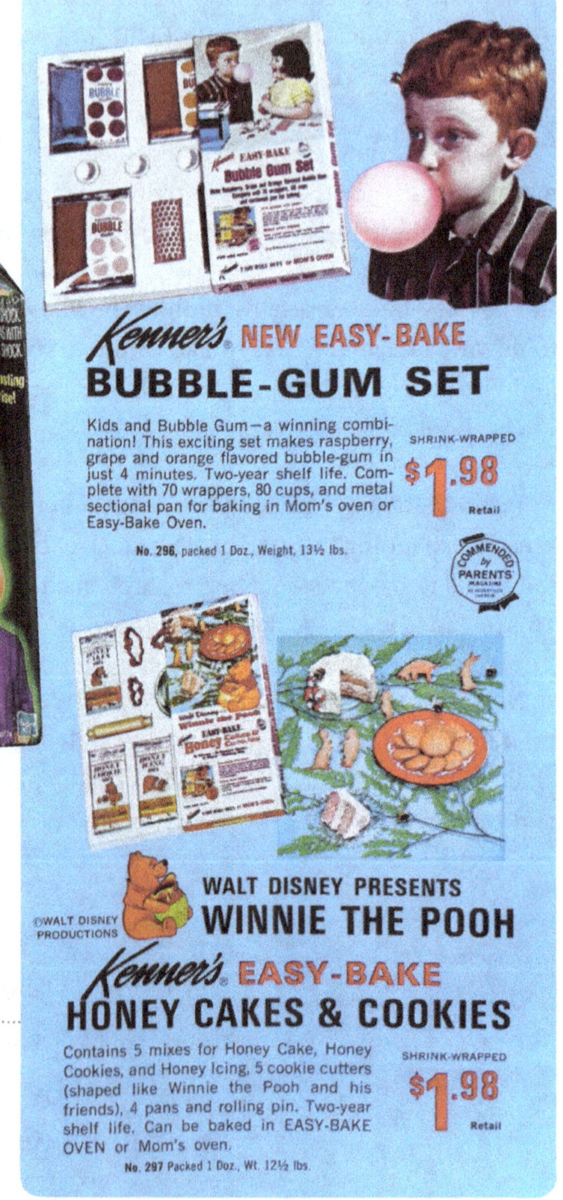

Kenner produced mix sets and oven add-ons—such as the Easy-Bake Corn Popper and the Easy-Bake Bubble Gum Set—that were designed to appeal more to boys. Attempts at cross-gender appeal can also be seen in the packaging of these items.

Hasbro took a different approach by relying on its cross-brand merchandising to expand the oven's appeal to boys; for example, with mix sets branded with Scooby-Doo! and SpongeBob SquarePants. Hasbro also released two ovens designed with boys in mind: The Queasy Bake Cookerator in 2002/2003, and the Easy-Bake Real-Meal Oven, sold between 2003 and 2006.

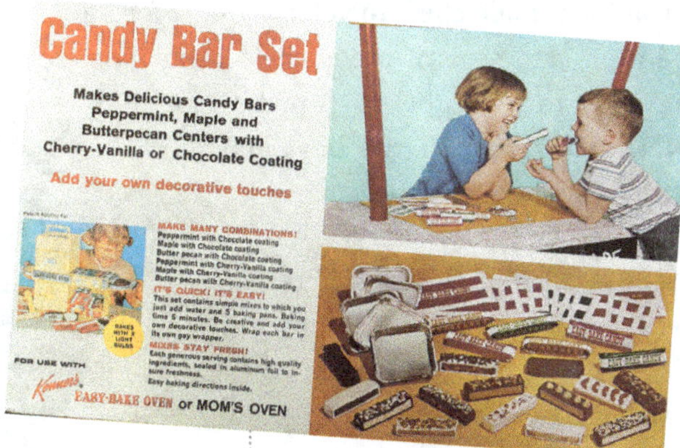

Kenner's candy bar mix sets were marketed to both boys and girls.

For one reason or another, all of these attempts failed to gain a foothold in the competitive toy market; the Easy-Bake Oven has never developed substantial enough appeal among boys to warrant much change in the female-focused marketing strategy.

Gender Politics Go Viral

In December 2012, a 13-year-old girl from New Jersey named McKenna Pope attracted mass-media attention to this topic with a petition on the website change.org aimed at convincing Hasbro to produce a gender-neutral Easy-Bake Oven. Inspired by her four-year-old brother asking for the toy, McKenna and her petition went viral. Hasbro responded by revealing that it already had a silver, black, and blue oven in the works with the intent to advertise it to both girls and boys.

Many interests latched on to the opportunity that this media debate provided. Bobby Flay was the first of a number of

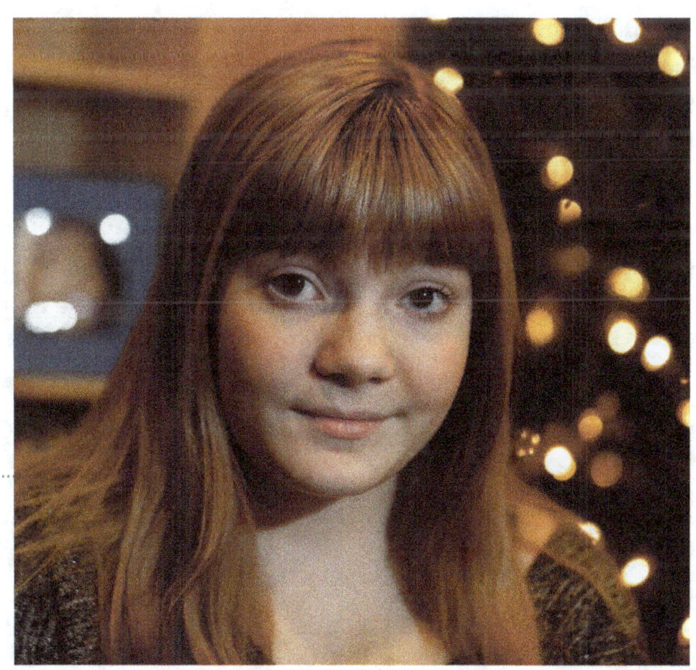

McKenna Pope presented Hasbro with a petition containing over 45,000 signatures for a gender-neutral Easy-Bake Oven.

prominent male chefs to voice support for the petition, and several other chefs posted a video to YouTube in support of McKenna, saying, "Little boys and little girls can all be chefs!"

CNN, The Associated Press, MSNBC, Good Morning America, *The Washington Post*, and the *Los Angeles Times* all covered the story, and Hasbro eventually invited McKenna for a personal visit to its headquarters for the reveal of the new gender-neutral oven. The revamped Easy-Bake Ultimate Oven—released in 2013—"celebrates 50 years of making sweet memories" and is marketed to "chefs in training".

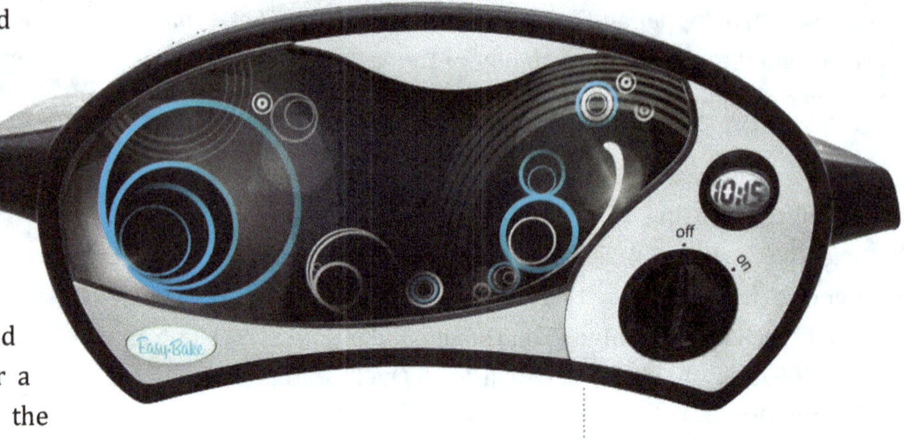

The 2013 Easy-Bake Ultimate Oven in gender-neutral colors.

Cooks versus Chefs

The language chosen to market the new toy oven is notable. Throughout history, the marketing communications surrounding the Easy-Bake Oven has focused on girls, who are described in the literature as "cooks", "little cooks", "junior cooks", and "little homemakers". But when the target market shifts toward boys, the language changes and the child is referred to with the professional title, "chef", or "chef in training".

This trend is also present in the Baker of the Year Contest mentioned later in this chapter. In 2004, the contest was renamed to Chef of the Year to promote the Easy-Bake Meal Oven (capable of cooking baked goods as well as pizzas and other entrées). Perhaps not coincidentally, that was the first and only year that the contest was won by a boy.

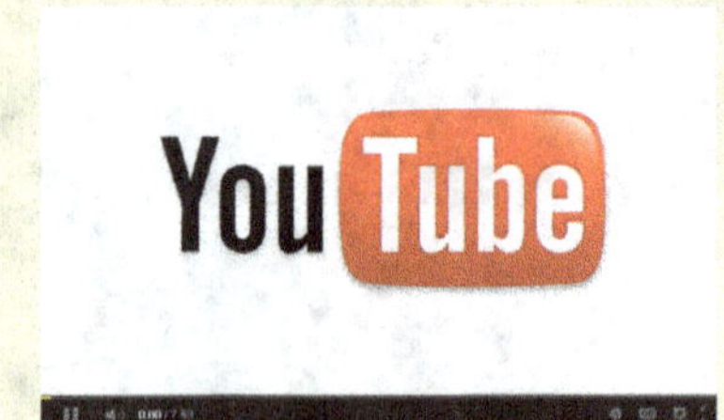

Did you know?

View the chefs' video in support of McKenna's petition—and many other Easy-Bake Oven related videos—at youtube.com/lightbulbbaking.

Silent Actor

T he Easy-Bake Oven has cemented its pop culture icon status by landing a variety of non-speaking parts in network and cable television shows, including Friends, Fringe, Psych, Queer as Folk, Seinfeld, and Six Feet Under.

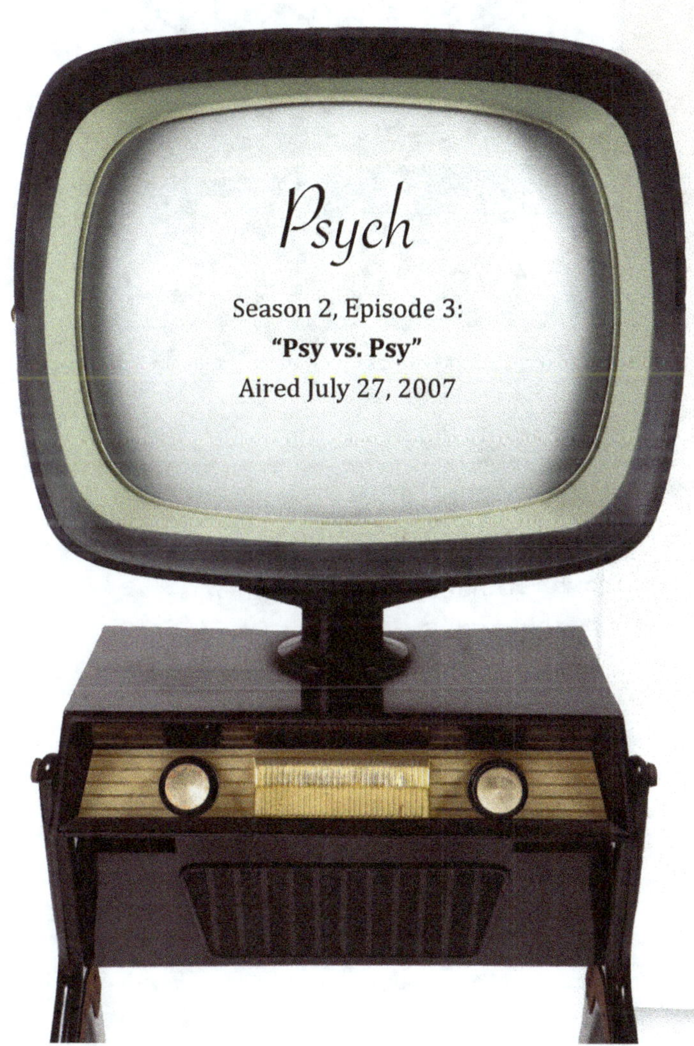

PSYCH HEADQUARTERS

Shawn, wearing an apron and potholders, offers Gus a pineapple upside-down cake, which he baked for 19 hours in his Easy-Bake Oven.

SHAWN

First of all - and I think I can say this with a fair amount of certainty - there is definitely something not right about this cake.

GUS

Maybe, because it was baked in a child's oven?

SHAWN

We're talking about a deluxe Easy-Bake Oven, Gus. I paid over three hundred dollars for it on eBay. This is hardly a toy!

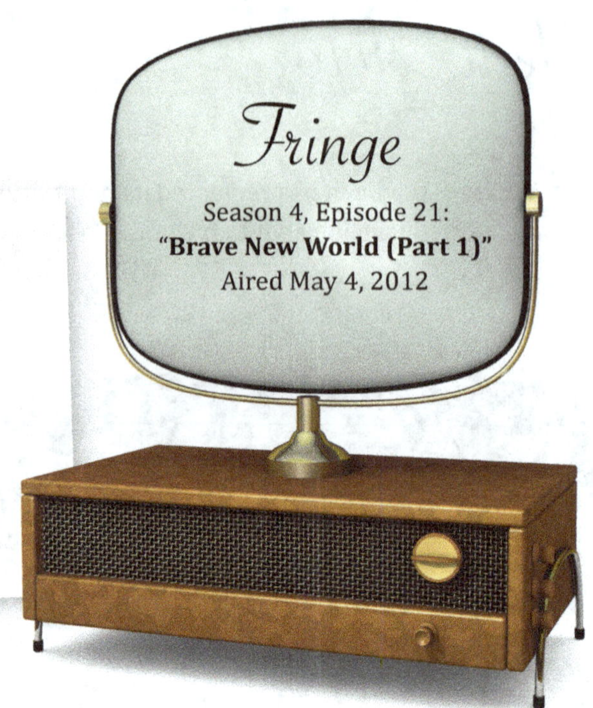

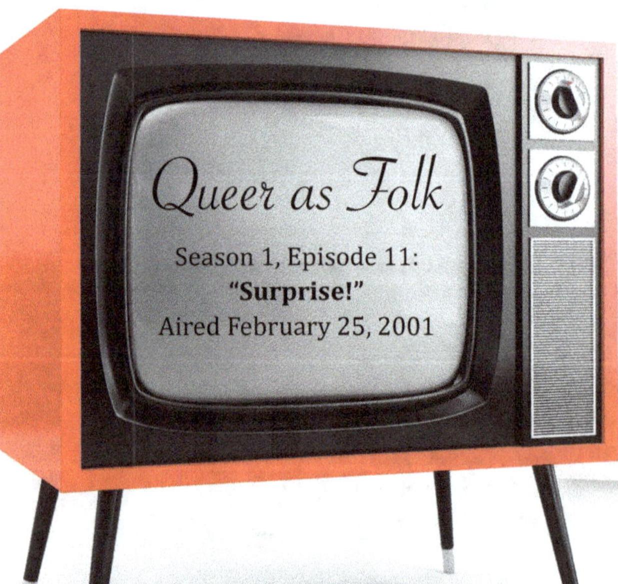

CLUB BABYLON

Brian throws Michael a surprise 30th birthday party and Emmett buys Michael a vintage Easy-Bake Oven, telling him that "every gay boy wanted an Easy-Bake Oven".

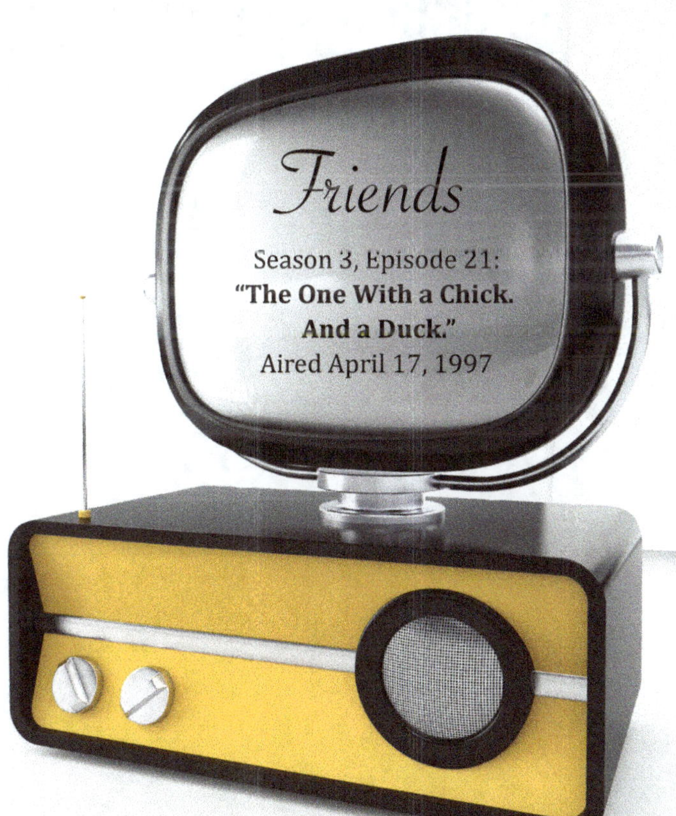

MONICA AND RACHEL'S APARTMENT

Pete buys a restaurant and offers
Monica a job as head chef; she's unsure
whether to take it, since she feels no
attraction to him.

MONICA

Can you believe he just offered
me a restaurant?

RACHEL

What a jerk! You want me to
kick his ass?

MONICA

I mean this has been, like,
my dream, since I got my first
Easy-Bake Oven and opened Easy
Monica's Bakery.

BACKSTORY

Jerry's new girlfriend, Celia, has inherited
a classic toy collection from her late
father. She won't let Jerry touch the toys,
let alone play with them, so he concocts
a scheme to render her senseless with a
combination of turkey, wine, and boring home
movies of George. Elaine is taken aback at
his behavior until she hears Celia's toy
collection includes an Easy-Bake Oven.

CELIA'S APARTMENT

(Celia at the dinner table, passed out again.
We hear a ding from the Easy-Bake Oven.
Elaine, Jerry and George are sitting on the
floor around the coffee table full of toys.)

                    ELAINE

Who wants a cupcake?

                    GEORGE

Oh, me, me, me, me, me!

                    JERRY

You know that batter is, like, 30
years old.

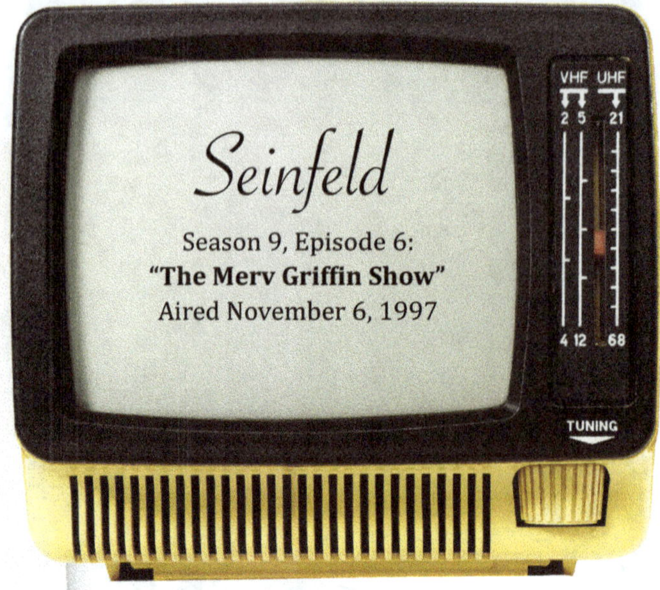

BACKSTORY

Marshall buys Lily an Easy-Bake Oven for Christmas. Lily is surprised because she always wanted one as a child, but has never told Marshall. Marshall reveals that the suggestion came from Ted, who remembered that she told him about it when they were at college.

LILY:

Merry Christmas! What's in the box?

MARSHALL:

Only the best present for the best girl ever. It took me all day to track it down.

LILY:

Oh my God, an Easy-Bake Oven! I've wanted one of these ever since I was a little girl, and this exact model. I never told you that, how did you know?

[Flashback to college in 1998 in a smokey dorm room]

LILY:

When I was a kid, all I wanted was an Easy-Bake Oven. I begged and I begged, all I got was a stupid Lego set because my feminist Mom didn't want me conforming to traditional gender roles.

TED:

Easy-Bake Oven … that's what I'm going to call my van!

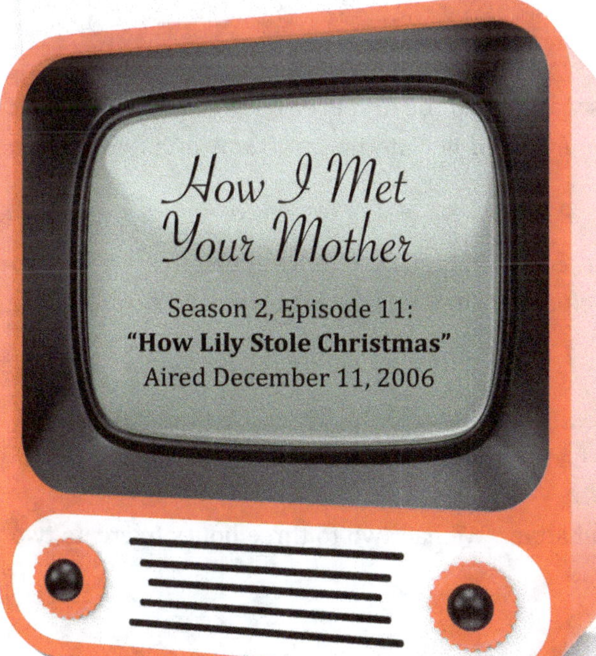

Baker of the Year

Since 1998, Hasbro has run five "Baker of the Year" contests, each tied to a milestone and aimed at children ages eight to 12. In 1998, the contest celebrated the Easy-Bake Oven's 35th anniversary. Hasbro rang in the new millennium with the next contest in 2000. The 2003 and 2009 contests celebrated the toy's 40th and 45th anniversaries respectively. The 2004 contest was unique, as it was timed with the release of the Easy-Bake Real Meal Oven and was expanded from baking recipes to include meals and was renamed to "Chef of the Year".

Part of a marketing campaign aimed at families, the contests created buzz around the Easy-Bake Oven among young cooks and

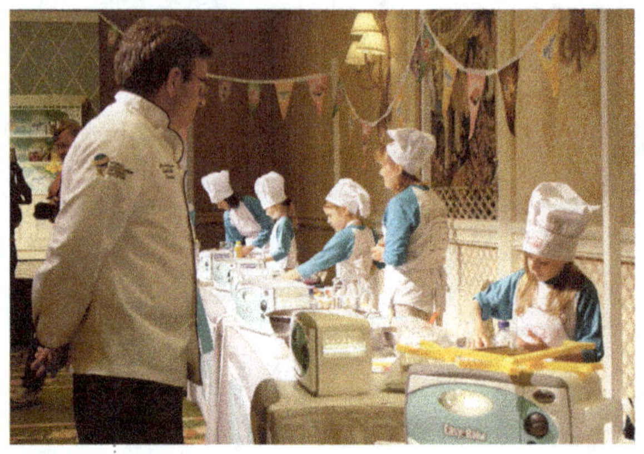

A judge observes the competition during the 2009 Easy-Bake Baker of the Year Contest.

Catching Up with Lindsey Thompson

In 1998, 9-year old Lindsey Thompson of Little Rock, Arkansas was named the first ever Easy-Bake Baker of the Year for her Toffee Trifle Cake. She entered the contest at the urging of her mother, who saw an ad for it in a magazine.

Her recipe was "easy-bake-ified" from a recipe of a friend of Thompson's mother. Each entrant had to send Hasbro a videotape of him or herself talking about and preparing the recipe on camera. "That was almost a deal breaker because I was very nervous on camera," Thompson said.

Each finalist received two plane tickets to New York City to attend the bake-off. The Thompsons made a family holiday of it: "We flew to New York a few days early. It helped me be less nervous for the day of the event."

The bake-off took place at the Four Seasons Hotel in midtown Manhattan. "We had two to three hours to create two their parents. By highlighting milestones in the toy's history, the contests also reinforced the oven's longevity and stature in the toy market.

Preparing for and entering the contest was often a family affair as contenders tested recipes, prepared their submissions to Hasbro, and obtained parents' permission to enter. Finalists (typically five, but seven in 2004) were flown to an exciting location to compete for the title.

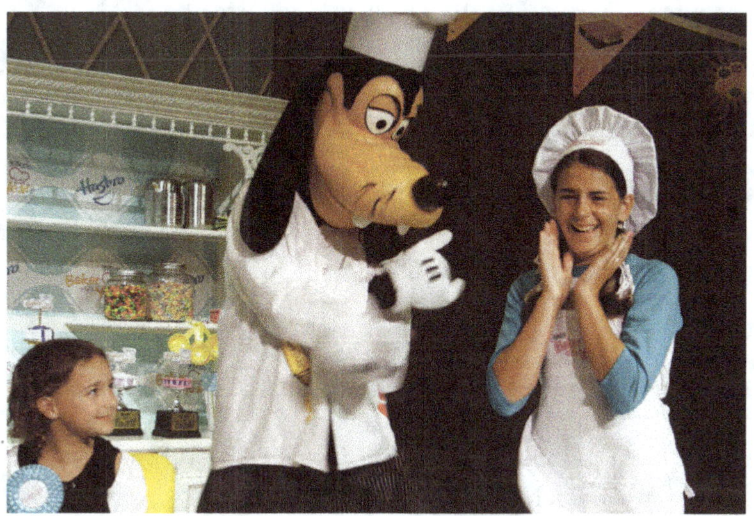

Catherine Ralston reacts as she is announced winner of the 2009 Easy Bake Baker of the Year Contest.

versions of our dessert—one for the judges to taste and another for presentation," Thompson recalls. While baking, the five finalists were periodically interrupted to answer questions from the judges, Hasbro representatives, and reporters.

As winner, Thompson received a $5,000 savings bond and made an appearance the next morning on the *Good Morning America* show, recreating her winning recipe on camera. Other television appearances over the next year included the Nashville, TN-based *Crook & Chase* show, *The Howie Mandel Show*, and a particularly memorable *The Tonight Show* with Jay Leno. "A Bill Clinton look-a-like was on The Tonight Show that same night and my Mom actually introduced me to him *as* Bill Clinton. I remember being really nervous that he was the real president!"

Now 24 years old and a Fulbright scholar, Thompson recalls initially being drawn to the Easy-Bake Oven after seeing a television commercial. "When I had mixes, I would bake up a storm and then put it away for a while until another set of mixes made their way into the house."

The prizes benefited the child's family as well. The first four contests awarded each winner with a $5,000 savings bond and Easy-Bake Oven supplies. Runners up received $1,000 savings bonds, and all five finalists were treated to a trip to New York City. The most recent contest, held in 2009, flew finalists to Disney World and awarded the winner a culinary-inspired trip for four to San Francisco.

Contest Winners

1998:   Lindsey Thompson, 9 years old
Recipe: Toffee Trifle Cake

2000:   Alexandra Stewart, 8 years old
Recipe: Chocolate Mousse Cake

2003:   Olia Wall, 9 years old
Recipe: Marshmallow Cloud on a Heart

2004:   John McCune, 9 years old
Recipe: Easy-Bake Carrot Cake

2009:   Catherine Ralston, 12 years old
Recipe: Queen of Hearts Strawberry Tart

Four Seasons Hotel Executive Chef, Susan Weaver, offers advice to Alexandra Stewart during the Easy-Bake Baker of the Year 2000 finals in New York.

Winner's trophy from the 2009 Easy-Bake Baker of the Year contest.

A Real Character

Over its 50-year life, the Easy-Bake Oven has made cameo appearances in a number of books and articles about vintage and classic toys. But the oven itself has also been the primary subject of three books.

In 1999, Dutton Children's Books, a division of Penguin Putnam Books for Young Readers, produced *The Official Easy-Bake Cookbook.* Aimed at kids, this 58-page guide offers 60 "kitchen-tested" recipes that use both pre-packaged Easy-Bake mixes as well as standard ingredients found in most kitchens.

Three years later, Reader's Digest Children's Books published the *Easy-Bake Party Planner.* This 30-page guide provided kids aged eight and up with recipes and baking advice for using the Easy-Bake Oven to throw a party for their friends. In addition to tips on planning the menu, the book also came with reusable decorating stencils and blank recipe cards.

The *Easy-Bake Oven Gourmet* from Running Press was released for the Easy-Bake Oven's 40th anniversary in 2003. This 128-page homage by author David Hoffman provides a visual timeline into the toy's storied past and presents unique recipes created especially for the oven by 26 world-class chefs.

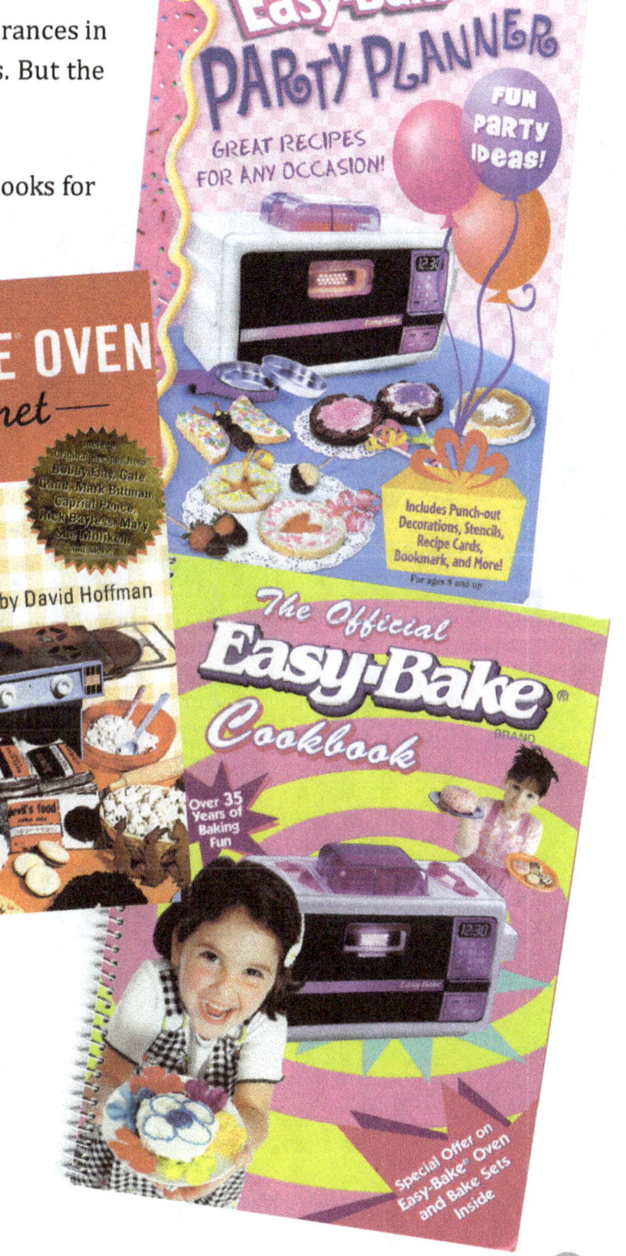

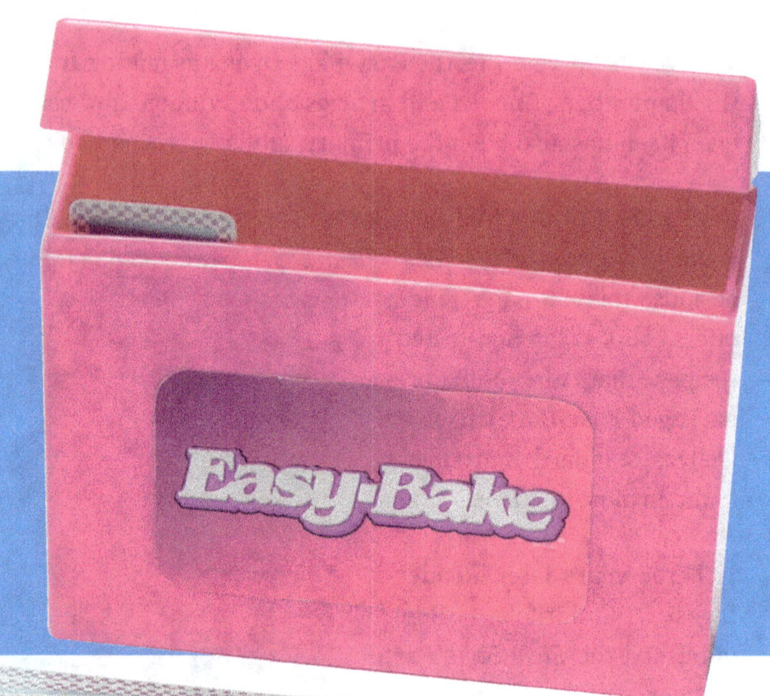

Easy-Bake
SMOOTHIES
CHOCOLATE CHIP COOKIES

Chapter 7

Recipe Box

*E*very Easy-Bake Oven comes equipped with several just-add-water mixes that make it easy for young bakers to learn the fundamentals of baking popular items such as cakes, cookies, and fudge. Refill mixes have also always been available and sold separately from the oven. Over the past 50 years, these bake sets have proven to be such a hit with consumers that more than 130 million mixes have been sold to date.

Baking Outside the Box

Initially, Kenner—and then Hasbro—encouraged exploration by packaging a cookbook with each oven so that amateur bakers could further hone their skills by

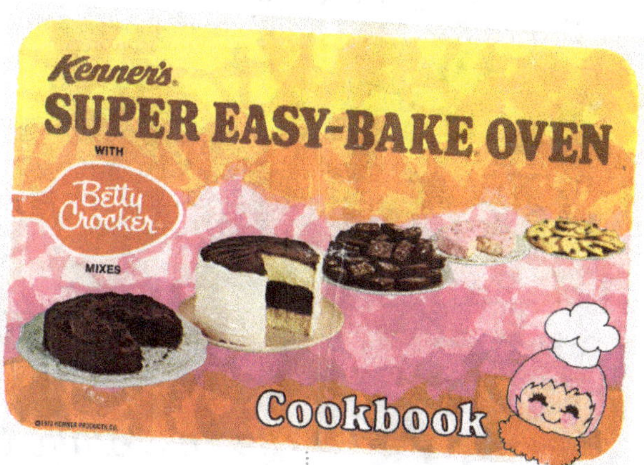

An original Betty Crocker Cookbook shipped with the Super Easy-Bake Oven.

creating original recipes using ingredients found in a typical kitchen.

In recent years, however, Hasbro has discouraged baking outside the box. Documents packaged with the Easy-Bake Ultimate Oven today state that young bakers should use only the mixes that have been specifically formulated for use in the oven. Nevertheless, a long tradition of Easy-Bake experimentation is a memorable part of the toy's history.

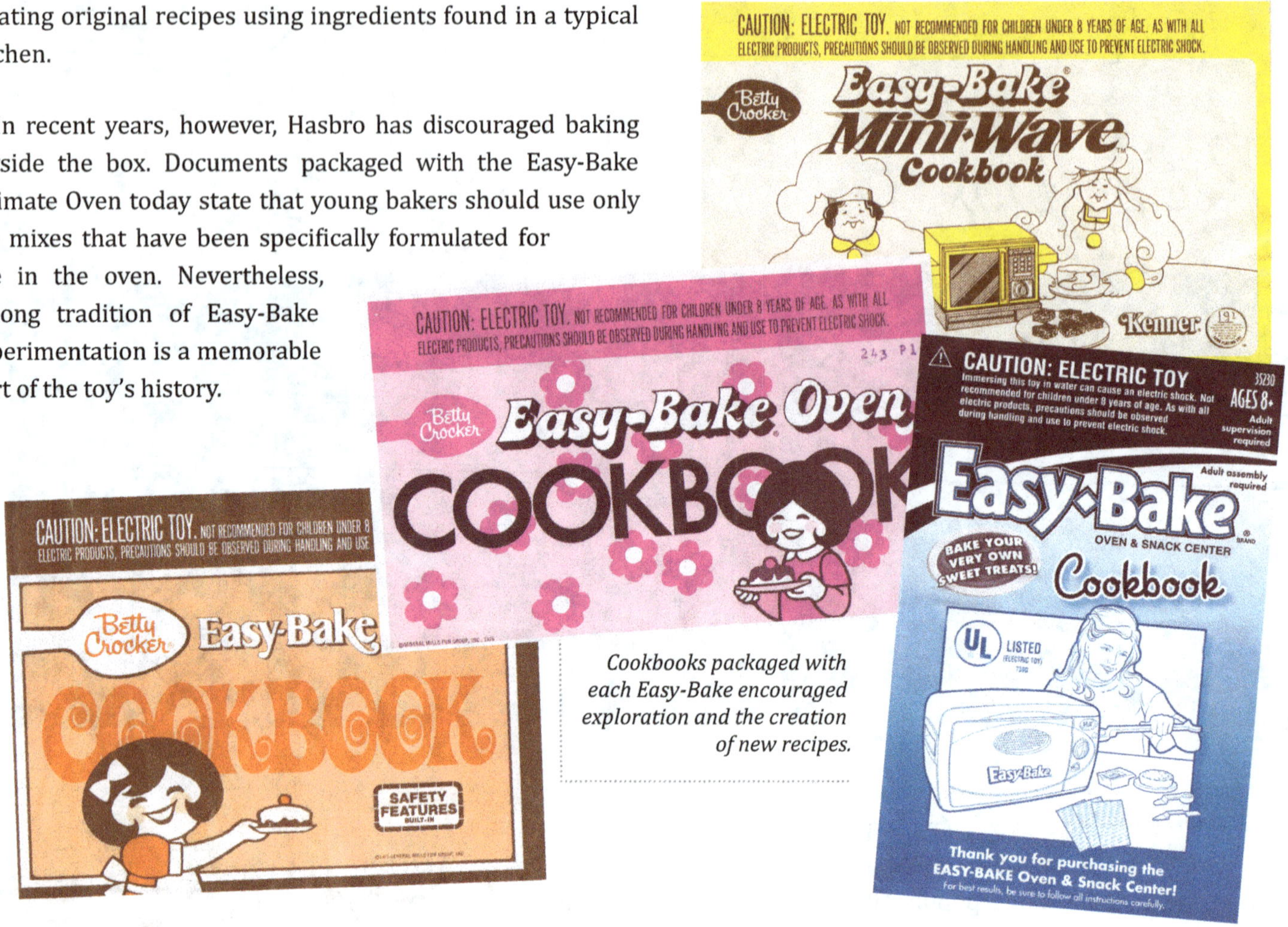

Cookbooks packaged with each Easy-Bake encouraged exploration and the creation of new recipes.

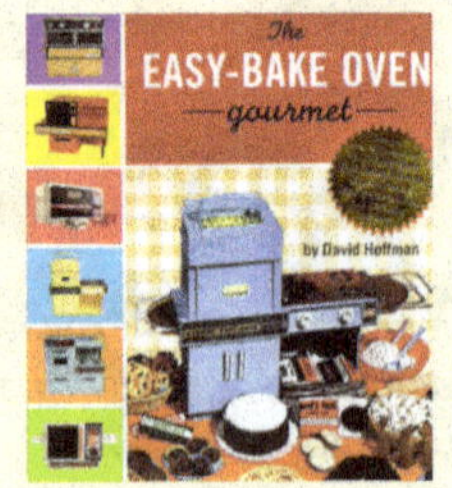

Did you know?

The Easy-Bake Oven Gourmet by David Hoffman includes original recipes from 26 world-class chefs, all prepared using the Easy-Bake Oven.

Classic Recipes

1960s

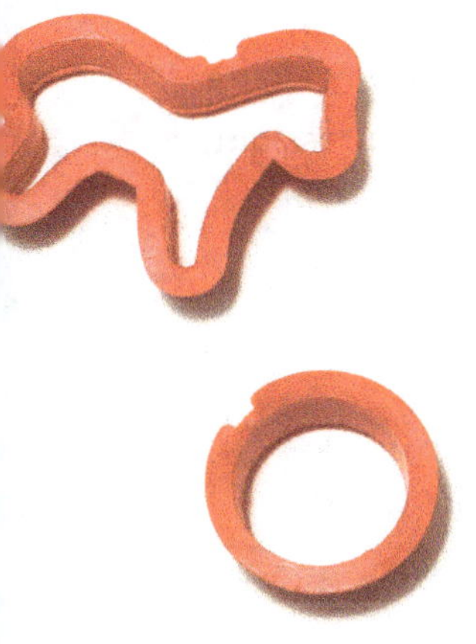

Snow Mounds

Makes 10-12 cookies

CREAM: 6 teaspoons shortening or soft butter
3 teaspoons confectioner's sugar

BLEND IN: ⅛ teaspoon vanilla
¼ cup flour
Dash of salt

ADD: 2 tablespoons finely chopped walnuts

Mix well and shape into 1 inch balls. Place 3 on greased Easy-Bake pan. Flatten slightly. Bake *5 minutes*. When cool, roll in confectioner's sugar.

Crazy Cake

MIX: 4 ½ teaspoons flour
3 teaspoons sugar
¼ teaspoon cocoa
⅛ teaspoon baking soda
Dash of salt

Place in greased pan.

ADD: ⅛ teaspoon vanilla
⅛ teaspoon vinegar
1 ½ teaspoons salad oil

Place 1 tablespoon (3 teaspoons) water over all ingredients and mix well with a fork, but do not beat. Bake *10 minutes*.

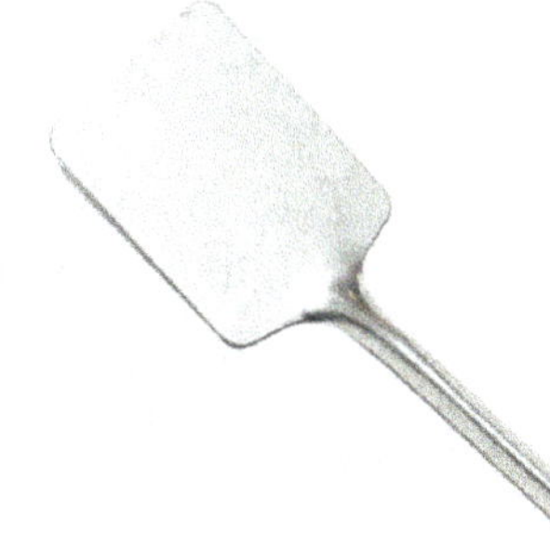

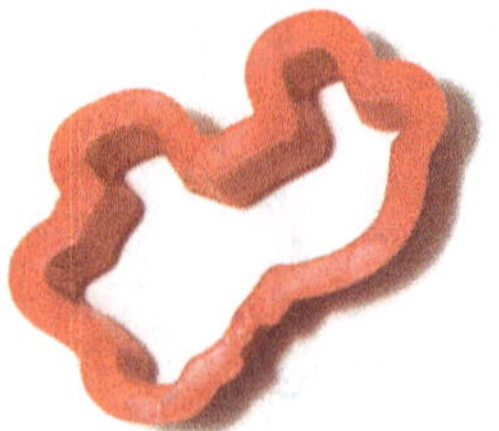

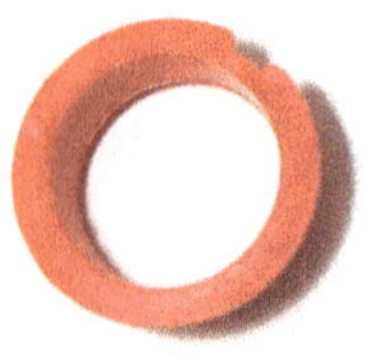

Peanut Butter Cookies

¼ cup Gold Medal Flour
1 tablespoon soft butter or margarine
1 tablespoon peanut butter
2 teaspoons sugar

In a bowl, mix all ingredients thoroughly to make dough. With your fingers, shape the dough into ½-inch balls. Place 4 of the balls in pan; use fingertips to press down gently. Press tines of fork into each cookie to make imprint. Bake about *6 minutes.* Cool. Bake remaining balls 4 at a time. *16 cookies.*

Jam Dandies

3 tablespoons flour
1 tablespoon crushed Country Corn Flakes cereal
1 tablespoon soft butter or margarine
1 teaspoon sugar
2 teaspoons raspberry jam

In a bowl, mix flour, cereal, butter, and sugar until crumbly. Reserve 2 tablespoons of the crumbly square mixture. Press remaining mixture firmly into pan. Spread with jam. Sprinkle reserved crumbly mixture over jam; press gently with fingers. Bake *18 minutes.* Cool. Cut into wedges.

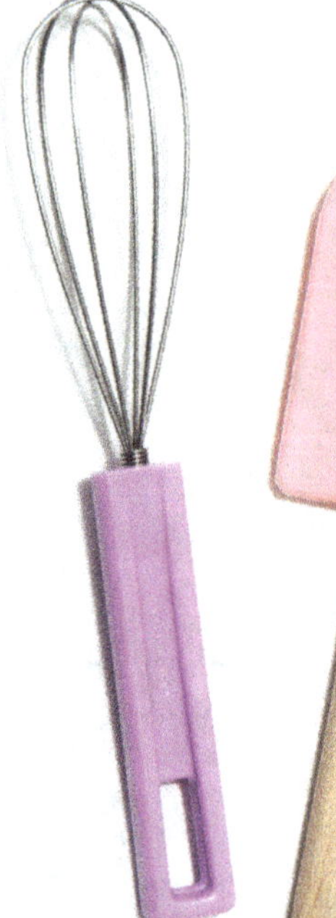

Sugar Buttons

⅓ cup Gold Medal Flour
2 tablespoons soft butter or margarine
2 teaspoons sugar

In bowl, mix flour, butter and sugar thoroughly. With your fingers, shape dough into ½-inch balls. Place 4 balls in pan; use finger tips to press down gently. (Cookies will have cracks at edges.) Sprinkle with sugar. Bake *10 minutes* or until light brown. Cool. Bake remaining balls, 4 at a time. *16 cookies*.

Cinnamon Coffee Cake

2 tablespoons Bisquick baking mix
2 teaspoons milk
½ teaspoon granulated sugar

Ingredients you will need for topping:
1 teaspoon Bisquick baking mix
1 teaspoon brown sugar
⅛ teaspoon cinnamon
½ teaspoon soft butter or margarine

Grease pan with butter or margarine. In bowl, mix 1 teaspoon baking mix, the brown sugar, cinnamon, and butter thoroughly; set aside. In another bowl, mix 2 tablespoons baking mix, the milk, and granulated sugar. Spread in pan. Sprinkle the cinnamon mixture over the top. Bake *13 minutes*. Cool in cooling chamber. Cut into wedges.

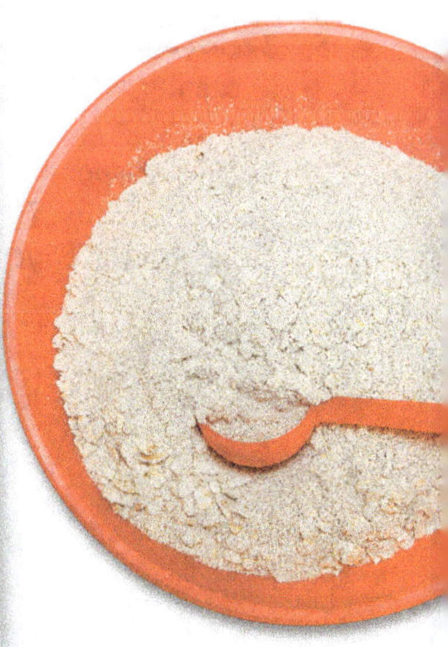

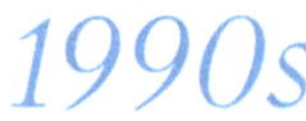

Krispie Treats

1 teaspoon of margarine or butter
2 teaspoons of Marshmallow Crème
Puffed rice cereal

Place margarine or butter and Marshmallow Crème in the warming cup. Put on top of oven and cover. Warm for *9 minutes* stirring occasionally. Half fill the other warming cup with puffed rice cereal. Thoroughly mix the puffed rice cereal with the warmed mixture of margarine/butter and Marshmallow Crème in a bowl. Take a small amount from the bowl and form a cookie shape. Place it on a plate. Refrigerate for about ½ hour or until firm.

Caramel Corn

2 teaspoons of caramel topping
½ cup unsalted popcorn

Place 2 teaspoons of caramel topping in the warming cup. Put on top of oven and cover. Warm for *9 minutes*. Drizzle the warm mixture over unsalted popcorn in a bowl. Stir the popcorn in the bowl to help coat it with the caramel.

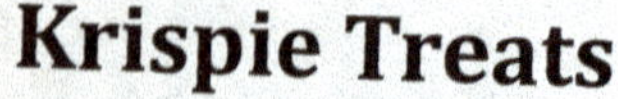

Award Winners

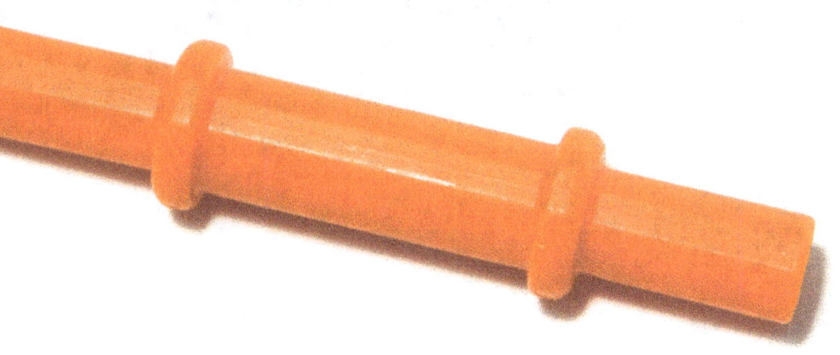

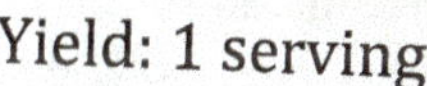

Toffee Trifle Cake

Yield: 1 serving

2 Easy-Bake Oven plain yellow cake mixes
1 small box vanilla instant pudding
1 ½ cups cold milk
1 small tub of Cool Whip, softened
2 Skor or Heath candy bars (crushed)

1. Make cakes according to directions. Let cool.

2. Mix milk and pudding.

3. Fold pudding and Cool Whip together.

4. In a trifle dish or glass bowl, layer the cake, then cover with some of
   the pudding mixture, then sprinkle ½ of the candy. Repeat layers. Chill
   until served.

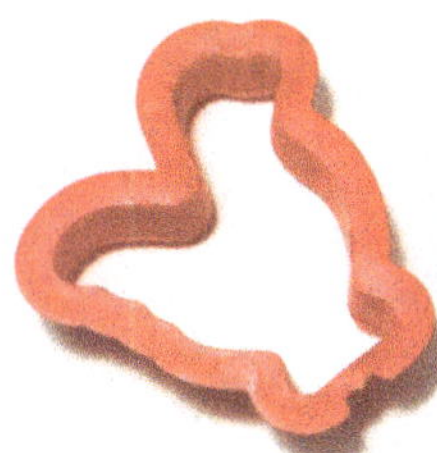

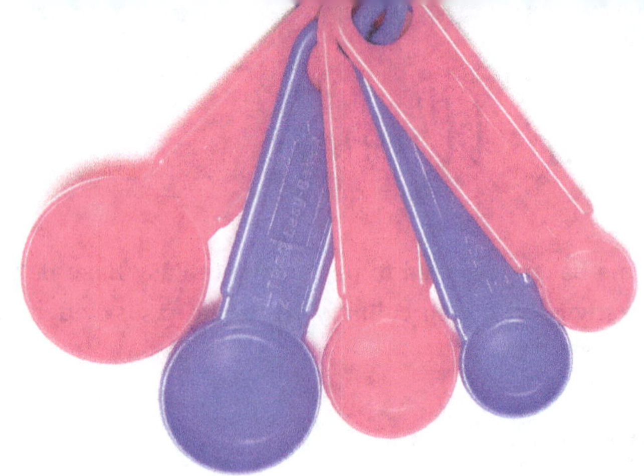

Chocolate Mousse Cake

2 Easy-Bake Oven brand chocolate cake mixes
2 Easy-Bake Oven brand chocolate icing mixes
1 package chocolate mousse mix
¼ cup crushed pecans
1 small package M&Ms
Whipped cream
1 small strawberry (optional)

Mix and bake cakes per package directions. Cool cakes completely. Mix icing per package directions. Mix mousse per package instructions. Ice sides of cakes. Roll each cake, icing side down, in crushed pecans. Spread mousse on top of one of the cakes until it is ½–inch thick. Ice the top of the other layer. Arrange cakes so that mousse is in the middle and the icing is on top. Sprinkle the top with whipped cream and, if desired, top with a small strawberry.

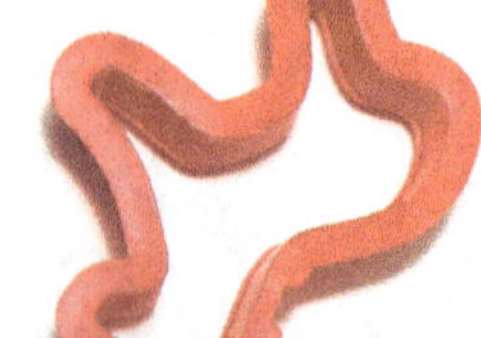

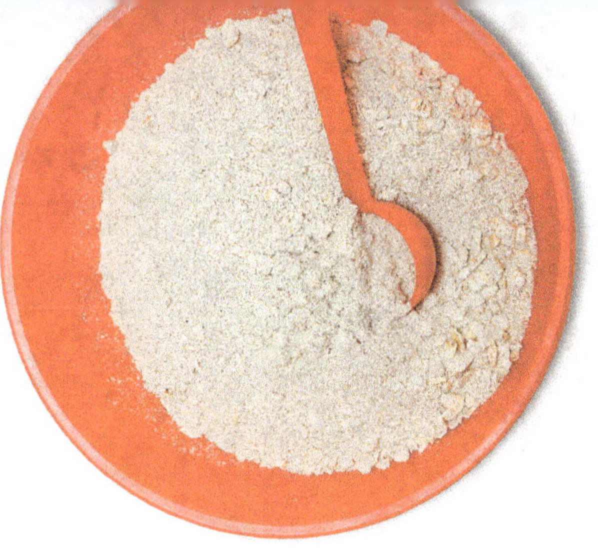

Marshmallow Cloud on a Heart

1 Easy-Bake Oven butterscotch chip cookie mix
1 Easy-Bake Oven blonde brownie mix
3 large marshmallows
Crushed peanut chocolate candies (M&Ms)

1. Mix cookie and brownie mixes according to directions.
2. Mix together in bowl and add 1 marshmallow (tear marshmallow into small pieces).
3. Place in greased round pan and bake for *15 minutes*.
4. Allow to cool and remove from pan.
5. Create into heart shape.
6. Melt 2 marshmallows in Easy-Bake warming tray, when soft and gooey, place on cookie heart.
7. Sprinkle with crushed peanut chocolate candies.

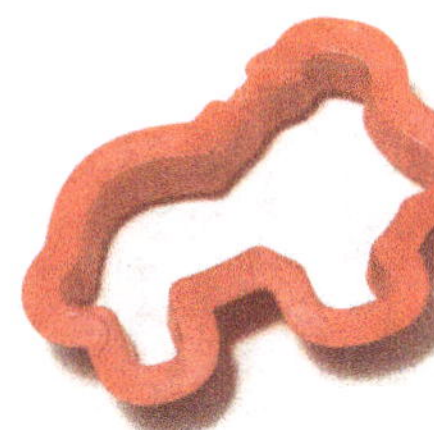

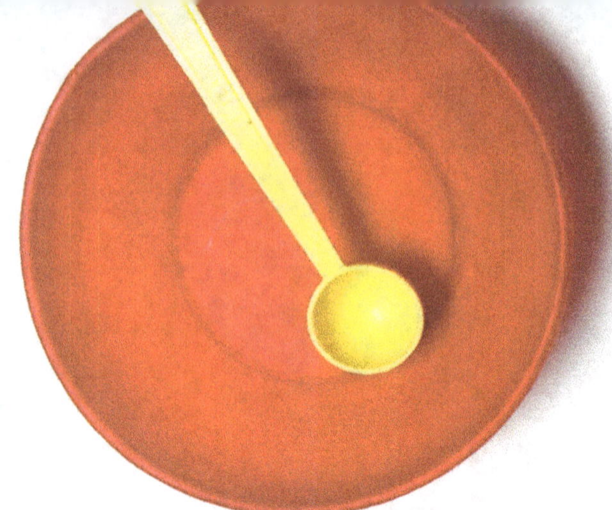

Easy-Bake Carrot Cake

Preheat Easy-Bake oven, grease and flour Easy-Bake pans.

Combine:
2 pkgs of Easy-Bake Oven yellow cake mix
2 pinches ground nutmeg
1 tbs. shredded carrots
2 tsp. drained crushed pineapple
2 tsp. prepared cook-n-serve vanilla pudding
2 ½ tsp. of water
⅛ tsp. ground cinnamon
2 pinches ground ginger
1 tsp. finely chopped pecans
1 tsp. real mayonnaise
1 tsp. of beaten egg

Combine all ingredients until completely mixed. Pour ½ of the mix into each of the two Easy-Bake pans. Bake cakes in an Easy-Bake Oven for *9 minutes* each. Remove from pan and allow cakes to cool. Ice around and between cake layers with a butter cream icing.

For icing:
2 cups powdered sugar
½ tsp. vanilla
4 tbs. softened butter
2 tbs. milk

Mix until creamy. Use a decorator bag to ice the cake.

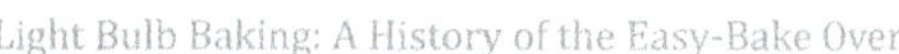

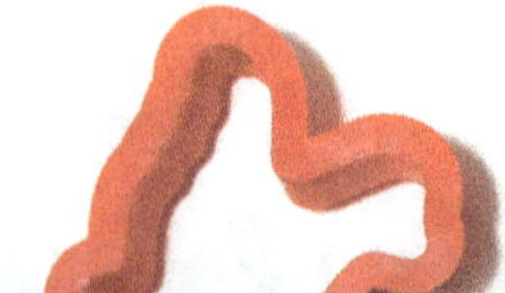

Queen of Hearts Strawberry Tart

Cooking spray
¾ teaspoon water
Flour for hands
Small white doily to put tart on
9 thin slices strawberry (outer red slices, from small strawberries—enough to cover tart)

1 package Easy-Bake Oven sugar cookie mix
⅛ teaspoon lemon extract
2 teaspoons lemon curd
Jumbo pink, white and red heart sprinkles

Preparation Instructions:

Heat Easy-Bake Oven for *15 minutes*. Spray round baking pan with cooking spray. Blend sugar cookie mix, water and lemon extract in a small bowl. Lightly flour your fingers. Spread batter in baking pan evenly, taking care not to come up on sides of pan.

Baking Instructions:

Place pan in Easy-Bake Oven baking chamber. Bake for *13 minutes*.

Cool for *10 minutes* in cooling chamber. Run a knife around edge of pan to loosen cookie. Turn out onto plate.

Use a heart shaped cookie cutter (3 inches across by 2 ½ inches long) to cut a heart shape. It should take up most of cookie round.

Spread top of heart with lemon curd and decorate with strawberries following heart pattern, in a single layer.

Tuck in sprinkles on tart, decoratively, as desired. Place doily on a small plate and top with tart.

Acknowledgments

When I envisioned writing *Light Bulb Baking*, I had no idea where the process of writing a non-fiction book would take me. In retrospect, I realize now that it was like baking a cake from scratch, albeit with a recipe that was honed over the course of two years.

The long and sometimes lonely hours at the keyboard were easily offset by the excitement of delving into history, interviewing a host of fascinating people, performing research in a variety of different locales, and the sheer thrill of collecting a toy that has played a key role in American pop culture.

Along the way, I put together a list of people who deserve both my thanks and gratitude.

Thanks To:

Don Vogel, for travelling with me on the road trip that stopped at The National Toy Hall of Fame and served as the inspiration for this project.

Andre Danis, Paul Dombowsky, Kim Douglas, Sue Erickson, Irving Gold, Gord Hiltz, Jacquelyn Hoult, Jody Jeffrey, Don Lapierre, Grant LoPatriello, Matt MacKeeman, Sean McCann, Barry Pratt, Steven Sousa and Melissa Stewart—all friends who provided feedback and support along the way.

Chris Georgoulias, a Kenner collector, for providing an abundance of resource material simply because I asked him too.

James Leach of The Brian Sutton-Smith Library and Archives of Play, and Michelle Dopp of Crain Communications, for sharing their research insights and skills.

Jill Peterson of The Jim Henson Company, for source material that made the book that much more interesting.

Lindsey Thompson, for recounting her experiences as the winner of the first Easy-Bake Baker of the Year contest.

Linda Bailey of the Cincinnati Museum Center, for providing insight into the city where Kenner grew and prospered.

Charlie Cummings, for sharing his stories and allowing me to talk to an honest-to-goodness toy inventor.

Special Thanks To:

Bob Steiner and Corky Steiner, who shed light on the Kenner legacy, shared their stories, filled in the blanks, and responded to every question I threw at them.

Denis Savoie, a true professional, who orchestrated multiple Easy-Bake Oven photo shoots and provided the book with a creative vision that equals that of the Easy-Bake Oven itself.

Maria Ford, a wildly talented editor and wordsmith, who believed in this project as much as I did, convinced me the story was significant enough to be taken seriously, and made it sing.

Daniel Leonard, for providing moral support, being enthusiastic even during times of renovation, and being my biggest fan.

My parents, especially my Mom, for providing me ample opportunity to explore my creative side as a child and never protesting while I was writing the book when yet another package containing an Easy-Bake Oven showed up on their doorstep.

Credits

Photography

enis Savoie of Savoie Photography and Design took all photographs in this book unless otherwise noted. Photo editing also by Denis Savoie. All original photography in this book is the property of the author and may not be reproduced without his permission.

All toys, ads, catalogs, books, and associated literature pictured within *Light Bulb Baking: A History of the Easy-Bake Oven* are from the author's collection, unless otherwise noted. Neither the author nor the publisher claim any copyright to the objects pictured herein.

Brilliant Thinking

p. 6 – pretzel courtesy of Renee Comet, National Cancer Institute/Wikimedia Commons
p. 9 – light bulb purchased from iStockphoto
p. 15 – one-dollar check courtesy of Jan Cummings
p. 15 – Charles Cummings courtesy of Jan Cummings
p. 16 – "*Home and Away*" comic strip courtesy of Steve Sicula

It's Kenner It's Fun!

p. 21 – Metropolitan Master Plan courtesy of the City of Cincinnati
p. 22 – Phil, Albert and Joseph Steiner courtesy of Corky Steiner
p. 22 – Albert Steiner Hall of Fame plaque courtesy of Corky Steiner
p. 25 – Easy-Bake commercial image courtesy of The Jim Henson Company
p. 26 – Kenner Street courtesy of Cincinnati Museum Center, Cincinnati, OH
p. 26 – Kroger Building courtesy of Cincinnati Museum Center, Cincinnati, OH
p. 27 – 2950 Robertson Avenue courtesy of LoopNet
p. 27 – 2940 Highland Avenue courtesy of LoopNet
p. 27 – 615 Elsinore Place courtesy of Catholic Health Partners
p. 27 – 912 Sycamore Street courtesy of David Day, Designer

Million-Dollar Baby

p. 110 – family watching television courtesy of National Archives and Records Administration

p. 114-115 – Easy-Bake commercial images courtesy of The Jim Henson Company

p. 119 – Jacob Javits Center photographed by author

p. 120 – The International Toy Center photographed by author

Pop Culture Icon

p. 124 – Betty Crocker photos and signature, used with permission of General Mills, Inc.

p. 126 – The Strong courtesy of the National Toy Hall of Fame at The Strong, Rochester, New York

p. 127 – Hall of Fame induction courtesy of Don Strand, the National Toy Hall of Fame at The Strong, Rochester, New York

p. 130 – VCR tape purchased from iStockphoto

p. 133 – McKenna Pope courtesy of Associated Press/Julio Cortez

p. 135-139 – televisions purchased from iStockphoto

p. 140 – judge observation courtesy of Jeff Houck, *The Tampa Tribune*

p. 141 – Catherine Ralston courtesy of Jeff Houck, *The Tampa Tribune*

p. 142 – Alexandra Stewart courtesy of United Press International

p. 142 – winner's trophy courtesy of Jeff Houck, *The Tampa Tribune*

Selected Bibliography

Books:

Carlisle, Rodney P., *Encyclopedia of Play in Today's Society, Volume 1*. Thousand Oaks, CA.: Sage, 2009.

Chudacoff, Howard P., *Children at Play: An American History*. New York: New York University Press, 2007.

Cummings, Janet, *A Toy Inventor's Story – Charles Arnold Cummings*. 07/03/13, http://www.bookemon.com/read-book/294150, 2013.

Eberle, Scott G., *Classic Toys of the National Toy Hall of Fame: Celebrating the Greatest Toys of All Time!* Philadelphia, PA.: Running Press, 2009.

Hoffman, David, *The Easy-Bake Oven Gourmet*. Philadelphia, PA.: Running Press, 2003.

Longest, David, *Collector's Toy Yearbook: 100 Years of Great Toys*. Paducah, KY.: Collector Books, 2007.

Marks, Susan, *Finding Betty Crocker: The Secret Life of America's First Lady of Food*. Minneapolis, MN.: University of Minnesota Press, 2007.

Mattson, Jennifer, *The Official Easy-Bake Cookbook*. New York: Dutton Children's Books, 1999.

McCallum, James T., *Irwin Toys: The Canadian Star Wars Connection*. Burlington, ON: Collectors Guide Publishing, 2000.

Mitchell, Claudia A., & Jacqueline Reid-Walsh. *Girl Culture: Studying Girl Culture: A Readers' Guide*. Santa Barbara, CA.: ABC-CLIO, 2008.

Reader's Digest Children's Publishing, Inc. *Easy-Bake Party Planner*. Pleasantville, NY, 2002.

Scott, Sharon M., *Toys and American Culture: An Encyclopedia*, Santa Barbara, CA.: ABC-CLIO, 2010.

Walsh, Tim, *Timeless Toys: classic toys and the playmakers who created them*. Kansas City, MO.: Andrews McMeel Pub., 2005.

Magazine, Newspaper and Internet Articles:

For reference purposes, the author used numerous editions of the toy trade publications *Playthings* and *Toy Book*. The *Playthings* archive located at the Brian Sutton-Smith Library & Archives of Play—part of The Strong museum in Rochester, NY—was an invaluable resource during the formative stages of the book.

Andriacco, Dan, "Toy production merges at Kenner." *The Cincinnati Post*, 06/04/83.

Ashdown, Simon, "Irwin Toy at 75." *Kidscreen*, 07/01/01. http://kidscreen.com/2001/07/01/30952-20010701/.

Associated Press, "2 Electric Toys Join Hall of Fame." *AP Online*, 11/10/06.

Associated Press, "Kansas youths to vie for Easy-Bake title." *The Topeka Capital-Journal Online*, 10/11/04. http://cjonline.com/stories/101104/kan_kanyouths.shtml.

Bhatnagar, Parija, "Toymakers getting booted from home?" CNN/Money, 11/12/04. http://money.cnn.com/2004/11/10/news/fortune500/toy_turmoil/.

Business Wire, "Catherine Ralston, Age 12, of New Albany, Ohio Takes the Cake at Hasbro's Easy-Bake 2009 'Baker of the Year' Contest." 05/08/09. http://www.businesswire.com/news/home/20090507006456/en/ADDING-MULTIMEDIA-Catherine-Ralston-Age-12-Albany.

Business Wire, "Hasbro's Beloved EASY-BAKE Brand Celebrates 50 Years of Baking Sweet Memories." 02/04/13. http://investor.hasbro.com/releasedetail.cfm?ReleaseID=737645.

Business Wire, "First Ever Boy Baker Wins Easy-Bake Chef of the Year Contest." 10/13/04. http://www.businesswire.com/news/home/20041013005748/en/Boy-Baker-Wins-Easy-Bake-Chef-Year-Contest.

Business Wire, "Little Rock's Lindsey Thompson Takes the Cake at the Easy-Bake 'Baker of the Year' National Finals." *The Free Library*, 10/9/98. http://www.thefreelibrary. com/Little Rock's Lindsey Thompson Takes the Cake at the Easy-Bake 'Baker...-a053073128.

Business Wire, "Hasbro Begins Search for EASY-BAKE 'Baker of the Year 2000'; Competition "Heats Up" As Second EASY-BAKE Kids Contest Gets Underway." 05/03/00. http://phx.corporate-ir.net/phoenix.zhtml?c=68329&p= irol-newsArticle_pf&ID=90702&highlight=.

Business Wire, "Hasbro's Easy-Bake Brand Selects Finalists for its 2009 "Baker of the Year" Contest." 04/07/09. http://www.businesswire.com/news/home/ 20090407005330/en/Hasbros-EASY-BAKE-Brand-Selects-Finalists-2009-Baker.

Business Wire, "Hasbro Celebrates 40 Years of EASY-BAKE with a Tasty Competition; America's Favorite Cooking Toy Mounts the Third 'Baker of the Year' Contest." 04/30/03. http://phx.corporate-ir.net/ phoenix.zhtml?c=68329&p=irol-newsArticlePR_ pf&ID=407223&highlight=.

Canadian Press, "Cancellation of Kenner deal will slash sales, Irwin says." *The Montreal Gazette*, 09/25/85.

CBC News, "Private firm buys Irwin Toy for $55 million." 03/05/01. http://www.cbc.ca/news/business/ story/2001/03/05/irwin010305.html.

Degarmo, Kelly, "Virtual Easy Bake oven keeps children happy, kitchens clean." *Bangor Daily News*, 03/05/99. Style Section.

Dobbin, Ben, "Lionel trains, Easy-Bake Oven inducted into US Toy Hall of Fame." *The America's Intelligent Wire*, 11/10/06

Dougherty, Nate., "Nominees announced for National Toy Hall of Fame." *Rochester Business Journal*, 09/11.

Ellis, Bryan, "Easy Bake Oven Turns 50." *Examiner.com*, 02/04/13. http://www.examiner.com/article/easy-bake-oven-turns-50.

Fasig, Lisa Biank. "Hasbro exits home of Play-Doh, G.I. Joe." *The Cincinnati Enquirer*. 10/13/00. Business Section.

"Fuzion Design pioneers Hasbro's new Easy-Bake Oven." *Providence Business News*. 08/15/11. http://www.pbn. com/Fuzion-Design-pioneers-Hasbros-new-Easy-Bake-Oven,60533.

Friedman, Stephen F., "Business: A Toy is Born." *Cincinnati Magazine*, 12/76.

Gibeau, Richard, "Kenner's top gun – President Mauer stays the course." *The Cincinnati Post*, 09/19/88.

Harrington, Jeff, "Cincinnati still home to Kenner." The *Cincinnati Enquirer*, 10/24/91.

"Hasbro's EASY-BAKE Oven Inducted into National Toy Hall of Fame." *Business Wire*, 11/9/06.

The Herald News - Joliet (IL). "Easy-Bake Oven is still cooking after 40 years." 06/03/03. HighBeam Research. http:// www.highbeam.com/doc/1N1-0FEBFDEF8753795A.html.

Jacoby, Steve, "Surviving the Toy Wars." *Cincinnati Magazine*, 12/00, 65-71, 109-110.

Jensen, Peter, "Empowered by two 100-watt bulbs." The *Baltimore Sun*, 12/99.

Jim Henson Company Archives, "6/3/1968 – 'Shoot Easy-Bake Oven Commercial'." *Jim Henson's Red Book*, The Jim Henson Company, 06/03/11. http://www.henson.com/ jimsredbook/2011/06/03/631968/.

"Kenner Announces Changes." *The Cincinnati Enquirer*, 04/04/85.

"Kenner pact with Canadian firm severed." *The Cincinnati Post*, 09/23/85.

"Kenner penetrates non-traditional outlets; display poles and prepack program give toy maker flexibility to vary market distribution. (1986-87 Directory Issue)." Playthings, 1986. *HighBeam Research*. http://www.highbeam.com/doc/1G1-4228831.html.

"Kenner Promotes Six To Top Executive Posts." The *Cincinnati Enquirer*, 10/4/73.

Leach, James, "Kids and Cooking: Playing with Fire." *Play Stuff Blog*, National Museum of Play, 05/10/11. http://www.museumofplay.org/blog/play-stuff/2011/05/kids-and-cooking-playing-with-fire/.

Locker, Melissa, "Top Chefs Join the Fight for a Gender-Neutral Easy-Bake Oven." *Time NewsFeed*, 12/14/12. http://newsfeed.time.com/2012/12/14/top-chefs-join-the-fight-for-a-gender-neutral-easy-bake-oven/.

Martin, Douglas, "Bernard Loomis, 82, Dies; Made Toys TV Stars." *New York Times*, 06/06/06. http://www.nytimes.com/2006/06/06/business/06loomis.html.

"New Easy-Bake Oven Recall Following Partial Finger Amputation; Consumers Urged to Return Toy Ovens." *United States Consumer Product Safety Commission*, 07/09/07. http://www.cpsc.gov/en/Recalls/2007/New-Easy-Bake-Oven-Recall-Following-Partial-Finger-Amputation-Consumers-Urged-to-Return-Toy-Ovens/.

News Limited Network Staff, "Teen says boys should be encouraged to use oven toy." *News Limited Network*, 12/4/12. http://www.news.com.au/lifestyle/parenting/teen-says-boys-should-be-encouraged-to-use-oven-toy/story-fnet08ui-1226529517800.

Owen, David, "Where Toys Come From." *Atlantic*, 10/86

Paramaguru, Kharuna, "How Children's Toys Are Getting a Gender Neutral Makeover for Christmas." *Time NewsFeed*, 12/6/12. http://newsfeed.time.com/2012/12/06/how-childrens-toys-are-getting-a-gender-neutral-makeover-for-christmas/.

Paramaguru, Kharuna, "Hasbro Reveals Plans for Gender Neutral Easy-Bake Oven." *Time NewsFeed*, 12/19/12. http://newsfeed.time.com/2012/12/19/hasbro-reveal-plans-for-gender-neutral-easy-bake-oven/.

Rhodes, Gary, "Kenner cuts costs, adds lines." *The Cincinnati Post*, 07/26/91.

Rieselman, Deborah, "UC alum Ronald Howes creates Easy Bake Oven." *UC Magazine. http://magazine.uc.edu/famousalumni/designers/EasyBake.html.*

Rossant, Juliette, "The Passing of 'Mr. Easy-Bake Oven.'" *Super Chef Blog*, 01/28/05. http://www.superchefblog.com/2005/01/passing-of-mr-easy-bake-oven.html.

Schifrin, Nick and Stone, Gigi, "Some Toys Are Just Better Than Others." *ABC News Online*, 11/9/06.

Smith, Michelle R., "Unisex Easy-Bake oven on the way" *Associated Press*, 12/17/12. http://news.yahoo.com/apnewsbreak-unisex-easy-bake-oven-way-215127263--finance.html.

Snyder Bulik, Beth, "Toy Makers Caught in New Gender Flap – But Are They at Fault?" *Advertising Age*, 12/18/12. http://adage.com/article/news/toy-makers-gender-flap-fault/238765/.

Specter, Michael, "Not All Fun and Games at 5th Ave Toy Center." *The New York Times*, 04/26/81. http://www.nytimes.com/1981/04/26/realestate/not-all-fun-and-games-at-5th-ave-toy-center.html.

Stammen, Ken. "HASBRO PLAY DAYS IN CITY ARE DONE. (BUSINESS)." The Cincinnati Post (Cincinnati, OH). Dialog LLC. 2000. *HighBeam Research*. 10/13/00. http://www.highbeam.com/doc/1G1-66099128.html.

Styles, William B. "Kenner Co. Big Gun Now in Toy Business" *The Cincinnati Enquirer*, 09/08/61.

Suess, Jeff, "Remember Kenner? It made Christmas toys fun" *Our History*, Cincinnati.com, 1/24/13. http://cincinnati.com/blogs/ourhistory/2013/01/24/remember-kenner-it-made-christmas-toys-fun/.

UPI, "Hasbro recalling Easy-Bake Ovens." UPI.com, 07/20/07. http://www.upi.com/Business_News/2007/07/20/Hasbro-recalling-Easy-Bake-ovens/UPI-68641184909206/.

United States Product Safety Commission. "Easy-Bake Ovens Recalled for Repair Due to Entrapment and Burn Hazards." 02/06/07. http://www.cpsc.gov/en/Recalls/2007/Easy-Bake-Ovens-Recalled-for-Repair-Due-to-Entrapment-and-Burn-Hazards/.

Walker, Dean, "When Fun's the Product, the Game Can Get Rough." *Executive*, 10/84.

Catalogs & Annual Reports:

For reference purposes, the author used numerous scans of Kenner & Hasbro toy catalogs used primarily by dealers. Chris Georgoulias graciously provided Kenner catalog scans dating from 1964-1990.

Scans of vintage Christmas catalogs were referenced from *wishbookweb.com*—an online catalog archive project

Publically available Annual Reports from Hasbro, Inc. and Irwin Toy Ltd. were also consulted.

Patents:

United States Patent #3,368,063—filed December 23, 1964
United States Patent #4,249,067—filed February 3, 1981

Interviews:

Cummings, Charles, former member, Advanced Concepts Group, Kenner Products, telephone interview, 08/11/13.

Gardiner, Lauren, former child actress, telephone interview, 08/26/13.

Kadysewski, Tony, Director of marketing and communications, Trion Industries, telephone interview, 09/10/13.

Posner, Marvin, former Executive Vice President of Sales & Marketing, Kenner Products, telephone interview, 07/16/13.

Steiner, Corky, former Vice President Sales, Latin America, telephone interview, 08/19/2013; on-going email correspondence.

Steiner, Robert, former President, Kenner Products, telephone interview, 02/09/13; on-going email correspondence.

Thompson, Lindsey, winner, 1998 Easy-Bake Baker of the Year contest, telephone interview, 07/25/13.

Online Resources

Stay on top of Easy-Bake Oven news and history at the *Light Bulb Baking* companion website and social media streams:

www.lightbulbbaking.com

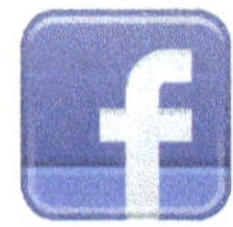 http://facebook.com/lightbulbbaking

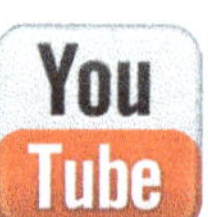 http://youtube.com/lightbulbbaking

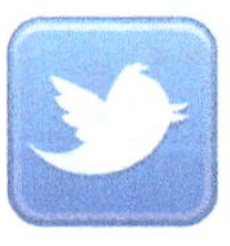 http://twitter.com/lightbulbbaking

 http://pinterest.com/lightbulbbaking

9 780099 174841 9